The whole works of Major Richardson Pack, ... in prose and verse. Now collected into one volume: with some account of his life and writings, drawn up by himself in the year M.DCC.XX.

Richardson Pack

ECCO
PRINT EDITIONS

Eighteenth Century
Collections Online
Print Editions

Gale ECCO Print Editions

Relive history with *Eighteenth Century Collections Online*, now available in print for the independent historian and collector. This series includes the most significant English-language and foreign-language works printed in Great Britain during the eighteenth century, and is organized in seven different subject areas including literature and language; medicine, science, and technology; and religion and philosophy. The collection also includes thousands of important works from the Americas.

The eighteenth century has been called "The Age of Enlightenment." It was a period of rapid advance in print culture and publishing, in world exploration, and in the rapid growth of science and technology – all of which had a profound impact on the political and cultural landscape. At the end of the century the American Revolution, French Revolution and Industrial Revolution, perhaps three of the most significant events in modern history, set in motion developments that eventually dominated world political, economic, and social life.

In a groundbreaking effort, Gale initiated a revolution of its own: digitization of epic proportions to preserve these invaluable works in the largest online archive of its kind. Contributions from major world libraries constitute over 175,000 original printed works. Scanned images of the actual pages, rather than transcriptions, recreate the works *as they first appeared.*

Now for the first time, these high-quality digital scans of original works are available via print-on-demand, making them readily accessible to libraries, students, independent scholars, and readers of all ages.

For our initial release we have created seven robust collections to form one the world's most comprehensive catalogs of 18th century works.

Initial Gale ECCO Print Editions collections include:

History and Geography
Rich in titles on English life and social history, this collection spans the world as it was known to eighteenth-century historians and explorers. Titles include a wealth of travel accounts and diaries, histories of nations from throughout the world, and maps and charts of a world that was still being discovered. Students of the War of American Independence will find fascinating accounts from the British side of conflict.

Social Science

Delve into what it was like to live during the eighteenth century by reading the first-hand accounts of everyday people, including city dwellers and farmers, businessmen and bankers, artisans and merchants, artists and their patrons, politicians and their constituents. Original texts make the American, French, and Industrial revolutions vividly contemporary.

Medicine, Science and Technology

Medical theory and practice of the 1700s developed rapidly, as is evidenced by the extensive collection, which includes descriptions of diseases, their conditions, and treatments. Books on science and technology, agriculture, military technology, natural philosophy, even cookbooks, are all contained here.

Literature and Language

Western literary study flows out of eighteenth-century works by Alexander Pope, Daniel Defoe, Henry Fielding, Frances Burney, Denis Diderot, Johann Gottfried Herder, Johann Wolfgang von Goethe, and others. Experience the birth of the modern novel, or compare the development of language using dictionaries and grammar discourses.

Religion and Philosophy

The Age of Enlightenment profoundly enriched religious and philosophical understanding and continues to influence present-day thinking. Works collected here include masterpieces by David Hume, Immanuel Kant, and Jean-Jacques Rousseau, as well as religious sermons and moral debates on the issues of the day, such as the slave trade. The Age of Reason saw conflict between Protestantism and Catholicism transformed into one between faith and logic -- a debate that continues in the twenty-first century.

Law and Reference

This collection reveals the history of English common law and Empire law in a vastly changing world of British expansion. Dominating the legal field is the *Commentaries of the Law of England* by Sir William Blackstone, which first appeared in 1765. Reference works such as almanacs and catalogues continue to educate us by revealing the day-to-day workings of society.

Fine Arts

The eighteenth-century fascination with Greek and Roman antiquity followed the systematic excavation of the ruins at Pompeii and Herculaneum in southern Italy; and after 1750 a neoclassical style dominated all artistic fields. The titles here trace developments in mostly English-language works on painting, sculpture, architecture, music, theater, and other disciplines. Instructional works on musical instruments, catalogs of art objects, comic operas, and more are also included.

The BiblioLife Network

This project was made possible in part by the BiblioLife Network (BLN), a project aimed at addressing some of the huge challenges facing book preservationists around the world. The BLN includes libraries, library networks, archives, subject matter experts, online communities and library service providers. We believe every book ever published should be available as a high-quality print reproduction; printed on-demand anywhere in the world. This insures the ongoing accessibility of the content and helps generate sustainable revenue for the libraries and organizations that work to preserve these important materials.

The following book is in the "public domain" and represents an authentic reproduction of the text as printed by the original publisher. While we have attempted to accurately maintain the integrity of the original work, there are sometimes problems with the original work or the micro-film from which the books were digitized. This can result in minor errors in reproduction. Possible imperfections include missing and blurred pages, poor pictures, markings and other reproduction issues beyond our control. Because this work is culturally important, we have made it available as part of our commitment to protecting, preserving, and promoting the world's literature.

GUIDE TO FOLD-OUTS MAPS and OVERSIZED IMAGES

The book you are reading was digitized from microfilm captured over the past thirty to forty years. Years after the creation of the original microfilm, the book was converted to digital files and made available in an online database.

In an online database, page images do not need to conform to the size restrictions found in a printed book. When converting these images back into a printed bound book, the page sizes are standardized in ways that maintain the detail of the original. For large images, such as fold-out maps, the original page image is split into two or more pages

Guidelines used to determine how to split the page image follows:

• Some images are split vertically; large images require vertical and horizontal splits.
• For horizontal splits, the content is split left to right.
• For vertical splits, the content is split from top to bottom.
• For both vertical and horizontal splits, the image is processed from top left to bottom right.

THE WHOLE
WORKS

OF MAJOR

Richardson Pack,

Late of BURY ST. EDMONDS
in the County of *SUFFOLK;*

In PROSE and VERSE.

Now Collected into one Volume   With some
Account of his Life and Writings, drawn
up by Himself in the Year M DCC XX.

LONDON·

Printed for E. CURLL in the *Strand,* 1729.

(Price 7 s. 6 d)

Academiæ Cantabrigiensis
Liber

MEMOIRS
Of the AUTHOR, and his Writings.

RICHARDSON PACK, was the Son of JOHN PACK, of *Stoke-Aſh* in *Suf-folk*, Eſq; who, in the Year 1697, was High Sheriff of that County.

HIS Mother was one of the Daughters and Co-heirs of *Robert Richardſon* of *Tudah*, in the County Palatine of *Durham*, a Gentleman of good Extraction, and well Allied in the *North* of *England*.

THE firſt Taſte that was given our Author of Letters, (after he had been kept a Year or two, but much to his Prejudice, with a Country School-Maſter) was at *Merchant-Taylor's-School*. From thence he was removed, between fifteen and ſixteen Years of Age, to St. *John*'s-College in *Oxford*. " About eighteen, his Father entered him of " the Middle-Temple, and fixed him in Cham-" bers there, deſigning him for the Profeſſion " of the Law. And by the peculiar Grace

A 2   " of

" of the Treafurer and Benchers of that Ho-
" nourable Society, he was at eight Terms
" ftanding, admitted Barrifter, when he was
" little more than twenty Years Old   But
" a Sedentary Life agreeing as ill with his
" Health, as a Formal one fuited at that
" time with his Inclinations, he did not long
" purfue thofe Studies; and after fome little
" Rambling in his Thoughts, he at length
" determined his View to the Army, where
" he flattered himfelf he fhould meet with
" Scenes of more Freedom as well as Action.

" HIS firft Command was that of a Com-
" pany of Foot, in the Year 1705.

" IN 1710, the Regiment in which he
" ferved, was one of thofe Two, of *Englifh*
" Foot, that were with Maiefchal *Starem-*
" *bergh*, at the Battle of *Villa Viciofa*, in
" *Spain*, the Day after General *Stanhope*,
" and the Troops under his Command, were
" taken Prifoners at *Brighuega;* where the
" Major being Killed, and he the Eldeft Cap-
" tain, and upon the Spot, his Grace the
" Duke of *Argyll* confirmed his juft Preten-
" fions to that Vacancy, by his Commiffion,
" immediately on his Arrival in that King-
" dom.

                     " IT

" IT was that Occasion which first intro-
" duced our Author to the good Fortune of
" being known to that truly noble and ex-
" cellent Person, with whose Protection and
" Patronage he has ever since been honoured.

" THE Ambition he had to celebrate the
" Duke of *Argyll's* Heroic Virtues, at a time
" when it was grown Popular to traduce them,
" and his desire of expressing in some Mea-
" sure his Gratitude for the many Marks he
" had received of his Grace's Favour, gave
" Birth to the best of his Performances he has
" obliged the World with. What other Pieces
" he has wrote in Verse, are for the most Part
" the unlaboured Result of Love or Friend-
" ship, and the Amusement of those few so-
" litary Intervals, in a Life that seldom wanted
" either serious Business, or social Pleasures,
" of one kind or other, intirely to fill up the
" Circle."

HERE ends the Major's Paper. The
Pieces referred to in this short *Memoire* were
first printed in the Year 1718, and Dedicated
to Colonel *Stanhope* The Volume contained
a Hundred twenty-six Pages, ending with A
Soldier's Prayer The whole Impression sold
off within three Months, and upon its being

immediately

immediately reprinted, the Major was pleaſed to enlarge the Second Edition, with *An* ESSAY *on the* ROMAN *Elegiac Poets*, and ſome Tranſlations from thoſe Authors; alſo ſome MEMOIRS *of the* LIFE *and* DEATH *of* Mr. *Wycherley.*

IN 1719, He publiſhed the LIFE of *Pomponius Atticus,* with Remarks. Addreſſed to his Grace the Duke of *Argyll.*

IN 1720, He publiſhed *Religion* and *Philoſophy,* a Tale. With five other ſmall Pieces.

IN 1725, He publiſhed a *New Collection* of Poetical Miſcellanies, to which he prefixed the LIVES of *Miltiades* and *Cymon,* from *Cornelius Nepos,* (as he had before done that of *Atticus*) This Second Volume he Dedicated, likewiſe, to the Duke of *Argyll,* dated from *Exeter,* where he was at that time with his Regiment, and from whence he ſent me the following Letter concerning the firſt Copy of Verſes, in this *New Collection,* AD LIBELLUM.

Mr.

EXETER, *May* 25th, 1725.

Mr. CURLL,

YOU may wonder perhaps how I came to change my Opinion fo often about *one Copy of Verfes*, but the Caution I have always had with regard to Ladies, makes me fometimes too fcrupuloufly Nice; as I have found in refpect to the Inclofed, which a *near Relation* of the *Fair One* to whom it is addreffed, has thought not too Particular, while her Name is concealed. I therefore defire it may be printed juft as you find it here Tranfcribed. I cannot fuppofe you can have printed, as yet, the Copy as I fent it you laft altered, but even if you had, that muft be fuppreffed, for this is infinitely better, only my Scrupulofity would not let me fo freely indulge my Genius as I ought.

Sir

Sir *J D* * has writ me word that a *Favourite Toaft of mine* is going to be *Married.* I wifh they may all fucceed in the fame Way. I defire you will not any longer delay the publifhing my Book. *Adieu* This is the laft Paper of Verfes you will have from your Friend, and Servant,

RICHARDSON PACK.

SINCE his *Second Collection*, the *Major* has only publifhed the following Copy of Verfes on the KING's *Acceffion*, fent under Cover to the Earl of *Scarborough*; and foon after, inftead of a Summons to Court, he received One to attend the Command of his Regiment which was marched from *Exeter* to *Scotland*; where that Country, which was his Averfion when Living, proved to be the Scene of his Death in the Winter of 1728, and of his Age, about the feven and fortieth Year,

* *Jermyn Davei.*

TO

TO THE

EARL

OF

SCARBOROUGH.

From my Houfe in Bury St. Edmonds,
October 13, 1727.

A T COURT Unknown, or, what is Worfe, I fear
Known only not to have a PATRON *There,*
I Live, MY LORD, with an inglorious Fate,
In *Country-Quarters* Hid, or *This Retreat.*
Yet when, revifiting my little Neft,
My Wings at liberty, my Cares at reft,

In chearful Innocence I fit and fing;

Methinks I'm Happier than the Happieft King.

But peevifh Thoughts, alas! fomeumes invade

The foft Recefles of my *Fav'rite Shade*

Whoe'er hath Merit, ftill hath fome Defign.

And Virtue, when Neglected, will Repine.

The Mufe too takes in This Difgrace a Part;

Pretends Her Own, as well as My Defert.

If doubly Arm'd You can't Advance, 'tis Hard

What! not fucceed as *Soldier,* nor as *Bard?*

Strait to the PALACE She refolves to Hie

But Heav'n knows *how* This STRANGER muft *Apply.*

If SCARB'ROUGH yet fome lucky Hour wou'd Chufe,

(Sure All are not Unlucky to the MUSE)

To recommend This Orphan to the Throne;

The Caufe can't Fail, which HE vouchfafes to Own.

Whilft afar off She Blufhing, Trembling, lies,

THE KING, MY LORD, may bid the VIRGIN Rife,

And She, like ESTHER, thus, find Favour in His Eyes.

                                        TO

TO THE
KING.

WHILE CAM and ISIS at Your Royal Feet
Offer'd, GREAT SIR, th' immortal Fruits of
Wit;
While *Rev'rend Bards* proclaim'd your Sacred Fame,
And the *Young Laureat Tribe* invok'd your Name;
At humble Distance from th' Harmonious Throng,
To gentle Strains I tun'd some Rural Song,
Whose *unambitious Airs*, at best, pretend
To cheer in Solitude a pensive Friend.
Profane it seem'd in Me to join the Choir,
And with rude Hands attempt APOLLO's Lyre.

But since You hourly spread your Gracious Light,
And chase, where-e'er You Go, the Clouds of Night;
Since your auspicious Rays diffus'd on All,
Sustain the Great, and animate the Small,

The

The moſt Remote your Infl'ence ſhou'd confeſs,

All Hearts ſhou d gratulate, Each Tongue ſhou'd bleſs.

After th Applauſe of Nobler Poets, then

Vouchſafe t'accept the Homage of his Pen,

Whoſe Boſom glows with an unuſual Flame,

While *Loyalty* inſpires, and *You're* the Theme;

Who raviſh'd ſees the Joyful Times retriev'd,

When Your *Bleſt* SIRE, and Mighty WILLIAM liv'd.

In YOU *Their diff rent Virtues* are Compleat;

Gentle as GEORGE, as Mighty WILLIAM *Great.*

Not *Phaeton-like,* by raſh Ambition hurl'd,

Too Young YOU Drove the Chariot of the World;

But Form'd by Nature, and Improv'd by Pains,

Explor'd the Road, e'er yet YOU *ſhook* the Reins.

For Empire Born, but Rais'd by juſt Degrees,

Experience taught You both to *Rule* and *Pleaſe;*

And like a skill'd Phyſician, wiſely-ſure,

You Felt the NATIONS Pulſe, You meant to Cure.

Believe

Believe me, SIR, (and Frown not too Severe,
That thus the MUSE familiar greets your Ear)
No Method better can Secure your Throne,
Than still to *Know* your Subjects, and be *Known*.
The Gen'rous BRITONS, Honest, Open, Bold,
Ill bear that *Courtiers* shou'd Their KING withhold:
With Veneration they *His Presence* Wait,
And think *His Person* truly makes *His State*.
Shou'd now the *Faithless* doubt Your *Right Divine*,
And, as the Jews of old, demand a *Sign*;
What *Ampler* can of GOD's *Vicegerent* be,
Than so much *Mildness* with such *Majesty* !

Revolving those Unhappy Kingdoms Fate,
Where *Depredations* make the *Sov'raign* Great;
Where Impious Slaves by Adulation rise,
And KINGS are Flatter'd into DEITIES,
At once both Prince and People we Deplore,
Nor know which GOD Permits to suffer more

The

The *Monarch's blinded* by that *Incenfe-fmoke;*
And the *Gall'd Subject groans* beneath the *Yoke.*
But You, GREAT PRINCE ' by LAW maintain your *Sway,*
And We by *Duty* and by *Choice Obey*

SOV'RAIGN of *Hearts*' Whofe Dread, yet lov'd,
    Commands
Extend o'er diftant Seas and various Lands,
What Other Province *fairer Tribute* Yields
Of flowing Wealth, than fruitful ALBION's Fields?
While You with *Juftice*, SIR, and *Mercy* Reign,
You *Shine* not on a *Barren Land* in vain.
What nobler Sight can entertain your Eyes,
Than a Glad Nation's *willing Sacrifice?*
Which Glorying in a MONARCH, *Brave* and *Good,*
For Him exhaufts her *Treafures* and her *Blood.*
Her Sons to *Freedom* born, with *Plenty* fed,
Eat not in *fervile Fear* precarious Bread:
Rich in their Father's, or their Own Increafe,
To *War's* rough Storms prefer the Calms of *Peace·*
                                        Yet

Yet Aim'd ne'er fail to Scourge their *Country*'s Foes
And Scorn all Chains but what Themselves impose. '

Sooth'd by your *Care,* and CAROLINA's Smile,
The Factions ceafe, which lately Griev'd *our Ifle:*
And under future Ills She ne'er can Faint,
Supported by a HERO and a SAINT.
But Heaven propitious feems to have Defign'd
Our Blifs not only Great, but Unconfin'd.
While FRED'RICK, and a long and glorious Train
Of Royal Iffue fhall o'er BRITAIN Reign,
While *Princely Virgins,* with collat'ral Grace,
Wear *Bridal Crowns,* ftill Deftin'd to *Your Race*

THE
TABLE.

A 2

The TABLE.

The TABLE.

A

The TABLE.

BOOKS

BOOKS *Printed for* E. CURLL.

the Lady JANE GRAY. Adorn'd with Cuts   Price 1 s.
Both by Mr YOUNG, Fellow of *All-Souls* College,
Oxon.

VI. ESTHER Queen of *Persia*   A Poem in Two
Books   By Mr *Henley* of St *John*'s College, *Camb.*
Price 1 s 6 d

VII. Mr. PRIOR's second Collection of Poems.
Price 1 s

VIII MUSÆ BRITANNICÆ è *Poematis varii Argumenti
vel hactenus ineditis, vel sparsim editis & rarissimis con-
stantes.   Pret 2 s. 6 d

IX. BOILEAU's *Lutrin*   In SIX Cantos.   Adorned
with Cuts.   Price 1 s. 6 d.

X ————Art of Poetry   Price 1 s

XI Mr. SEWELL's Poems on several Occasions 8vo.
Price 1 s 6 d

XII POEMS.   By Mr JOHN PHILIPS, late Student
of *Christ Church, Oxon*   With his Life by Mr. SEWELL.
Price 1 s

XIII The CONFEDERATES   A Farce. By Mr *Joseph
Gay*   Price 1 s

XIV. POEMS   By Mr POMFRET (Author of the
Choice)   Price 2 s.

XV Poems   By Mr. REYNARDSON, late of *Ba-
liol* College, *Oxon*   Price 1 s 6 d

XVI MUSCIPULA, *five Cambro Muo Machia.   Authore* E HOLDSWORTH, *è Coll Magd Oxon.*   With an
English Translation by Mr. COBB, late of *Trinity* College *Cambr*   Price 1 s

XVII MAC-DERMOT ·   Or, The *Irish* Fortune-
Hunter   A Poem, in SIX *Cantos*   Price 1 s

XVIII The Art of Dress   A Poem   By Mr *Bre-
val*   Price 1 s

XIX. *Letters, Poems,* and *Tales* ; Amorous, Saty-
rical, and Gallant   Which pass'd between Dr. *Swift,*
Mrs *Anne Long,* and several Persons of Distinction.
Price 2 s

XX The *Hoop-Petticoat*   A Poem in Two Books.
By Mr *Joseph Gay*   Price 1

To The Honourable

Coll. *William Stanhope*

His Majesty's Envoy Extraordinary *and* Plenipotentiary *at the Court of* MADRID.

SEVERAL of the Pieces That compose This little COLLECTION have had the good Fortune *formerly* to *Please* You in *Private*: And You have not,

B   I am

I am perſuaded, ſo much of the PUBLICK MINISTER to *Forget an Old Acquaintance.* Knowing, as I do, the Generoſity and Franknefs of Your natural Temper, I Flatter my ſelf, it will be no difagreeable Change to You from the Formal *Compliments*, and Diſſembled *Civilities*, that you daily fee paſs between *Courts*, to turn your Eyes upon the Sincerer *Profeſſions* of Real *Love*, and Diſintereſted *Friendſhip.* If I may claim any Degree of Merit as an *Author*, it is to have writ upon ſcarce any one *Subject* with which I was not *paſſionately* affected, and That was not capable in the *ſame* Manner to affect other People. This too will, I believe, diſtin-

guiſh

guifh the following *Tranflations*
from the *cold* and *lifelefs* ones
That have come from many
Hands Which have undertaken
that Work rather as their *Task*
than their *Choice*. There is one
Part, I own, of the Prefent I
take leave to fend You, the Publication of which may feem to
want an Excufe; I mean, the
Two Letters upon STUDY and
CONVERSATION. But if every
one had the fame equitable Dif-
pofition I can promife my felf
in You, there would be need of
no other Apology than what I
made in the Beginning of the
Firft ESSAY, where I fufficiently Explained at what *Level* I
Aimed; Who have often, as You
know, (for to a Friend One
would

would own the Truth) had occasion for a *Guide*, as much as Any of my Neighbours. These *Sketches* were drawn at the Request, and for the sole Use of an EXCELLENT YOUTH whom You Knew, and Loved: (For who could *Know* Him without *Loving* Him?) HE soon, indeed, out-grew any *Instructions* I could pretend to suggest to Him ; and, had He *Lived*, might have given, in HIMSELF, the brightest EXAMPLE. The Value He set upon Them, makes me think THEY may not be entirely *Useless*, at least to the *Younger Class* of READERS; for which Reason they have taken their Place among the rest of These Papers. What Fate

may

may attend this MISCELLANY in *Print*, I am not able to Judge; but the Reception it hath found in *Manuscript* from some of the First Rank in Both Sexes, gives me a Confidence that every *Peevish Critick* will not have Credit enough to put it out of Countenance. I am in no Pain upon That Account; but it is with a great deal of *Pleasure* that I have *Now* a Publick Occasion, to make known to the World, the perfect *Esteem* I have always had for your *Person*, and my *grateful Resentments* of the many *Favours* with which You have Distinguished Me; and, at the same Time, to Assure You of my warmest *Wishes*, that You may meet

with

vi *DEDICATION.*

with all the *Success* that Cou-
RAGE, INTEGRITY, HONOUR,
and GOOD SENSE can Merit.

I am, with the greatest *Respect*, and with equal *Reason*,

S I R,

Your most Obliged,

most Faithful, and

most Humble Servant,

London,
June 23. 1718.

RICHARDSON PACK.

To Major PACK, *upon Reading his* POEMS.

SWay'd by the vulgar Tide (forgive the Wrong)
   I thought before I Heard your pow'rful Song,
In noisy *War* the MUSE's Voice was Mute,
Nor hop'd to find the *Trumpet* near the *Lute*.
But now I See, from Thy melodious Lays,
The *Laurel* well may mingle with the *Bays*;
The *Warrior's Oak* may tremble on the *Crest*,
And yet the *Lover's Myrtle* shade the *Breast*.

   MINERVA thus in HOMER's Camp is seen,
Now the Maid Threatens with a Warlike Mien,
Now in soft Words Perswades the giddy Throng,
And melts in Musick on ULYSSES' Tongue.
So on the Bosom of the THAMES unite
The Fruits of gentle *Peace,* and Pomp of *Fight*.

Here

Here Breathe The Spicy Gumms from *India*'s Shores,
In Thunder there the *Royal Navy* Roars.

   May BRITAIN never want such Sons as You,
To Fight her Battles, and Record them too.
TYRTÆUS so led SPARTA's Soldiers on,
Then sung the Trophies which Himself had won.
Be this thy Double Praise ; while We commend
The WARS you Write, the FREEDOM you Defend.

G. SEWELL.

ORIGI-

ORIGINAL POEMS

AND

TRANSLATIONS.

❧❧❧❧❧❧❧❧❧❧❧❧❧❧❧❧❧

ELEGY.

Sylvia to Amintor.

Excute Virgineo conceptas Pectore flammas,
Si potes, infelix. Si possem, sanior essem.
At trahit invitam nova vis, aliudque cupido,
Mens aliud suadet. Video meliora, proboque,
Deteriora sequor. —— —Ovid.

Behold, *Amintor*, an abandon'd Maid,
  By Love and You to Misery betray'd!
With tend'rest Vows, and fond bewitching Art,
You press'd on ev'ry side, my easy Heart;

B   Till

Till, having thrown the weak Intrenchments down,
You Plunder'd firſt, then Left the naked Town.
Was it for this I all the World Forſook,
And in your Arms my wiſh'd *Aſylum* Took:
To be, like ſome cheap Flower, unkindly torn
From my fix'd Root, then flung away in Scorn?
Ill-fated Paſſion! oh unequal Lot!
So long Purſu'd, am I ſo ſoon Forgot?
Sure all our Sex are born to ſuffer Pain,
Either from Falſhood, or from cold Diſdain.
When Old, or Ugly, Men our Faces ſhun:
If Young and Handſome, we're too oft undone.

Ye happier Virgins, whoſe unblemiſh'd Fame
Has ne'er been ſullied by the guilty Flame;
By my Example warn'd, avoid with Care
All cloſe Engagements in Love's fatal War!
Tho' long uninjur'd you maintain the Fight,
You'll find your only Safety's in your Flight.
The Foe all Stratagems and Methods tries:
Who Force eſcape, are taken by Surprize.

On

On Wings of Down his treach'rous Arrows fly :
Ah ! guard each Avenue, or else you Die.
Trust not the flight Defence of Female Pride,
Nor in your boasted Honour much confide.
So Still the Motion, and so Smooth the Dart,
It stole unfelt into my heedless Heart.
The subtle Poison lurk'd a while conceal'd :
But soon the Symptoms the Disease reveal'd.
A sad afflictive melancholy Pain
Throbb'd at my Breast, and beat in ev'ry Vein.
My heaving Bosom swell'd with sudden Sighs,
And Tears unbidden trickled from my Eyes.
In restless Fervours languishing I lay,
Dreaming all Night, and raving all the Day.
Yet this, methinks, with ease I could sustain,
Abjure my Freedom, and embrace my Chain,
Would but *Amintor* one kind Look bestow
To sooth my Grief, and mitigate my Woe.
One flatt'ring Smile would scatter all my Fears,
As Shadows vanish when the Sun appears.
So, if the Weight of some unfriendly Storm
Crush the pale *Hyacinth*, his Charms deform,

He

He hangs his Head, and seems awhile to mourn,
Till the bright Ruler of the Day return :
But soon as e'er he feels his Genial Fire,
With kindly Warmth his tender Leaves inspire ;
Strait he Revives with the same Purple Grace ;
And the chill Dews no longer cloud his Face,
But, ah ! This Image no Resemblance bears,
Amintor still is false, and *Sylvia* still despairs.

Like some misguided Traveller that strays
Through pathless Woods, and unfrequented Ways,
My Soul, deluded from her Native Seat,
Finds no kind Shelter, no secure Retreat.
Safe while I follow'd Virtue's steady Light :
Depriv'd of That, I'm left in endless Night.
What shall I do ? Ah, whither shall I turn ?
In lawless Fires must I for ever burn ?
Nor Peace, nor Innocence again return ?
Ah no ! All other Ills some Cure may find ;
But there's no Med'cine for a Love-sick Mind.
Death only can my mortal Anguish end,
And Nature's Enemy must be my Friend.

Unge-

Ungen'rous Lord, from Whom thy Wretched Slave
Flies for Relief to the relentless Grave!
But when my Afhes in their Urn are laid,
Who fcorn'd me Living, will lament me Dead.
My Suff'rings cannot fail at length to move
Your Mind to Pity, though averfe to Love.

AMIN-

AMINTOR *to* SYLVIA.

UNjuſtly, *Sylvia*, you my Coldneſs Blame :
  I wiſh, my Dear, that I were ſtill the Same.
But Nature ſeconds not my fond Deſires ;
The Oil once ſpent, o' courſe the Lamp expires.
Love's Food is Luſcious, and too apt to fill ;
And 'tis the Devil to eat againſt one's Will!
Your wanton *Cupid*'s an Inſatiate Gueſt,
And Thinks that ev'ry Meal muſt be a Feaſt.
I play'd my Part as ably as I cou'd ,
But thou'rt, i' faith, too Hard for Fleſh and Blood.
Have Conſcience, Fair One, and the *Vanquiſh'd* ſpare ;
Grant a ſhort Truce — divert a while the War —
Draw off your Forces from a ravag'd Land,
And ſeek ſome Wealthier Province to command.

Nor

Nor live ingloriously a vulgar Name,
Content at one poor Stream to flake your Flame,
Who, like the glorious Ruler of the Day,
Demand, to quench your Fires, at leaft a Sea.
Your Beauty too fhould, like his Beams defign'd
A Gen'ral Good, be to no One Confin'd.
Conceal not then the Luftre of your Charms;
Open to All the Heaven within your Arms,
Mankind for this alone the Gods Adore,
Becaufe their Bounty's Equal to their Pow'r.

Writ

Writ at SEA *in* 1709, *to a Friend on Board the Admiral.*

TO you, dear *Cotton,* who on Board
   Have all that Land, or Seas afford,
And, if you pleafe, in Fortune's Spight,
May laugh from Morning until Night,
Poor *Pack* in doleful Cabbin fhut,
No Bigger than the Cynick's Hut,
Makes bold to fend this homely Greeting,
Hoping, e'er long, a Happy Meeting

  The Moon has thrice renew'd her Prime,
(Aid me, fome friendly Mufe, with Rhime !)
Since firft our Redcoats and their Trulls,
Were ftow'd on Board thefe rotten Hulls,
          Where

Where We, condemn'd to Dirt and Fleas,
Live, God knows, little at our Eafe,
For all we're cramm'd with Pork and Peafe.
Oft have I wifh'd the Coxcomb damn'd,
Who weary of his Native Land,
Firft fell'd for Mafts the Mountain Pine,
And fpoil'd good honeft Beef with Brine.
'Tis true, whilft we indulg'd in Claret,
I made fome kind o' Shift to bear it.
But what Defenfe againft the *Hip*-----
Now we're reduc'd from Wine to *Flip?*
Nay more, I Fear I fhall e'er long
Have neither Liquor fmall or ftrong,
To quench my Thirft, or cool my Tongue.
Unlefs, my Dear, I can prevail,
With you to Beg, or elfe —— to Steal,
A Dozen or Two of Wine or Ale.
May you fucceed! and fo Farewel.

To JOHN CREED *of* Oundle *in* Northamptonſhire, *Eſq*;

Mombrio in Catalonia, Oct. 9. 1709

Hile you, dear *Creed*, ſecure at Land,
    Enjoy your Fortune at Command ;
And, careleſs of the Wind and Tide,
Anchor'd at *Oundle* ſafely ride :
I have been rowling on the Ocean,
Sick as I'd taken Pill or Potion.
Coup'd up within a narrow Cabbin,
(Grave as a Monk, or ancient Rabbin)
I led a Life ſo odd and lazy,
By *Jove* it almoſt made me crazy.
Inſtead of Men of Converſation,
Mix'd with a *Wapping* Generation,
The Filth and Scum of all the Nation,

Rogues

Rogues without Souls, or other Fire,
Than what their Brandy did infpire ;
I guzled Flip, or viler Liquor,
And drunk and fmoak'd like Country Vicar.
But, Thanks to Heav'n, that Plague is o'er ;
And I'm got fafe again a Shore ;
Where, free from Sicknefs, and from Sorrow,
I'll Live to Day, and — Hang to Morrow,
For I'm the fame as heretofore ;
Juft as Extravagant and Poor :
Refolv'd to fpend the utmoft Farthing ;
And ne'er increafe my Pelf by ftarving:
But freely feed my Genial Fire,
Indulge each elegant Defire,
While Wit, and Mirth, and gen'rous Wine,
Shall all their happy Forces join,
To foften the rough Scene of War,
And find a Charm for ev'ry Care.

  Had I been Turn'd for Ways of Thriving,
(As my grave Father was Contriving)

E'er

E'er this you might have heard me Bawl
At *Weſtminſter*, or *Hicks's-Hall*.
I, at the *Temple* had been Plodding,
Inſtead of Plund'ring and Marauding.
But 'tis in vain to force the Mind,
Which way ſoever 'tis inclind :
Elſe I ſhould never ſpend my Time in
This trifling Dogrel Vein of Rhiming,
But in plain Proſe, and better Senſe
Tell you what News there is from hence.

   Our preſent Theatre of War
Lies chiefly here among the Fair :
How to ſubdue the Ladies Hearts ;
And manage *Cupid*'s pointed Darts.
Each Cavalier attacks his Dame,
And all our little Camp's in Flame.
The *Spaniards*, to their Coſt, may feel
Our Eyes are fatal as our Steel.
F—*e*'s Who, by Nature form'd for Love,
Alike does both the Sexes move,

                    With

With am'rous Airs and wanton Glances,
Tickles the young *Sennora*'s Fancies,
Whilft I, who turn'd of Six and twenty,
Find *Venus*' Treafure not fo Plenty,
With more Succefs, and better Grace
Supply the abfent Chaplain's Place ;
Admonifh Youth to fly from Vice,
Abftain from Whoring, Cards, and Dice,
And, like an Orthodox Divine,
Damn all Mens Sins, yet ftick to mine.

I rife each Day by Morning-Peep,
(For Hunger will not let me fleep)
Then in fat Chocolate I riot,
To bribe my Stomach to be quiet.
At Noon I twift at fuch a rate,
'Twould do you Good to fee me Eat.
The Priefts, who find me always Cramming,
Pray againft Herefy and Famine.
But how fhould Men be Stout and Warlike,
Who feed on nought but Fifh and Garlick.

'Tis

'Tis Beef and Pork fupport the War,
And not their Fafting, nor their Pray'r.

When cooler Thoughts by chance prevail,
Sometimes from Company I fteal,
With *Horace*, *Virgil* and *Tibullus*,
Or That moft pleafant Droll *Catullus*,
In private I enjoy the Night,
And reap both Profit and Delight.

Thus in a merry idle Scene,
I make a Shift to fteer between
Th' Extremes of Folly, or of Vice,
And hope in time I may grow Wife :
Then worn a little of my Mettle,
I'll e'en go Home, and Wive, and Settle.

A

A PASTORAL.

In Imitation of VIRGIL's II*d Eclogue.*

YOung *Corydon*, a poor inamour'd Swain,
The Fair *Miranda* lov'd, but lov'd in vain.
With Gifts he brib'd her , and with Songs he ſtrove
To Tune her Heart to the ſoft Notes of Love.
But ſtill ſucceſsleſs the fond Shepherd woo'd :
The Wanton faſter fled, the more purſu'd.

With Grief and Shame, and hot Deſire he preſs'd,
(Tyrants that rul'd by Turns within his Breaſt.)
Penſive and Sad he ſought the ſilent Grove ;
And thus in artleſs Numbers mourn'd his Love.
Ungrateful Nymph, and oh too rudely Coy !
Thy fierce Unkindneſs will my Life deſtroy.
No Tongue can ſpeak the Torments I endure ;
So deep the Wound that I deſpair of Cure

Fool

Fool that I am, on certain Fate to run,
And court the Mischief that I ought to shun!
The Flocks and Herds oppress'd with sultry Heat,
To the thick Shades, and cooling Springs retreat;
And the green Lizard, and the painted Snake
Find a kind Refuge in some neighb'ring Brake.
But where, alas! can wretched I retire?
No Shades can cool, no Streams can quench my Fire.
Careless and unconcern'd I could have born
Dorinda's Hate, or *Sacharissa*'s Scorn.
Those vulgar Beauties scarce our Passions move:
But you inspire me with the Rage of Love,
Yet know, Fond Maid, tho' so divinely Fair,
That with'ring Time will all thy Charms impair.
How gay the Lilly, and how sweet the Rose,
When the young Months their Virgin Bloom disclose!
But soon as e'er they feel the chilling Frost,
Their Leaves are blasted, and their Odours lost.
Consider Beauty will not always last,
Then lay out ev'ry happy Hour in haste.
That lovely Face proclaims a gentler Mind:
The God who form'd you Fair, design'd you Kind.

Return,

Return, dear Fugitive, return again;
And Bless, at last, thy much-enduring Swain.
Regard your Lover with impartial Eyes;
And see that Wealth, which you unknown despise.
Here mantling Vines the rising Hills adorn,
There the glad Vallies smile with rip'ning Corn.
My num'rous Flocks o'er-spread the flow'ry Plains,
And I'm the Envy of my Fellow Swains.
Content already with my present Store,
For your Sake only I could wish for more.
Secure and happy in yon little Cell,
Like *Sylvan* Gods we might together dwell.
With chearful Hounds we'd rise by Morning Dawn
To course the Hare, or chase the nimble Fawn.
In Rural Sports, and harmless Wanton Play,
Unmark'd the swift-wing'd Hours would glide away.
No busy Cares shou'd our soft Thoughts annoy,
But all our Life be Gentleness and Joy.
Ah *Coridon!* thy airy Hopes restrain,
Nor feast with flatt'ring Dreams thy Mind in vain.
Int'rest, you see, prevails o'er all Mankind;
And Gold so *Dazzles*, that it makes *Love* Blind.

D

Thy

Thy Wealthier Rival, tho' Deform'd and Old.
Does thy Heart's Darling from thy Arms withold
Go, prune thy Vines, or tend thy woolly Care;
Nor waste thy Youth in Mourning and Despair.
Let no false Raptures discompose thy Mind,
Forget the Cruel, and embrace the Kind.

The

The Praise of SULPITIA.

From TIBULLUS, Book IV. Eleg. II

FOrſake, Great God of War ! thy Native Skies,
   A brighter Heaven is in *Sulpitia*'s Eyes.
To Grace thy Feſtival, behold her Dreſt
In all the ſhining Glories of the *Eaſt.*
On the Soft Pomp indulge thy raviſh'd Sight,
Nor fear leſt *Venus* grudge the chaſte Delight.
But, Thou impetuous Warrior well beware ;
Thy Arms will ſcarce defend me from the Fair.
When *Cupid* would ſome am'rous God inflame,
He ſteals his Fire from this Celeſtial Dame.
The chearful *Graces,* and the ſportive *Loves,*
Attend the Beauteous Maid, where'er ſhe moves :
With ſecret Harmony each Act compoſe,
And give a happy Turn to all ſhe does.
Whether in artful Pleats ſhe brades her Hair,
Or lets it looſely Wanton in the Air :

Whe-

Whether with Purple Pride she robes her Vest,

Or neatly Plain seems negligently Drest :

Alike there does through ev'ry Manner shine,

A Grace Peculiar, and a Form Divine.

Vertumnus so a thousand Dresses wears,

And Charming still in All the youthful God appears.

This matchless Fair is worthy to enjoy

Whatever Art, or Nature can supply.

For her the *Tyrian* shou'd employ his Care,

For her Alone the costly Fleece prepare

For her the Sun in bless'd *Arabia*'s Soil,

Shall ripen Gums, and Incense, Spice, and Oil.

For her Both *Indies* shall their Treasures bring :

For her our Roses blow, our Violets spring.

For her the Muses shall young Bards inspire,

For her *Apollo* tune his Vocal Lyre.

Unnumber'd Years may she their Toil prolong,

No nobler Subject can adorn their Song.

To

To D. C. *when very* YOUNG.

IF to be Gay, well-humour'd, Witty,
  Youthful, Agreeable, and Pretty,
Attracts the Eye, and wins the Mind;
Then what Refiftance can you find,
Whom Heaven has form'd with ev'ry Grace,
A fprightly Soul, an Angel's Face ?
Yet fhall I, gentle Boy, impart,
What Kindnefs dictates from my Heart.
Something there is that's ftill requir'd,
To make my *Campbell* more admir'd.
Nature but half the Work has done;
Art muft compleat what She begun.
The richeft Oar has fome Allay,
'Till Labour does the Mafs refine;
The Fire muft Purge the Drofs away,
E'er the Intrinfick Bullion fhine.

So you by Study, Obfervation,
Ufeful and well-bred Converfation,
Muft drefs your Mind, correct your Tafte,
And give your Thoughts a jufter Caft :
Muft polifh the rough Draught of Nature ;
Re-touch, and foften ev'ry Feature :
Set in true Light, each *Trait* will Shine,
And the whole Piece will look Divine,
A Genius like to yours fhou'd aim,
To merit more than common Fame ;
Shou'd ftrive in all Things to excel ;
In Judging right, and Acting well :
Ambitious ftill to pleafe the Beft,
Defpifing all the Vulgar reft.
Think not, I mean by this Advice,
To cenfure Pleafure as a Vice.
My Lyre to fofter Notes is ftrung.—
I laugh at thofe myfterious Fools,
Who live inflav'd to former Rules,
And under a conftrain'd Difguife,
By looking Grave wou'd pafs for Wife.

Reaʃon tho' ʃhe forbids Exceʃs,
Yet blames Severity no leʃs.
She, like a *Maid*, our Fancy warms
With Modeʃt, but Obliging Charms :
With decent Pride diʃdains to tread
The Paths that to Diʃhonour lead :
But ʃafe from Danger, far from Noiʃe,
Revels in ʃilent real Joys ;
Such as true Friendʃhip does inʃpire,
Or Love's more active nobler Fire.

The

The Third ELEGY of the Third BOOK of TIBULLUS.

Quid poteſt cœlum votis impleſſe Neæra ?
Blandaque cum multâ thura dediſſe prece ?

WHY to the Gods do I my Vows repeat ?
With Incenſe bribe them, and with
Pray'r intreat ?
Is it, *Neæra*, that thou may'ſt behold
Me tread on Marble under Roofs of Gold ?
That *Bacchus* would a joyful Vintage yield ?
Or *Ceres* crown the Labours of the Field ?
No, (Only Bleſſing!) 'tis for thy Return,
The ſacred Fires on ev'ry Altar burn.
In thy Embraces let me happy Live,
'Tis all that I would ask, or Heav'n can give :

There

There to refign my lateft Gafp of Breath,
Clafp'd in my Arms, when feiz'd by thofe of Death.
Not Heaps of treafur'd Gold allure my Eye ;
The *Phrygian* Column, or the *Tyrian* Dye ;
Not awful Bow'rs, like facred * Groves defign'd,
That ftrike Religious Rev'rence on the Mind ;
Not all the Pomp that gazing Crowds admire,
The gawdy Equipage , and rich Attire :
Thefe Envy raife.   Nor can the lab'ring Mind
Affur'd Repofe in their Poffeffion find.
Fortune, who governs with Defpotick Sway,
Refumes to Morrow, what fhe gave to Day.
Poor be my Lot ! Inglorious be my State !
Blefs'd with thy Prefence, I'll abfolve my Fate.
But if thy Abfence I muft ftill bemoan,
What Gift of Life can for the Lofs attone ?
The Wealth of Kings would be too mean a Price ;
On Crowns lefs Splendor waits than on thy Eyes.
Pride and Ambition vulgar Souls may fire,
But Love's the Empire to which I afpire.

---

* A Great Part of the *Religious Service* of the *Ancients* was
performed in *Groves* Dedicated to their *Peculiar Divinities.*

E   *Satur-*

Saturnian Juno! hear thy Suppliant's Pray'r,
And thou, O *Venus!* aid a Lover's Care.
Haften the happy and the welcome Day,
That fhall *Neæra* to my Arms convey.
Or, if the Fates averfe with fullen Pride,
Mock my fond Paffion, and my Hopes deride,
Deep let me drink of the *Lethæan* Wave,
And dark Oblivion hide me in the Grave.

The

The Twelfth ELEGY *of the Second* BOOK *of* PROPERTIUS.

Quicunque ille fuit, Puerum qui pinxit Amorem,
Nonne putas miras hunc habuisse manus?

WHO first drew *Cupid* a young Boy, and Blind,
    With Skill, no doubt, the Moral Piece defign'd.
He faw how Lovers with fond Childifh Play
Lavifh in idle Cares their Hours away.
His Airy Wings the Artift too expreft,
Flutt'ring in wanton Sport from Breaft to Breaft.
(For fo our Hopes no conftant Meafures know,
And Tides of Joy alternate ebb and flow,)
And arm'd his little Hands with pointed Darts,
To fhew his Tyranny o'er human Hearts.
With fatal Certainty he draws his Bow,
And unobferv'd directs the filent Blow.

Too

Too well I kenn how each fell Arrow Stings,
But sure the Wanderer has loft his Wings.
For Settled here, he Rages in my Breaft,
And my poor wearied Soul can find no Reft.
Ah ceafe a wretched Spectre to invade !
Attack fome blooming Youth, or haughty Maid :
Me thy old Servant, and thy Poet fpare ;
Elfe who fhall fing the Triumphs of thy War ?
My Mufe opprefs'd, now fcarce one Note can raife,
Reftore my Liberty, I'll Sound thy Praife.
I will defcribe Thy *Cynthia*'s Air and Mien,
Thofe Eyes, That Shape, That Grace in Motion feen.
Harmonious Beauty fhall my Song infpire ;
And Love's bright Torch fhall fet the World on Fire.

The

The Fourth ELEGY *of the Fourth* BOOK *of* TIBULLUS.

To PHOEBUS.

Huc ades, & teneræ morbos expelle puellæ,
Huc ades, intonfâ Phœbe *fuperbe comâ.*

PHæbus defcend, thy radiant Locks difplay'd,
Come and relieve the fweet complaining Maid.
Truft me, make Hafte: She well deferves thy Care:
Who would not be Phyfician to the Fair ?
Revive the fading Rofes on her Cheek ;
Revive the drooping Lillies on her Neck :
And far to Winds commit, and diftant Seas
Each Rebel Atom that difturbs her Eafe.

Come

Come, Sacred Sire! and bring each pow'rful Juice,
Each pow'rful Sound thy * double Skill can chuse.
Nor wound the *Youth* who mourns her doubtful State,
And with unnumber'd Vows wou'd bribe her Fate.
One while he Prays: Anon, if she Complains,
Distracted he Blasphemes, and Heaven Araigns.
But fear no Foes, *Cerinthus*, from above:
The Gods will all Befriend the Cause of Love.
Weep then no more, thy Tears were only Due,
Were she grown Cold, Indiff'rent, or Untrue:
But well thou know'st, for Thee alone she Lives;
Nor minds th'officious Crowd besides that Grieves
Propitious *Phœbus* ! Show'r thy Blessings down.
Preserve Two Lovers Lives in saving One.
So, when the grateful Pair their Praise shall join,
And hand in hand Approach thy hallow'd Shrine,
The thronging *Sanctities* of Heaven shall Own,
No Arts worth Envying but Thine alone.

- *Apollo* was the God of *Musick* and of *Medicine.*

To

To my Dear FRIEND, *Captain* DAVID CAMPBELL.

Cividadella in *Minorca*, Nov. 1712.

Writ upon the Reduction *of some* Regiments *in That* Island, *where, by the* Singular Humanity *of the* Ministry, *the* Officers *were Detained upon* Half-Pay, *when they could scarce live, with* Decency, *upon* Whole

Hen *Campbell*, on the Banks of *Thames*,
Mixt with the *Beaus* and shining *Dames*,
The sweet Variety you prove
Of Wit, and Wine, and happy Love,
Reflect a little on this Scene, ︿
The Seat of Poverty and Spleen ;
And while gay Pleasure fills your Mind,
Pity those Friends you left behind,

Who

Who, banifh'd from the Fair and Young,
Muft Live Unbleft, and Dye Unfung.

In vain kind Nature would employ
Her baffled Aid to give me Joy :
In vain each Pulfe proclaims aloud,
The gen'rous Fire that warms my Blood :
To Rocks, alas ! or defart Plains,
(Far from the Nymphs and tuneful Swains)
Confin'd, I mourn my Vigor loft,
By Love forfook, by Fortune croft.
No Verdant Beauty cheers my Sight ;
No feather'd Choirs my Ear delight ;
No *Park*, nor *Play*, nor fond Amour,
Amufe one tedious lonefome Hour ;
But the fame Round ftill wears away,
In Sleep the Night, in Sloth the Day.

How partial is the Hand of Fate !
Who roul in Wealth, and ride in State !
See we not fome, like Infects Born,
Our Sex' Difgrace, the other's Scorn,

Yet

Yet favour'd by capricious Chance,
By Springs unseen their Steps advance ;
Mount to the Top of Fortune's Wheel,
Made happy ev'n against their Will ?
While the brave Youth, whose Counsels aim
By vertuous Acts to merit Fame,
In fruitless Toils consumes his Days,
And neither meets Reward or Praise.
Others, whom Beauty's Pow'r controuls,
Form'd with soft-impassion'd Souls,
(And oh my Heart is tend'rer far
Then Sighs of pitying Virgins are)
Address in vain the cruel Boy,
Feel all his Pains, nor taste the Joy.
The Gods of their own Bliss secure,
Neglect the Ills which we endure.

If all our Piety's not vain,
If long Intreaty Heav'n can gain ;
E'er yet my Noon of Life be past,
E'er gath'ring Clouds my Sun o'ercast,

F   Let

Let me, ye Pow'rs ! fuccefsful prove
In my Ambition, and my Love.
My Active, Reftlefs, Fiery Mind,
Can ill fubmit to be confin'd :
Urg'd by Defires perhaps too great,
I fain, methinks, would tempt my Fate :
But if the Spear, and cumb'rous Shield
Too weighty are for me to wield ;
If fhut out from the Lifts of Fame,
I'm doom'd to live without a Name :
Grant me, at leaft, This one Requeft,
(And that, alone, will make me Bleft)
Redeem me from a long Defpair,
And make my Charmer Kind as Fair.

To

To his Grace the Duke of ARGYLL.

Port-Mabon, Jan 1ſt 1713.

ARGYLL, deriv'd from Royal Blood,
  My ſureſt Guard, my ſweeteſt Good ;
O that inſpir'd with happy Skill,
And Force proportion'd to my Zeal,
In laſting Verſe I cou'd Proclaim
Thy matchleſs Worth, thy growing Fame !
Like Thee ſhould be my num'rous Song,
Exact yet Eaſy, Smooth tho' Strong.
But the ſmall Genius I could boaſt,
Shipwreck'd on this dull Shore, is loſt.
My baniſh'd Melancholy Muſe,
Condemn'd to live a poor Recluſe,
Mourns her neglected Charms decay'd,
And moults her Wings, and droops her Head.

When

When *Horace* by the *Tyber*'s Flood
Sung young *Augustus*, Great and Good,
His chearful Hours with Pleasure fraught,
Enlarg'd his Soul, and tun'd his Thought
Gay od'rous Flow'rs his Temples crown'd;
The Loves and Graces play'd around,
The Purple *Chian* flush'd his Wit;
He laugh'd, he lov'd, he sung, he writ.
Th' immortal Offspring of his Lyre,
Conceiv'd in Energy and Fire,
Still Triumphs over Age and Time,
Beautiful, Noble and Sublime!

So, if my lucky Star would smile,
If Landed on the *British Isle,*
Within some little snug Retreat,
At length I could my Wishes meet:
On *Thames*' fair Banks supinely laid,
Beneath a spreading Poplar's Shade,
By no uneasy Passions press'd,
(Which now in Crowds insult my Breast)
                                        Tho'

Tho' far unequal to his Strain,
I might not fing perhaps in vain.
Smit with Ambition of thy Praife,
I'd ftrive my feeble Notes to raife.
Thy Sight new Vigour wou'd infufe,
The Heroe is the Poet's Mufe.
Not the fhrill *Lark*, when Morn does fpring,
Should higher Soar, or fweeter Sing.
The lift'ning Groves fhould blefs my Choice,
And Eccho learn to fpeak my Voice.
This Merit I'll, however, claim,
To Love, tho' not Adorn thy Name.

Upon Religious SOLITUDE.

*Occasioned by Reading the Infcription on the Tomb
of* CASIMIR *King of* Poland, *who Abdicated
his Crown, and fpent the Remainder of his
Days in the Abbey of St.* Germain's *at* Paris,
where he lyes Interred

MAN, foolish Man! made wretched by his
(Will,
Confcious of Good, yet ftill declines to Ill.
Reafon in vain directs our wand'ring Choice :
Each Paffion turns us with her Syren Voice
Through Airy Vifions (giddy with the Round)
Our Fancy leads us o'er inchanted Ground
Till tir'd at length with Change, and out of Breath,
We clofe the Scene, and fhut up all in Death.

But ah ! how Blefs'd are they, and only they,
Who Nature's wife Inftructions can obey ·

Who

Who within Bounds their Appetites confine;
Nor drink too deep of Pleasure's heady Wine:
Who free from Bus'ness too the Leisure find
To dress the little Garden of their Mind
That Grateful Tillage best rewards our Pains:
Sweet is the Labour, certain are the Gains.
The rising Harvest never mocks our Toil,
Secure of Fruit, if we manure the Soil.

Cities and Courts, with false Allurements bright,
Mislead the Judgment by their dazzling Light.
Our Envy sometimes we on those bestow,
Whom we our Pity rather should allow.
Gay Looks too oft the sadned Heart belye,
And the loud Laugh is follow'd by a Sigh.
Not all the Charms of the luxurious East,
Can quell the Tumults of a troubled Breast.
Musick and Wine in vain exert their Pow'r:
The Musick grates our Ears, the Wine turns sow'r.
Nor Beauty Love, nor Wit can Mirth excite;
Dull lags the Day, and joyless is the Night.

Ye

Ye bold Difturbers of Mankind be warn'd !
Dear cofts the Glory, which your Guilt has earn'd.
Fortune, a while, deceitfully may fmile,
And with fmooth Hopes your fecret Feaıs beguile ;
But Horrour will fucceed, and dire Remorfe —
Nor Strength can check, nor Skill elude their Force ⎞
They board the Three-deck'd Ship, and back the ⎬
                       [Warriour-Horfe. ⎠

    Greatnefs, at beft, when by juft Aıts puıfu'd,
Is but a paıtial and unequal Good.
Thofe needful Caıes that do the Throne fecure,
Give Princes Pains which Peafants ne'er endure
Sick of this Evil, CASIMIR retir'd,
And gave the Kingdom back his Aıms acquir'd.
He faw the tempting Luftıe of a Crown,
But felt its Weight, and laid the Burthen down.
Pride, Cruelty, Contempt of Sacred Things,
(The ufual Minifters of Conqu'ring Kings)
Banifh'd by him, to grace his future Reign,
Faith, Hope, and Charity were all his Train.
                            Hail,

Hail, gentle Piety ! (unmingled Joy !)
Whose Fullness satisfies, but ne'er can cloy :
Spread thy soft Wings o'er my devoted Breast,
And settle There, an everlasting Guest !
Not cooling Breezes to the languid Swain,
To Winter Sunshine, or to Summer Rain ;
To sinking Mariners the Friendly Hand,
That bears 'em up, and guides 'em safe to Land ;
Bring half the Comfort, or the Welcome find,
As thy Accesses to a Shipwreck'd Mind

An

IPSWICH, *April* 1714.

An EPISTLE *from a Half-Pay*
Officer in the Country to his Friend
in London, *upon Reading the Ad-*
dreſs of the Two Houſes, to thank
her Majeſty for the Safe, Honourable, *and* Advantageous PEACE.

O Dulces comitum valete cœtus.
Longè quos ſimul à domo profectos,
Diverſe variæ viæ reportant.   Catull.

CUrſe on the Star, dear *Harry*, that betray'd
  My Choice from Law, Divinity, or Trade,
To turn a Rambling Brother o' the Blade !

C.

Of all Profeſſions ſure the worſt is War.
How whimſical our Fortune ! how Bizarre !
This Week we ſhine in Scarlet, and in Gold :
The next the Cloak is pawn'd — The Watch is ſold.
To Day we are Company for any Lord :
To Morrow not a Soul will take our Word.
Like Meteors rais'd in a tempeſtous Sky,
A while we Glitter, then obſcurely Dye.
   Muſt Heroes ſuffer ſuch Diſgrace as This ?
   O Curſt Effects of Honourable Peace !

I, who not long ago indulg'd my Hours
In witty Commerce, or in ſoft Amours ;
And in rich *Mulſo, Volney,* or *Champaigne,*
Ador'd each Night the Beauties then in Reign ;
(Till, Arms ſubmitting to the Awful Gown,
Our Troops were forc'd to abdicate the Town,)
Muſt now Retire, and Languiſh out my Days
Far from the Roads of Pleaſure, or of Praiſe :
Quit ſweet *Hyde-Park* for dull Provincial Air ;
And change the Play-Houſe for a Country-Fair :

With

With fneaking Parfons beaftly Bumpers quaff,
At low Conceits, and vile Conundrums laugh;
Toaft to the Church, and talk of Right Divine:
And Herd with Squires--more noify than their Swine

Muft Heroes fuffer fuch Difgrace as This?
O Curft Effects of Honourable Peace!

.

There was a Time--O! yes there was a Time--
(E'er Poverty made Luxury a Crime,)
When Marigolds in Porridge were a Jeft;
And Soups were us'd to introduce the Feaft.
Then French Ragouts were Orthodox and Good
And Trufles held no Herefy in Food.
Nor to eat Mackarel was judg'd High-Treafon,
Tho' Goosberries as yet were not in Seafon.
But under *H—ley*'s frugal Difpenfation.
Thefe Vanities require a Reformation.
Scourg'd by his Wand, and Humbled by his Sway,
I've learn'd to fuit my Diet to my Pay;
And Now can fanctify, with folemn Face,
A heavy Dumpling with a formal Grace.

In Aukward Plenty flovenly I Dine :
And nappy Ale fupplies the want of Wine.
No nice *Dyferts* my learned Palate pleafe.
To fill up Chinks —a Slice of *Suffolk Cheefe.*
　And muft then Heroes Nibble *Suffolk-Cheefe?*
O *Curft Effects of* Honourable Peace '

But ah ' the hardeft Part is ftill behind----
The Fair too, Gentle *Harry,* prove Unkind.
Think then how wretchedly my Life muft pafs!
For what's this World, my Friend, without a Lafs?
Poor be my Lot, Inglorious be my State,
Give me but---Woman, I'll abfolve my Fate.
But 'tis in vain.————
Th' ungrateful Sex, as fenfelefs as unjuft,
To Feed their Pride, will even ftarve their Luft.
And fool'd by Equipage and empty Show,
Quit the Tough Souldier for the Lathy Beau.
I, who fo oft my forward Zeal have fhow'd,
And in their Service fpent my warmeft Blood,

Am

Am Now reduc'd, (hard Fate!) for want of Pelf,
To fight the Jesuit's Battle by my self.

Must Heroes suffer such Disgrace as This?
O Curst Effects of Honourable Peace!

The Fourth Eclogue of VIRGIL *Imitated.*

SIcilian *Muse* exalt thy tuneful Voice:
Not always make the Woods and Groves
(thy Choice.

Or, if that humbler Theme you still pursue,
Make the Groves worthy of a Consul's View.

---

* This ECLOGUE was Composed in Honour of CAIUS
ASINUS POLLIO, under whose *Consulship*, and by whose
happy *Mediation* the Famous PEACE of PUTEOLI had
been lately Concluded, and ROME thereby Delivered
from the Pressures under which it had Laboured while
SEXTUS POMPEIUS (who was before possessed of SI-
CILY, and at War with OCTAVIANUS and ANTHONY)
had by means of his Fleet, cut off all Provisio~ from the
the City. POLLIO having a SON Born to him at That
Time, The POET Celebrates His *Nativity* with all the
Glorious Circumstances that were the Consequence of so
Fortunate a Conjuncture, and to Adorn His Subject Bor-
roweth many Things besides from the SYBILLINE *Pro-*
phecies That have been since Applied by the Piety of some
FATHERS of the CHURCH to the Birth of CHRIST

The

The Time is come the *Sybil* long Foretold,
Reftoring the *Saturnian* Age of Gold.
Again *Aftræa* is return'd to Earth :
And a new Race defcends of Heav'nly Birth.
O Chafte *Lucina* ! thy kind Aid Beftow ;
(Lo ! Thy *Apollo* rules the World below)
Difcharge the Mother of her pregnant Load,
And quick Reveal to Light the Infant God.
And Thou O *Pollio* ! chofe by fmiling Fate,
From thy great Confulfhip fhall give this *Æra* Date.
If any Seeds of Vice fhall dare appear, ⎰
Thy bright Example, and fuccefsful Care, ⎱
Shall free the World at once from Guilt, and Fear.
Th' Illuftrious Babe for future Sway decreed,
Belov'd by Gods, the Life of Gods fhall lead :
Long with Hereditary Virtues Reign ;
And late Afcend his Native Skies again.

The Grateful Earth to greet her Infant King,
Shall facred Wreaths of Circling Ivy bring :
While *Flora* decks with various Art the Ground,
And *Zephyrs* fcatter Her Perfumes around.

At

At thy *Approach*, bleft B o y ! fhall ftrait remove
Each *rougher Kind* that's *Enemy* to *Love*.
The *Prowling Wolf* no more fhall *hunt* for *Prey*;
The *Ox* and *Lion* fhall together *play*;
The *Serpent* lofe his *Sting*, each pois'nous *Weed*
Shall *die*, and S y r i a n *Rofes flourifh* in their
(Stead.

But When, contemplating thy *Father's Praife*,
Thy *ripen'd Thought* fhall *Emulation* raife
To *urge* Thy *Fate* the fame *Heroic Ways*,
The *dreary Wafte* fhall rife with *wavy Corn*;
The *blufhing Grape* in Clufters load the *Thorn*;
And *Pearls* of *Honey-Dew* the *rugged Oak* adorn.
Yet ftill *fome Footfteps* fhall of *Fraud* remain.
The *greedy Mariner*, in hopes of *Gain*,
Shall tempt the *Dangers* of the *faithlefs Main*,
Cities with *Walls* fhall be incompafs'd round;
Troops fhall *embark*, and *Martial Trumpets* found;

H   *Greece*

GREECE shall again a new ACHILLES boast,
And TROY once more lament *her Glory* lost.

   But as thy *firmer Years* to *Manhood* rise,
The *Port* no more shall hear the *Sailor*'s Cries;
Traffick shall cease, alike in ev'ry Land
All things shall be produc'd by NATURE's boun-
                              (teous Hand.
The sharpned *Share* no more shall vex the *Soil*,
Nor the luxuriant *Vine* demand the *Pruner*'s Toil.
The lusty *Hind* no more shall yoke the *Ox*,
Nor for the TYRIAN *Merchant* sheer his *Flocks*.
Unborrow'd *Lustre* shall the *Fleece* adorn,
And native *Gold* and *Purple* shall be *Shorn*.
In FATE's *eternal Volume* 'tis *decreed*.
And the glad Years come rowling on with happy
                              (*Speed*.

   Advance; and to thy destin'd Honours move,
O *Darling Care!* O *genuine Seed of* JOVE!
                              Aloft

Aloft behold the *Gods* inthron'd in *State*,
While *Heaven* inclines beneath the *glorious*
(*Weight.*
Gay looks the *Earth* ; the *Skies* ferenely *fair* ;
Calm are the *Seas*, and *Breezes* fan the *Air*.
Each *jarring Element* forgets its *Rage*,
Pleas'd with the Profpect of the *coming Age*.

O ! that Kind *Heaven*, propitious to my *Vow*,
Would to my *Life* fo long a *Space* allow :
To celebrate the *Bleffings* of thy *Reign* !
Not *Thracian* ORPHEUS with his pow'rful *Strain*,
Nor LINUS fhould the envy'd *Prize* obtain :
Though each great *Parent* did their *Sons* infpire,
And PHOEBUS with CALLIOPE confpire.
Should PAN's own *Song* be with my *Numbers* try'd,
And his own ARCADY the *Prize* decide ;
Ev'n PAN himfelf, who with my *Numbers* vy'd,
Should lofe the *Prize*, tho' ARCADY decide.

See !

See! fee! thy MOTHER * *Smiles*, Aufpicious
BOY!
She owns her Ten Months Qualms o'erpaid with
(Joy.
The *Parents Frowns* the haplefs Child fhould
(dread :
† No GOD fhall grace his *Board*, nor GODDESS
(blefs his *Bed*.

---

* The ANCIENTS took the *Omen* of the Future *Good* or *Ill*
Fortune of CHILDREN from the *Kind* or *Sullen Regards* of the
MOTHER upon the INFANT's being prefented to her foon
after its *Birth*   And in the fame manner looked upon it as a
Sign of a *Lucky Genius* in the CHILD   if it could *Diftinguifh*,
and, as it were, *Acknowledge* the *Fondnefs* of the PARENT
† This COMMINATION relates to the *APOTHEOSIS* of
the HEATHENS   which confifted in the HERO's being
Admitted, after his *Tranfiation*, to the *Mafs* of the GODS, and
the *Embraces* of fome GODDESS

TO HIS
Grace the Duke of ARGYIL.

APRIL 1714.

WHILE You, my LORD, by *Birth* and
(*Virtue* Great,

Depend not on the giddy Turns of State,

Nor aw'd by *Threats*, nor by vain *Flatt'ry* sway'd,

Can tamely see your *Country*'s Cause Betray'd;

But *Brave* and *Wise* with equal Merit claim

The *Gen'ral*'s Triumph, and the *Patriot*'s Fame:

In *Camps* ador'd, in *Senates* too rever'd;

By good Men *honour'd*, and by bad Men *fear'd:*

Tho' far retir'd from the ambitious Throng,

Soft Images alone employ *my Song*,

The

The *Muse* inamour'd with thy fair Renown,
Quits her lov'd *Groves* to feek the bufy *Town*.

When with impartial Eyes we COURTS furvey,
And fee what *Infects* in That *Sun-fhine* play;
How *Vice* and *Folly* moft Preferments fhare;
And what *dull Rogues* are *thoughtlefs Monarch.*

(Care;

What *Mimick Nobles* do the *Robe* difgrace,
From *Dunghils* rais'd to *Dignity* and *Place*;
Such upftart Giants, who were Pigmies born,
Tempt not our *Envy*, but provoke our *Scorn*.
Thofe Titles only true Refpect can give,
Which bold Exploits, or gen'rous Acts atchieve:
When Men, fuperior by a Right of Fate,
(But ah! how far unlike the *Vulgar Great*)
With Dauntlefs Courage, and a Godlike Mind,
By *Arts* improve, or *Arms* relieve Mankind.
This be thy Praife---who, while the *Star* you wear,
Are lefs diftinguifh'd by That Mark you bear,

Of

Of *Royal Favour* on your *Noble Breaſt*,

Than by a *Soul* of ev'ry *Grace* poſſeſs'd.

Aſpiring, Gallant, Liberal, and *Good,*

Each Action blazons your illuſtrious Blood,

Which through ſucceſſive *Heroes* ſtill has run,

But ne'er before with ſuch *Advantage* ſhone.

The Beams your *Youthful Dawn* did firſt diſplay,

Foretold the Brightneſs of your *Future Day.*

Early you enter'd on the World's great Stage ;

Saw, and Deſpis'd the Follies of the Age :

Forſaking *Pleaſure,* and Diſdaining *Reſt,*

The Thirſt of *Glory* fir'd your daring Breaſt.

Expos'd to *Dangers,* and Inur'd to *Care,*

You firſt Deſerv'd the *Lawrel* which you wear ;

For the *Fair Prize* you Thought no *Labours* hard.

When *Honour* call'd, to *ſuffer* was *Reward.*

Unſatisfy'd, tho' Foremoſt in the Race

As you *advanc'd,* you *quick'ned* ſtill your Pace ;

Till

Till long *Experience*, and superior *Sense*,

Gain'd you, at last, your *just Preheminence*

FORTUNE, *Fantastick* in her *Choice*, we find

Rarely to those, whom *Nature* Favours, *Kind:*

But here *Both Blessings* we behold compleat,

In You those *Winding Streams* united meet.

By just Degrees acquainted with it's Weight,

Your *Virtue* sinks not underneath your *State.*

No *Luxury* betrays your Thoughts to *Ease.*

No Starts of *Fancy* on your *Judgment* seize.

No *Pride* insults ; no *Vanity* prevails.

Justice and *Candour* poize the equal Scales.

Tho' *Foe* to All whose Pow'r affects *Excess,*

You stoop, like *Heav'n,* to hearken to *Distress.*

Kind without *Affectation* or *Disguise,*

Your *Heart* makes good the Promise of your *Eyes.*

False Heroes, rais'd by undeserv'd Success,

Jealous of Others *Merit,* make it Less.

You,

You, like the SUN, *essentially* are Bright,

Lend to the meaner Orbs a Portion of your Light :

Aid the young Vigour of a rising Name ;

Point out the Quarry, and provoke to Fame.

Possess'd of all for which fond Mortals toil,

You fear no *Rival*, and can want no *Foil*.

In various Lands your *Skill* and *Valour* long

Supply'd fresh Wonders to the Poet's Song.

The proud IBERIAN, and the faithless GAUL,

Have seen their Tow'rs beneath your Thunder fall.

Where e'er you steer'd, successful prosp'rous Gales

Favour'd your Course, and fill'd your spreading

(Sails.

But *now* the surly Drum, and sprightly Fife,

No longer wake the drowsy World to Strife :

PEACE is ordain'd. ———

And O ! that *diff'rent Wars* did not succeed,

And *Civil Fury* make the Nation bleed,

While *Faction* does in ev'ry Place declaim,

And *Malice* blots out the Records of *Fame*.

I   No

No *Faith* is kept, no *Quarter* is allow'd,

Among thefe *Ruffian Champions* of the Crowd.

Each *hot-brain'd Fool* pleads Merit, if he can

Draw his vile Pen, and ftab fome *envy'd Man.*

Enough my *Mufe* — Reftrain thy juft Difdain —

Thy Bus'nefs is to *Praife,* and not *Complain.*

And you, MY LORD, in confcious Virtue bold,

Carelefs and unconcern'd the *Storm* behold,

Firm as the deathlefs Gods you keep your Courfe ,

Drive through the Waves, and Baffle all their Force.

Vain their Attempts ! who wou'd the Man invade,

Whofe *Arm* muft Conquer, and whofe *Voice* Per-

(fuade-

(For BRITAIN's *Annals* fhall with Pride record

Your *Tongue* no lefs victorious than your *Sword.*

That *pow'rful Eloquence* muft needs fucceed,

Where *Art* and *Nature* both united plead :

Where *Strength* and *Beauty* do the *Charm* compofe,

Keen as the *Thiftle, Sweeter* than the *Rofe.*)

With

With double Weapons you your Foes engage,
Convince their *Reason*, or Disarm their *Rage*
Unlike the num'rous Herd of senseless *Braves*,
Who, Tools to *Statesmen*, or their *Fortune*'s Slaves,
Hire out for low Rewards their Health and Ease,
The *Plagues of War*, or *Lumber of a Peace*.
In either State you challenge our Esteem ;
The *Soldier*'s Darling, and the *Gownsman*'s Theme.
MINERVA so at ATHENS was confess'd,
With *Olive* crown'd, or in bright *Armour* dress'd.

Amidst the Cares, the Hurry and the Strife,
That fill the busy Scenes of *Publick Life*,
Your GRACE too sometimes does the Leisure find.
With *gentler* Arts to entertain your Mind.
Tho' train'd to *nobler Wars*, you don't disdain
To listen to the *Combats of the Plain* :
The *Trumpet*'s Clangor, and the *Cannon*'s Noise,
Drown not the *Music* of the *Shepherd*'s Voice.

Few

Few in this dull degen'rate Iron Age,

Who boaſt the *Martial,* ſhare the *Tuneful* Rage.

In You great *Nature* ſhew'd herſelf profuſe ;

And form'd at once a *Hero* and a *Muſe.*

To *either Laurel* you have juſt pretence ;

Your COUNTRY's *Ornament,* and her *Defence.*

Fragment

Fragment of a LETTER

To the HONOURABLE

Mr. JAMES BRUDENELL.
1714.

CUrse on the *lazy, frowning, treach'rous Tribe!*
Who meanly wou'd our *Freedom* circumscribe;
And bred Themselves in *Slav'ry* and in *Vice,*
Would proftitute our *Reafon* to their *Lies.*
Miftake me not —— with *Reverence* I Bow,
And bend my humbled Heart *devoutly* low
To *Thofe good Men,* who *zealous* but *fincere,*
Serve at the ALTAR with Religious Fear,
Practife th' *Aufterities* they gravely Teach,
And in their *Lives* as well as *Sermons* Preach.
Such are the *Guardian Angels* of Mankind;
All muft adore their *Light* who are not *Blind.*

BUt

But when some sawcy *Pedant* of the Schools

Would bridle *Senates* by Fantastick Rules ;

When *Mother* C H u R C H turns *Bawd* to Regal
(Pow'r,

That her black Locusts may the Land devour,

Each honest BRITON should assert his Right,

And put those *Spiritual Dragoons* to Flight.

Too fully did a *late Example* show

What ill Effects from *Superstition* flow.

Our *Laws* and *Treaties* were become a Jest,

And *blind Obedience* was the only *Test.*

Some *Prigg Divine* was ready still at hand,

With *spread Phylactery,* and *well-starch'd Band,*

(The solemn Ensigns of the Fop's Command)

To Recommend the Folly to the Land.

All Orders and Degrees of Men infected,

Acted as the smooth *Hypocrites* directed

Laymen and *Priests* were huddled in the Cry,

And *Atheists* wrangled for a *Mystery.*

Ev'n

Ev'n *Whores* wou'd Cant *Religion* (so they mock'd
(her!

And lewdly TOASTED to the CHURCH and *Doctor*;

Rail'd at the *Taxes*, grumbled at the *War*;

While *Love* (poor Things!) was but their second
(Care;

For when Oppress'd with *Miseries* like *These*,

How could they *Cultivate the Arts of Peace?*

On

On FRIENDSHIP.

To the HONOURABLE
Collonel WILLIAM STANHOPE.
1715.

SAY, Gentle STANHOPE, for Thou well can'ſt
(tell

The happy *Charms* that in True FRIENDSHIP
(dwell,

Say, why thoſe *Charms* ſo ſeldom long endure,

Why Few e'er Taſte the gen'rous *Bleſſing* Pure ;

But Moſt ſtill find that *Cordial Wine* of Life,

With fulſome *Flatt'ry* ſtum'd, or ſowr'd with *Strife*.

The Cauſe ſeems This : To Vanity reſign'd,

Fancy not *Reaſon* rules our wayward Mind.

We

We feek not *Virtue* in the Man we Love,
But fuch affect, who *Like* what we *Approve.*
With forc'd *Complacency*, and venal *Smiles,*
The *Harlot* thus, and *Parafite* Beguiles.
The dear Diffemblers we with *Pride* believe,
Nor think fuch *civil Creatures* can Deceive.
When *Young* Unfkilful in the World's falfe Arts,
Carelefs w'unlock to ev'ry Gueft our Hearts;
Till better Taught, we by Experience find,
Smooth Looks are *Artifice*, and *Vows* are *Wind.*
Then *Craftier* grown (as CULLIES turn to ROOKS)
We try, perhaps, the *Cheat* on other Folks,
Revenge the Suff'rings of our heedlefs *Youth*,
And to our *Int'reft* facrifice our *Truth.*

But *Virtue* in a FRIEND will not fuffice,
He fhould not only *Honeft* be, but *Wife.*
Difcreetly *Bold*, and mannerly *Severe*,
Averfe to *Court*, or to *Offend* the Ear,

K   *Cautious*

Cautious, to fkreen from *publick* View, or Shame,
Thofe Faults which he in *private* can't but Blame.
Some, who'd difdain to act a *treach'rous Part,*
Turn Villains out of *Gaiety of Heart* ;
And, to indulge their wanton *Ridicule,*
Will *Shock* a *modeft* Man to *Pleafe* a *Fool :*
For *Fools* are ever on the *laughing Side* ;
And nothing eafier is than to *Deride.*
The Pert *Buffoon,* for Mifchief only fit,
Is but, at beft, the *Jackanapes* of *Wit :*
And fometimes Lafh'd for his Impertinence,
The *Fop* proves merry at his own *Expence.*
Such coarfe rude Freedoms are not to be born.
Malice is lefs Provoking far than *Scorn.*

. FRIENDSHIP's the higheft *Elegance* of Mind,
Few know to *Relifh* Pleafure fo *refin'd.*
As POETRY can ne'er be Learn'd by *Art,*
(For Heav'n the tuneful Talent muft impart.)

So

So FRIENDSHIP feems a *Genius* to require,
Some *Spark* peculiar of *Celeftial* Fire,
To guide our *Choice* by its unerring Light,
And wing our *Paffions* in their noble Flight.
Where this bright Flame is kindled in the Soul,
It Mounts apace, and Spreads without controul.
The pregnant Seeds lye long perhaps conceal'd,
But O ! how fierce the Blaze, when once reveal'd !
Thus have we feen a fecret wondrous Charm,
At the firft View of one expos'd to Harm,
With fond Concern a *Stranger*'s Breaft alarm.
The Call of NATURE, he with Joy obey'd,
Nor waited for *Reflexion*'s flower Aid :
Swift as a Wifh with *Extacy* he mov'd ;
And hurry'd to embrace the *New belov'd.*

When we confider, in this *Mortal* State,
How None are fhelter'd from the Bolts of *Fate* ,
What fudden Storms arife within our Sphere,
And change the Face of the inverted Year ;

What

Methinks we should in *social Cares* unite,

Nor add our *Indolence* to FORTUNE's *Spite* ;

But by Compassion of our Brother's Woe,

Engage his Help against the common Foe.

And tho' alike the PULPIT and the STAGE,

Have both debauch'd to *Rage*, or *Vice*, the Age,

Yet e'en in *these flagitious factious* Days,

Some I could Name (and such as all must Praise)

Whom this *Benign*, this *Tender* Spirit sways.

To Merit *just*, to sad Misfortune *kind*,

Now *Pity* melts, now *Zeal* inflames their Mind.

But O ! in vain the grateful MUSE would aim

Her *Duty*, or their *Bounty* to proclaim ;

(To whom my Soul bends more devoutly low,

Than *Mitred Hypocrites* at Altars Bow)

My faint *Expressions* my *Ideas* wrong ;

My *Heart*'s ill represented by my *Tongue*.

Some *Features* seem to mock the *Painter*'s Skill.

'Tis hard to draw a STANHOPE, or ARGYLL.

Le CHEVALIER *sans soucis.*

I.

LET *Whig* and *Tory*, WILL, Debate,
        And in Defence of *Church* or *State*
                Proclaim their *zealous Folly*;
While we, ingenious for our Eafe,
Contrive our own *dear felves* to pleafe,
                And banifh *Melancholy.*

II. The

II.

The GAY the WITTY and the FAIR,

Are all the *Parties* worth our Care;

　　　The Reſt would but *Enſlave* Us.

Let Us adore the GOD of *Wine*,

Submit to BEAUTY's *Right Divine*,

　　　And truſt to *Chance* to ſave Us.

In

In Imitation of CATULLUS, ad Seipsum.

Mifer CATULLE *definas ineptire,*
Et, quod vides periffe, perditum ducas.

PRithee, PACK, the *Strife* give over,
    Yield a *Game* you can't recover.
Once, 'tis true, thy *Days* were *Fair,*
Free from *Clouds* of jealous *Care* ;
When the lovely loving MAID
All thy *Vows* with *Warmth* repaid ;
With a Thoufand Ways of *Toying,*
Still *Inviting,* never *Cloying.*
Once, indeed, thy *Days* were *Fair,*
Free from *Clouds* of jealous *Care* ;
But fince grown *Coquet* and *Vain,*
She rejects thee with *Difdain.*

Quit the *Fickle*, *Falſe*, *Ingrate* ;

And revenge her *Scorn* with *Hate*.

Well ! from hence I'll break my *Chains*.

Lᴏᴠᴇ adieu, and all thy *Pains !*

Lᴇsʙɪᴀ too, perhaps, may *Mourn*,

When *Neglected*, in her *Turn* ;

When ſhe ſits whole Nights *Alone*,

Sought by *Few*, *Believ'd* by *None*.

Who will now that *Boſom* Preſs,

Mad with *Joy*, and *ſweet Exceſs* ?

Who will *Mark* thoſe *Lips* with *Kiſſes* ?

Who *Diſſolve* in *riper Bliſſes* ?

Well ! at length I've broke my *Chains*.

Lᴏᴠᴇ adieu, and all thy *Pains !*

The LOVER'S *Parting.*
To a French *Air.*

I.

SHE. HARK! the Trumpet founds to Arms,
   O fatal Noife!
 Hark! the Trumpet founds to Arms,
   Adieu my Joys!
 Ah! the thoufand Fears I prove,
 For thy *Life,* and for my *Love.*

II.

HE. Ceafe thy Plaints, and dry thy Tears,
   My Charming Maid!
 Ceafe thy Plaints, and dry thy Tears,
   Nor Fate upbraid.
 Heav'n that makes Mankind its Care,
 Guards the *Brave* to ferve the *Fair.*
   L   STANZA

STANZAS.

To the Tune of COLIN'S COMPLAINT.

I.

YE NYMPHS who frequent those sweet Plains,
  Where THAME's gentle Current doth glide,
Who whilom have heard my glad *Strains*,
Nor grateful *Attention* deny'd.
With Pity, ye FAIR, O reflect
On the cruel *Reverse* of my *Fate* !
See *Constancy* paid with *Neglect*,
And *Fondness* rewarded with *Hate* !

II.

How *joyous* and *gay* was each *Hour*,
How wing'd with soft *Pleasures* They fled,
E'er shipwreck'd on HUMBER's dull Shore,
By LOVE my poor *Heart* was betray'd'

Fo

For there the *Deceiver* doth dwell,

Whofe Charms have fo long been my Theme:

In *Beauty* the MAID doth excel,

But is *Fickle* and *Wild* as the *Stream.*

III.

If Averfe to my *Courtſhip* at firſt,

SHE had *check'd* my *fond infant Defire,*

Her *Coldneſs* had left me leſs *curſt,*

And, perhaps, had *extinguiſh'd* my *Fire.*

But a thouſand *falſe Arts* SHE employ'd,

(*Ingenious* and *wanton* in *Ill*)

The *Paſſion* SHE *nurs'd* SHE *deſtroy'd*;

And only *Created* to *Kill.*

IV.

Yet tho' SHE *delights* in my *Smart,*

Tho' SHE *robs* me of all I held *Dear,*

Revenge is below a *brave Heart,*

I wiſh *Her* a *Lot* leſs *fevere.*

May

May the *Swain* S H E ſhall Crown with Succeſs,

By his *Kindneſs* Deſerve to be *priz'd* :

'Twould *Double*, methinks, my *Diſtreſs*,

At laſt to ſee H E R too *Deſpis'd*.

To Lady KATHARINE MANNERS.

Upon her Commending and Singing the foregoing
STANZAS.

INſpir'd by LOVE, *my tender artleſs Strains*
 Have oft, in *lonely Shades*, amus'd the *Swains:*
But ſhunn'd to venture on a *Publick Scene,*
The COXCOMB's *Envy,* or the CRITICK's *Spleen,*
Now *more aſſur'd* the *modeſt* POET *Writes,*
Since YOU vouchſafe to *Sing* what HE *Indites.*
When *BRITAIN's faireſt* NYMPH approves my
        (*Lays,*
Dull were Their *Cenſure,* and as *vain* Their *Praiſe.*
Your *Favour's* all the *Fame* my VERSE wou'd
         (boaſt;
The MUSE will ſhare the *Merit* of the TOAST.
          To

To Mr. ADDISON.

Occasioned by the News of the Victory obtained over the REBELS *in* Scotland, *by his Grace the Duke of* ARGYLL.

On Eagles Wings Immortal Scandals *fly,*
But Virtuous *Actions are but Born and* Die.
Dryd. Juv

H OW long shall, *ADDISON,* thy charm-
(ing *Lyre*

Hang up *unstrung* amid the *tuneful Quire* ;

T H o u ! Who with ev'ry *Master-Stroke* of *Art*

To *Love* can sooth, or rouse to *Rage* the Heart ?

One *Labour* more at least, sweet P o E T, yield ;

And sing DUNBLAIN, as well as BLENHEIM Field.

GER-

GERMANIA *there* was fav'd by CHURCHILL's
(Deed;
And BRITAIN *here* by CAMPBELL's Arm was
(freed.
Who can to CAMPBELL's *Worth* a *Verse* refuse?
What *Nobler Subject* for a PATRIOT-MUSE?
Of late the *Bigotry* of our *dull Times*,
Had funk the *Dignity* of *Sacred Rhimes*.
Mock-Triumphs only then fupply'd our Scenes :
Pacifick-GENERALS and *Pious*-QUEENS.
O vindicate the *Majefty* of *Verfe* !
And loftier *Things* in loftier *Song* Rehearfe.
Defcribe ARGYLL in all his *Glories* drefs'd ;
A *Godlike Soul* in *Human Shape* confefs'd :
Like Fair ADONIS *Beautiful* and *Young* ;
Like Great ALCIDES *Valorous* and *Strong* :
In CAMPS *Experienc'd*, and in COURTS *Refin'd* ,
Like FATE *Refolv'd*, and yet as WOMAN *Kind*.
If HEAV'N, *indulgent* to my *duteous Zeal*,
Had blefs'd me with fome *Portion* of *Thy Skill*,

In

In *Verse Immortal* fhould the HERO *fhine*,

And *MILTON's Thunder* had been *drown'd* in *mine*.

But I, alas! a *lower Theme* muft chufe,

(An *Ardent*, but an *Unfuccefsful* MUSE!)

Content in *humbler Numbers* to *commend*

The *Gen'rous* PATRON, and the *Tender* FRIEND.

A Bur.

A Burlesque Imitation of the First Ode of HORACE.

To my Friend Captain ANTHONY HINTON.

HINTON, whose *happy-humour'd* FACE
Proclaims thy *gen'rous jovial* RACE;
Frequent thou haft obferv'd at *Feafts*,
The various *Taftes* of diff'rent *Guefts*.
This 'SQUIRE in VENISON is a *Glutton*;
That fwears the Prince of Meats is MUTTON.
EAST-SAXONS ftick by *kindred* VEAL,
And PORK to TAR is DUCK and TEAL.
H ——— S will forfake good BEEF and MUSTARD,
To run a muck at *filthy* CUSTARD;
And THEE I've feen, with *Paunch* of YEOMAN,
Quilt CHEESECAKES like a very WOMAN.

M   PUD-

PUDDING the PARSON ftill *commends,*

Aud DUMPLING too has many *Friends.*

Yet oft in vain an honeft HOST,

May lavifh forth *Boil'd, Bak'd,* and *Roaft :*

Some *travell'd* FOP, more *Nice* than *Wife,*

Shall *wholfome Luxury* defpife,

And rife from Table in Difdain,

For want of RAGOUTS and CHAMPAIN.

To me, whom Frugal NATURE meant

A Fool on *eafier Terms* content,

Nought comes amifs that Fate affigns,

SOUPS, HASHES, FRICASSES, and CHINES :

But, fince each Man will chufe his *Difh,*

If I too might indulge my *Wifh,*

When in the circling Annual Dance

NOVEMBER fhall her *Ides* advance,

To grace my BIRTH-DAY ev'ry Year,

TURKEY fhall Crown my *Bill of Fare.*

The

The RETREAT.

To ✶ ✶ ✶ ✶ ✶ ✶

WHILST within the *silent Grove*,
Favour'd by *Auspicous* LOVE,
YOU in PEACEFUL TRIUMPHS *Reign*,
All the *Trophies* all the *Spoils*,
(Tho' so *Pompous*) seem but *Vain*,
That *Reward* the WARRIOR's *Toils*.

See the *chearful Hours* advance,
Unmolested in their *Dance* !
Busy Hopes, and *Anxious Care*
Change not *here* by turns the *Scene :*
All your DAYS are *cloudless-Fair ;*
All your EV'NINGS are *Serene.*

On

On Bright *CYNTHIA's Bosom* laid,
CYNTHIA for *Inchantment* made!
Through a *World* of *Sweets* you *rove*,
Unconfin'd as *wanton Air* :
When did e'er AMBITION prove
Joys so *Tempting*, so *Sincere* ?

Let the *Storms* of *adverse* FATE,
Fright the RICH, and *Shake* the GREAT ;
Let the WAVES *tumultuous rise* ;
In *That* HARBOUR YOU're *Secure* :
Hid from FORTUNE's *prying Eyes*,
HE's most HAPPY, who's OBSCURE.

ESSAYS

ESSAYS

ON

Study *and* Converſation.

In Two LETTERS

TO

DAVID CAMPBELL, Eſq;

Who deſired me to give him ſome
RULES in Writing for his future
CONDUCT.

ESSAYS

ON

STUDY and CONVERSATION.

LETTER I.

Of STUDY.

 I P S W I C H, *June* 1714

Can never enough Applaud the Resolution you have taken, my Dearest *CAMPBELL*, to distinguish your self from the Herd of idle young Fellows about the Town, by making a right Use of That Leisure you at present enjoy, to the Improvement of your REASON, and the

Form-

Forming of your M A N N E R S. The U N D E R-
S T A N D I N G, like *a tender* P L A N T, requires
Pains to *Raife* it, and Care to *Preferve* it. Yours
hath, 'tis true, all the Signs of *Health* one can
defire, and if we may guefs at the *Fruit* that is
to be expected from its *riper Seafons* by the *Blof-
foms* it puts forth in its *Spring*, your Friends have
a great deal to Hope, and little to Fear for you.
Yet this ought not to tempt you to Negligence,
or Supinenefs : It fhould the rather encourage
your Induftry in continuing to cultivate it, that
it may Grow, and Spread, and Flourifh, and
become, in Time, not only an *Ornament* to
Your Self, but a *Shelter* to *Others*.

N o w there are *Two Ways* only by which we
can Pretend to Advance Ourfelves in *general
Knowledge*, namely, by S t u d y and C o n-
v e r s a t i o n. When we joyn *Both Thefe*
together, we give the laft Perfection to our
. *Judgments :* But if we truft to Either of Them
fingly, we are fure to be Mifled. They who
live fhut up in their Clofets, and fecluded from
the Commerce of Mankind, can have but very
narrow and contracted Views of Things. They
will be apt upon all Occafions, from *probable
Suggeftions*, to make *Univerfal Conclufions* ; and
Fond of the Schemes they had erected in their

own

own Heads, get an Habit of *Pofitivenefs*, *Mo-rofenefs*, and *Self-fufficiency*. On the other Side, when We give up all our Time to Company, We grow, by Degrees, as it were *Strangers to our own Thoughts*; Change our *Opinion* as we do our *Acquaintance*, and, Governed lefs by *Principle* than *Example*, frequently Sacrifice *Virtue* and *good Senfe* to *Complacency* and *Fafhion*. It is ne-ceffary now and then to *Retire*, that we may *Re-cruit* our Minds by *Books*, and it is as ufeful fometimes to mingle in *Society*, to *Exercife* them by *Difcourfe*. But if We Over-charge them with the *Firft*, We fhall abound with *Crudities:* If We are conftantly engaged in the *Latter*, We muft be foon *Exhaufted*. The Want of Difcretion in *This Point*, is the Caufe we meet with fo many SCHOLARS who are PEDANTS, and fo many MEN *of* FORTUNE who are BLOCK-HEADS

BUT Reflexions at large have feldom any other Effect than to Amufe. We muft make our Applications Directly, when we intend they fhould take Place. I fhall therefore lay out the reft of my Thoughts on this Subject with regard to *Your particular Circumftances* and *Genius*. I fhall confider you as *a young Gentleman*, who

N   have

have no Defign to devote your felf either to
L E T T E R S, or B U S I N E S S, as your *Profeffi-*
on , but who would indulge your *Tafte* for the
One by *Reading*, and improve your *Talent* for
the Other by *Obfervation* ; who would not be
altogether an idle Dreamer in the *Philofophical*,
nor a reftlefs Adventurer in the *Ambitious* World
One who, upon the whole, prefer *good Senfe* to
Learning, *Prudence* to *Politicks*, *Agreeablenefs*
to *Popularity*. This is the *Idea* I have form'd of
YOU , and according to *This Plan* I fhall Pro-
pofe the *Materials* that feem to me the moft Proper for your Purpofe.

T O begin then with the *Firft Article*, That
of S T U D Y. The B O O K S I would recommend to your Perufal, as moft fubfervient to the
Ends above-mentioned, are of *the following Kinds :*
DIVINITY, *MORALITY*, *NATURAL*
and *CIVIL HISTORY*, *LOGIC*, *RHE-*
TORIC, *POETRY*, and the *lighter Compo-*
fitions of *WIT* and *GALLANTRY*. I fhall
juft Touch upon each of *Thefe Heads*, and, having marked out the *Roads* through which you
are to *Travel*, will leave it to your own *Choice*,
where to make your longeft *Stay*, and exercife
your greateft *Curiofity*.

I. DI-

I. DIVINITY is the *Knowledge of those Matters* which RELIGION makes *necessary* for us to *Believe* and *Practise*. And *This* certainly Deserves *our most serious Attention.* It is justly thought a *Disgrace*, and is always found an *Inconvenience* to be *Ignorant* of the LAWS of one's COUNTRY. But much more *Scandalous* is the *Neglect*, more *Fatal* will be the *Consequences*, if we live in *Ignorance*, or *Contempt* of those of GOD; and such we should esteem RELIGION to be. The many *Sects*, indeed, that have prevailed by Turns, or at the same Time in different Parts of the World, so inconsistent with EACH OTHER, and yet ALL asserted with *equal Confidence* and *Pretence* to DIVINE AUTHORITY, have inclined some Men, in all Ages, to look upon RELIGION as the *Craft* of *Priests*, or an *Invention* of designing *Politicians*. But THESE UNBELIEVERS have, for the most Part, been found to be Men of light Minds, and profligate Manners. The Vanity of the IDOL should not make us Renounce the DEITY. And supposing even that the Being of a PROVIDENCE were a Thing in doubt, on whatever side of the *Question* the *Truth* may lie, the *Importance* of it is such, that we ought, at least, to allow it *a fair Enquiry*.

N 2

RE-

RELIGION may be divided into *Natural*
and *Revealed* The Former hath been more
generally Agreed among Mankind than the Latter. But They who have Leisure and Abilities
should search into the *Principles* of BOTH ; and
not owe their *Opinions* to *Chance*, or the *Fashion*
of the *Place* where they Live. There are two
Treatises, one writ by Bishop *WILKINS*, the
other by Archbishop *TILLOTSON* (which
stands at the Beginning of his Works) That may
supply the Want of all others upon the First
Head. And in These you will find all the Proofs
the Nature of the Subject can admit, urged with
such clear and solid Reasoning, as cannot, I
think, fail to establish your Mind without wa-
vering. As to *Revealed* RELIGION (I mean
the *Christian*) GROTIUS hath undertaken to
defend the *Truth*, and *LOCKE* the *Reasonableness* of its *Institution* and *Doctrine*. Besides These,
you will do well to read *DU PIN* upon the
Canon of the SCRIPTURES, and then proceed
to *Examine* and *Compare* the SCRIPTURES
Themselves , and, where you shall be at a loss
about the Sense, consult the *Commentators* ; a-
mong whom *POOLE, HAMMOND* and
WHITBY,, are reckoned in the first Class.
How-

However, give not up your Belief implicitly to
to any of their Interpretations, but follow your
own Reason in the laft Refort. From hence
you may defcend to take a View of the Conftitution of the C H U R C H of *E N G L A N D*
in its *Articles* and *Catechifm.* Several Learned Pens have been employed in giving Ex-
pofitions of Both ; as Bifhop *B U R N E T T*, Bifhop *B E V E R I D G E*, and Archbifhop *WAKE.*
It will not be amifs likewife to Read thofe Authors who have diftinguifhed themfelves upon the
Points in Controverfy between the *Eftablifhed
Church* and the *Roman Catholicks*, or any other
Diffenters. Archbifhop *T I L L O T S O N* hath,
with great Sharpnefs of Wit, and Strength of
Argument, managed the War againft the *Papifts* ;
and the *Cafes of the* L O N D O N *Divines* (of
which Dr. *B E N N E T* hath publifhed an excellent Abridgment) are a Magazine where the moft
ufeful Weapons may be found that can be employed againft the *Nonconformifts.*

II. M O R A L I T Y treats of What is *Fit*,
What is *Decent*, What is *Commendable* in *this
World*, not What is *Neceffary* to *Salvation* in the
Next. It maketh *Virtue* the Effect of *Wifdom*,

and

and *Happiness* the Reward of *Virtue*. The Ancient HEATHENS, both POETS and PHILOSOPHERS, have left behind them many admirable *Monuments* of their *Wit* and *Learning* upon *This Topick*. The *Satires* and *Epistles* of *HORACE* are an Instance of One kind, and the *Offices* of *TULLY* are esteemed a Masterpiece in the Other. *THEOPHRASTUS, EPICTETUS, ANTONINUS,* and *SENECA,* are held in universal Veneration. These have all been *Naturalized*, and taught to speak *our* LANGUAGE. After these Reverenced Names of ANTIQUITY, I will take Leave to mention the MODERNS of our own NATION, who have Excelled in this Way, and insinuated their *Instructions* in the most *Familiar* and *Delightful* Manner, I mean the Authors of the TATLER, SPECTATOR, and GUARDIAN.

III. NATURAL HISTORY, is a Subject upon which I shall chiefly refer you to the *History of the Royal Society*, compiled by the Famous Bishop *SPRAT*, where you will meet with the best Account of the Use of *Natural* and *Experimental Philosophy*, delivered in a *Style* that is the the most perfect *Model of English Eloquence*. There are several other Pieces writ before and

since

since the Publication of that Work, by Members of the same Society, which are equally Curious and Useful.

IV. CIVIL HISTORY is, of all other Parts of Learning, the most agreeable Amusement to an idle Man, and the most instructive Entertainment to a Man of Business. Our Curiosity is perpetually Awakened by somewhat *New* and *Diverting* ; and the Remarkable *Examples* of *Persons*, and *Events* of *Things* that occur in Books of This Nature, Beheld in their true Springs of Action, suggest to us many profitable Reflections for our *Conduct* both in a *Publick*, and a *Private* Life. It is a common Complaint, that our Countrymen have succeeded worse in this sort of Writing than any other. Mr. *MILTON*, indeed, and Sir *WILLIAM TEMPLÉ* have cleared the Way, by their *Introductions*, to a *General History of* ENGLAND , and we have the Accounts of some particular *Reigns* from very good Pens, most of which are mentioned in the Preface to Sir *W. TEMPLE's Introduction* ; and the Number of those hath been lately augmented by the Noble Labours of the Lord Chancellor *CLARENDON*   But many Periods of our Story remain so Disguised, or Mangled in the

lame

lame or fabulous Relations that have been given
of them, that we are left extremely in the Dark
about thofe Times in Matters even of the greateft
Concern , and we want fome Comprehenfive Genius to go through the Whole, and thereby do
Juftice to a Nation, that hath not only Always
made a very confiderable Figure in the *Northern*
Quarter of the World, but hath, by Turns,
extended its Conqueft in almoft all the different
Parts of it.   To make what we have more Advantageous to You, I would advife you, when
you read the *Lives* of any of our K i n g s, to
read at the fame time the *Laws* that were made
during their Reign ; the *Wifdom* and *Greatnefs*
of a P r i n c e appearing as much by his *Infti-
tutions* at Home, as by his *Exploits* Abroad. You
ought likewife to acquaint your felf with the Hiftory of our Neighbouring Kingdoms and States ,
fuch more efpecially with whom we have been
long in *Alliance*, or *Commerce*. *MEZERAY's*
Hiftory of *France*, and *MARIANA's* of *Spain*,
are reputed the Beft.   The Life of *HENRY*
the Fourth of *France*, writ for the Ufe of *LEWIS*
the Fourteenth, by his Preceptor the Archbifhop
of *Paris*, is an incomparable Piece.   There are
feveral other Lives, writ by different Authors,
that may deferve your Perufal.   If you defire to
                                                    have

have a general View in a fmall Compafs, *PUF-FENDORF* will give it you in his *Introduction.* I pretend to fay nothing of the *Greek* and *Roman* Hiftorians, the Character of thofe few that are extant being commonly known, and the beft of them tranflated into *Englifh* or *French.* As for the *Originals,* you will not, I believe, find Lei-fure or Inclination to make your felf Mafter of them, efpecially the Firft. The Epitome of the *Roman Hiftory,* by Mr. *ECHARD,* and the *Antiquities* of *Rome* by Dr *KENNETT*; as likewife thofe of *Greece,* by Bifhop *POTTER,* ought to have a Place in your little Library, and will be of ufe to you in explaining many things that you may be at a Lofs, without their Affi-ftance, to underftand in the general Courfe of your Reading.

UNDER this Chapter of HISTORY, tho' in an inferior Order, may be ranked MEMOIRS, TREATIES of *Peace* or *Alliance,* LETTERS, and *Publick* ACTS of Minifters of *State,* of which there is greater Plenty in the *French* Language than in any other. Sir *W. TEMPLE,* and the Earl of *ARLINGTON*'s *Letters,* are of this kind in our *own.* The Obfervations upon the *Netherlands,* publifh'd by the Firft of thofe

O   Great

Great Men, difcover the Author's Penetration and Skill in *Politicks* ; but the many Changes that have fince happened in that *Republick*, both as to the Form of its *Government*, and the Extent of its *Dominions*, will oblige you to have Recourfe to later Accounts.

V. LOGICK is the Art of *Reafoning* , and I do not know a better Guide to fet you right in That Way than Mr. *LOCKE*'s *Effay* on *Humane Underftanding.* But you will do well to read the *Third Book* firft, That being more familiar to a young Beginner than the *Two Former.*

VI. RHETORICK is the Art of *Speaking Elegantly.* But the beft Method to attain that, is not, I think, to ftudy *Rules* , but to converfe with the *Writings*, and be Prefent frequently at the *Difcourfes* of the Greateft Mafters. We want not in our own Nation many Noble *Orators*, who have Triumphed at the *Bar*, in the *Senate*, and the *Pulpit*. I need not tell you who are looked upon as the Ornaments of the Two Firft. But You having been, perhaps, lefs inquifitive after thofe who have gained the moft Applaufe in the Laft, I fhall give you a Lift of fome Few (among many more that might be be named) who tho' they are not all Living, their Works will never Die , *viz.* Archbishop *TILLOTSON,* Sir *WILLIAM DAWES* the present Illustrious Archbishop of *York,* the Learned and Excellent Bishop *SMALRIDGE,* the late Bishop *SPRAT,* Mr. *YOUNG,* Dr. *BRADY.* Bishop *BURNETT,* Dr *SCOTT* Bishop *ATTERBURY,* and Dr. *CRADOCK,* (see his incomparable *Sermon* on *Providence,* preached before King *CHARLES* II.) If you would go farther, and desire to know what were the mighty Talents that made *CICERO* and *DEMOSTHENES* so Powerful in their own Countries, and so Admired in all others, Read the *Comparisons* of the Judicious *RAPIN,* and his Treatise of *Eloquence,* where you will find an Extract of all that is valuable in the Books of the Ancient *Rhetoricians.*

VII. Of POETRY, considered as an *Art,* I shall say nothing, there having been so many Excellent Writers who have treated of it under its several Species.   I will only Point out to you some of the principal Poets of our *own,* and the FRENCH *Nation,* and leave you to satisfy your Enquiry more at large from *DRYDEN, BOSSU, DACIER, RAPIN, ROSCOM-MON,* and *POPE.*

THE firſt in Dignity among our POETS in the *Epic* Way is without diſpute *MILTON*; but in reading Him, you muſt give a more than ordinary Attention The Height of the Subject, the Variety of Learning that is interſperſed through the whole Work, the Obſoleteneſs of many of his Terms, and the Length of his Periods, will ſoon make him grow Tedious to an Indiligent Reader, but the longer you *Contemplate*, the more you will *Admire* his *Beauties*. After you have carefully peruſed Him, and made your *own Remarks*, which always ſet down in Writing, though you fling them away afterwards (for it will, ſhould it be of no other Advantage, teach you to expreſs your Thoughts *clearly* and *pertinently*) Read what has been publiſhed by the *Criticks*, who have writ either in his *Commendation*, or *Cenſure*. Thus you will have the Satisfaction to find your *Judgment* in ſome places *confirmed*, in others *informed*, and many *Hints* ſtarted that may be of Uſe to you in Reading him again. But if you conſult his *Criticks*, before you have impartially conſidered your *Author*, you will run the Hazard of being *Prejudiced*, or, however, will not be able to diſtinguiſh your *own Obſervations* from *Thoſe* of *other People*.

SPEN

SPENSER and *COWLEY* are P o e t s too of the *Heroic* Order ; an Account of the *Writings* of the Laſt hath been given us with his *Life*, by the Incomparable Biſhop *S P R A T*.

T h e F r e n c h have nothing that ever I heard to be worth Reading in this Kind.

T R A G E D Y may juſtly claim the next Honour to the *Epic* ;   and the Greateſt *Genius* we have had in this Way was certainly *S H A K E-S P E A R*. But he is not without His Faults. He often quits the *Buſkin* to trip about in *Pantoffles*. No Man could live in thoſe Days without his *Quibble*. S t a t e s m e n and B i s h o p s *Punn'd* for *Preferment* ; while the R o y a l E x a m p l e led them into That *Emulation* It is not therefore ſurprizing that *a Stage-Poet* ſhould fall in with the Humour of the *Court*. It is more to be wondered that he could Reach the admired Heights he did, and Where he will always reign unrival'd, than that he ſhould, in Complaiſance to the vicious Taſte of the Age, ſometimes Deſcend below himſelf.   In raiſing *Pity* (one of the great Ends of T R A G E D Y) *O T W A T* has ſhewn more Skill than any of his

Con-

Contemporaries. There is fomewhat inexpreffibly moving in the *Suffering* Parts of his *Orphan*, and his VENICE *Preferved.* And he hath that Characteriftick, that *HORACE* thinks fo neceffary to a Tragic Poet who would fucceed, that is, to feem *fincerely affected* by *thofe Paffions* which he intended to *excite* in his AUDIENCE. There are fome other late Authors, who are in every one's Hands, that enjoy a very juft Reputation for this kind of Writing. Among the FRENCH, *CORNEILLE* and *RACINE* have excelled.

FOR COMEDY, *BEN. JOHNSON, BEAUMONT* and *FLETCHER*, are celebrated Names. But to confefs the Truth to you, I have never read any of them fince I was able to judge of their Characters, fo have only mentioned them in Paffing.

CONGREVE of all the Moderns, feems to me to have the righteft Turn for COMEDY. In all his Plays there is a great deal of *Lively* and *Uncommon Humour*, and fuch as yet, for the moft part, is a *Picture* of *true Life.* Befides, he hath raifed the Vein of *Ridicule*, and made the STAGE, which had been too much proftituted

to

to the Mob, *edifying* to Persons of the first Condition.   And as his *Fable* is *Diverting,* so is it wrought according to the *strictest Rules.* *WY-CHERLY* abounds in *Wit* and *Satire.* *E-THEREGE* is *Polite.* SOUTHERN is remarkable for the *Purity* of his *Diction,* and *VANBRUGH's Dialogue* is extremely *Easy,* and *well-turn'd.*

MOLIERE is acknowledged the greatest Genius the F R E N C H have ever had for C o-m e d y.

F o r SATIRE, *DRYDEN,* *RO-CHESTER,* and *BOILEAU,* have excelled all the Moderns.   The First of which Great Men distinguished himself in almost every Kind of P o e s y, and, at the same Time, deserves no less to be admired for the *Correctness,* and *Harmony* of his P r o s e.   But in his P o e t i c a l *Works,* as his *Beauties* are allowed by all to be very *Great,* so his *Faults* are confessed by the most *Partial* to his *Fame* to be very *Numerous.*

U p o n the Subjects of L O V E and P A-N E G Y R I C K, Mr. *WALLER* hath writ
better

better than any Man.   He hath at once a *Fancy*
the moſt *elevated*, *Sentiments* the moſt *delicate*,
and a *Judgment* the moſt *correct* of all our Poets.
He was the Firſt who *reformed* our *Verſification*,
and his *Numbers* will *laſt* as long as our *Lan-*
guage.   Sir *JOHN DENHAM*'s *Cooper's Hill*
has rendered him Immortal.

THE DISPENSARY of Sir *SAMUEL*
GARTH hath *Loſt* and *Gain'd* in *every Edition*.
Almoſt every Thing he left out was a *Robbery*
from the Publick : Every Thing he Added hath
been an *Embelliſhment* to his *Poem*.

Mr. *PRIOR* hath joined to a natural good
Genius an happy *Imitation* of the *Ancients*, and
the moſt elaborate *Care* in his *Compoſitions*.
One may diſcover, that the *File* and the *Chiſſel*
have been often employed in bringing his Works
to the Perfection in which we now Behold
them.

Mr. *ADDISON* is Graceful, Eaſy, Natural, and Juſt   There is nothing Redundant ;
nothing that looks like Impropriety in him.   He
Shapes his Thoughts with the greateſt Exactneſs,
and yet they are the freeſt from Conſtraint that
can

can be. HIS CHARACTER of the ENGLISH POETS is a *fine Piece*, where he hath not only defcribed their feveral *Excellencies*, but imitated their different *Styles*. HIS POEM intitled *The* CAMPAIGN, his EPISTLE from *ITALY* to the late Earl of *HALIFAX*, his TRANSLATIONS from *OVID*, his *CATO*, his LATIN POEMS, and, in a word, every Thing we have of *His Fafhion*, fhews the *laft Hand* of a *Great* MASTER.

BUT there is a Noble Author whom I have not yet mentioned, whofe POEMS it would be Thought a *Difgrace* not to have *Read*, and a much *Greater* not to have *Read* THEM with *Admiration*. For The Man muft certainly be as *Infenfible* of the *Pleafures* of LOVE, as of the *Charms* of WIT, who can look on *MYRA* with *Indifference* ; or furvey the PROGRESS of *BEAUTY*, as Defcribed by MY LORD *LANS-DOWN*, without *Rapture*.

AMONG the MISCELLANIES that were publifhed by Mr. *DRYDEN*, there are many TRANSLATIONS, and fome ORIGINAL POEMS by very good Hands. But I remember *Three little* PIECES, that infinitely pleafed

P   me me when I read them. One is a SONG by the late Earl of *DORSET*, and begins thus, *May the Ambitious ever find*, &c. The other are Two LYRICS by the Earl of *ROCHESTER* 1 *An Imitation of* CORNELIUS GALLUS 2. APOLLO's *Lamentation for the Death of* HYACINTH. I own, I had rather have been the Author of *These Three Copies* of *Verses* than of All *TOM BROWNE*'s *Works*, tho' very Few of them are without *Wit* But a *CUPID*, or a *VENUS* of *RAPHAEL URBIN*, or *CORREGGIO*, is worth a whole A u c- t i o n of *modern* PRETENDERS.

VIII. I come now to confider the *laft Article* of the firft *General Head*, The *lighter Compofi- tions* of WIT and GALLANTRY.

A n d here I fhall content my felf with giv- ing you a few Reflections upon thofe *Authors*, who have been the moft fhining in this Way, among the MODERNS. At the Head of thefe, I think, I may juftly place *St. EVREMOND*. The Delicacy of whofe *Sentiments* in FRIEND- SHIP, in LOVE, in LUXURY; his happy Turn for *genteel* RAILLERY, his *courtly* MAN- NERS, the *Propriety*, *Clearnefs*, and *Beauty* of

his

his STYLE, are Proofs of an extraordinary *Genius*, an uncommon *Observation*, and a *Commerce* with the *First* of *Mankind* He who deserves the next Rank to him, is a *Countryman* of *his own*. One who was his *Contemporary*, and had been his *Friend* and *Fellow Adventurer* in LOVE and in WAR, I mean *BUSSI RA-BUTIN*, Author of *Les Amours de Gaule*; which Book, though it is writ pretty much in the *Spirit* of *Lewdness*, hath a Thoufand irrefiftible *Graces* that are *Chafte*, and *Unfullied*. The CHARACTERS are *Fine* and *Mafterly*, the RAILLERY *pleafantly fevere*, the RELATIONS full of entertaining *Variety*, and the LANGUAGE hath the utmoft *Purity*. But it is rare to meet with a *correct Copy*.

THERE is no *Sort* of WRITING in which a Man hath a freer Scope to fhew his WIT, his HUMOUR, or his GALLANTRY, than in his LETTERS: And of thefe the *French* have publifhed the *largeft Collections*. The AUTHOR I laft mentioned, hath left behind him no lefs than *Seven Volumes*, of which the *Firft Four*, particularly thofe addreffed to Madam *SEVIG NY* (whofe ANSWERS too have an equal *Merit*) are writ in the moft *natural*, *eafy*, and *un-*

affected

affected Manner, and may ferve for a *Pattern* of *juft Writing* to all who would fucceed in the *Familiar Way*. Nor muft I pafs by, on this Occa-fion, my *old Favourite VOITURE*, whofe *Manner*, though it be very *different* from That of the *Gentleman before-mentioned*, is no lefs *Gallant*. He is, I own, the AUTHOR in the World, who can always put me into *good Hu-mour*. The inimitable *Turns* of his *Wit*, even upon the moft *barren Subjects*, his *Droll-Mirth*, his *Quotations* fo *happily* applied, free from any of that *Pedantry* fo offenfive in moft others who mingle the *learned* LANGUAGES with their *own*, his *Skill* in that hardeft Part of GOOD BREEDING, *Complimenting the* LADIES (where he never runs into *common Place*) and *Flattering the* GREAT (where he never defcends to *Servility* or *Meannefs*,) in fhort, the *Gene-rofity*, as well as *Gaiety* of his SOUL, runs through all he writes, and makes one not only read him with *Admiration*, but *Affection*. I doubt not but the *Laft*, and this *Prefent Age*, hath produced many Perfons among *our felves*, whofe *Entertainments* in *this Kind*, had they been made *Publick*, might have vied with the *Beft* of thofe of our *Neighbour Nations*. But whether it be from the *Modefty* of the AUTHORS, who were content

tent with pleafing their *Friends* and *Miftreffes*, without the *Vanity* of letting the World into the *Secret* of their *Familiarities*, or *Intrigues* ; or from the *Genius* of our PEOPLE, who are generally *Grave*, and lefs *Inquifitive* after *Pieces* of WIT, than *the more ufeful Works of* REASON; or from whatever other *Caufe* it may proceed, fo it is, that the ENGLISH have not many *Collections* of FAMILIAR LETTERS that are of *any Value.* We have indeed fome *Few* of the *Witty* Lord ROCHESTER, but *Thofe* very *imperfect*, and *mangled.* I have feen fome *Others* in the MISCELLANEA AULICA that have a *right Turn* ; among which there are *Five* or *Six* writ by King CHARLES the Second, during *his Exile*, to Mr. BENNETT, afterwards Earl of ARLINGTON, That give a TRUE IMAGE of the *carelefs* and *difengaged Temper* of *That happy-humoured* MoNARCH. I will add to Thefe a fmall Volume of *Letters*, writ by the late *ingenious* Mr. WALSH, (whofe DEFENSE too of the FEMALE SEx added very much to the *Reputation* of his WIT, though not much, I believe, to his *Conquefts* among the LADIES.) But the Beft *Letters* I have met with in *our Tongue* are thofe of the celebrated Mrs. PHILIPS : They are Addreffed to

Sir

Sir *CHARLES COTTEREL*, *Grandfather*, I
suppose, to the *Gentleman* who bears that *Title*
at present.   As they are directed all to the
same Person, so they run *All* in the *same
Strain*, and seem to have been employed in the
Service of a *refined* and *generous* F R I E N D S H I P.
In a word, they are such as a W O M A N of *Spirit* and *Virtue* would write to a C O U R T I E R
of *Honour*, and *true Gallantry*.   I don't know
whether I have *Many* of *my Opinion*, but I must
declare they please *my Taste extremely*.   But if
you would be entertained with some that are
more *Luscious*, let me recommend to you the
SYLVIA and *PHILANDER* of Mrs. *BEHN*.

I am unwilling to Dwell longer on *This Subject*, lst at a Time, when I have been critici-
sing upon other *People*'s L E T T E R S, I should
grow *Tedious*, and want an *Excuse* for *my Own*.
I shall Defer to my next what I have farther
to offer to your Consideration: And am ever
with the greatest *Truth* and *Affection*,

Yours, R. P.

LETTER II.

OF

CONVERSATION.

Dear DAVY,

A N unforeseen Accident occasioned this *long Interval* between
my *Former* and *This Letter*, in
which I had promised to give
you my Thoughts upon the o-
ther *General Head*, under which
I had ranged the few *Rules* of *Advice* I proposed
for your Observation, namely, CONVER-
SATION. And here I shall only fling together a few occasional Reflections, without pre-
tending to treat a *Subject* in *Form*, THAT demands
a long Practice of the World, and the finest Dif-
cernment

cernment for the *just Management* of it. Some-
times it hath happened, that a *loose Hint* from a
F R I E N D hath had a quicker Effect upon the
Mind, than the *formal Precepts* of more *finished
Discourses*, which are often composed in *Ostenta-
tion* rather of the W R I T E R's *Wit*, than for the
Benefit of the R E A D E R.   But to proceed:

T H E R E is certainly nothing that hangs so
strong a Biass upon our *Inclinations*, or *Under-
standings*, as CONVERSATION. The *Thoughts*
of an A U T H O R many Times escape us in a
transient Reading , and when we allow them a
closer Attention, the *Impressions* they make are
Faint, in Comparison of *Those* that are accompa-
nied with *Action*.   The very *Humours* and *Passions* of the *Persons* with whom we constantly
associate, *mingle*, as it were, with *our Souls* ;
and we *slide insensibly* into their *Principles* and
Practices.

I T hath been observed of *ATTICUS, CI-
CERO*, and *HORTENSIUS*, the Three
Wisest Men in their Time among the R O M A N S,
that the same Persons, who were their *Friends*
in their *old Age*, had been their *Familiars* in
their *Youth*. The *Habitudes* we make at *our*
first

first setting out, have, doubtleſs, a very great Influence on *our future Journey*. But how difficult
is the *Choice?* How eaſy the *Miſtake?* While
PLEASURE, PREJUDICE, and FLATTERY
all conſpire to *Blind us*.

I. THE Purſuit of PLEASURE, during *our
Youth*, doth very much pervert us in the *Choice*
of our COMPANIONS. Our *Deſires* are *then*
the *Strongeſt* and moſt *Violent*; and we *oppoſe*,
or *run counter* to every Thing that ſeems to
Baulk them. We *wantonly refuſe* as *Flat* and
Taſteleſs, tho' never ſo *Sound* and *Nouriſhing*,
whatever doth not *tickle* our *capricious Appetites.*
Thus the MAN of BUSINESS ſhall paſs for a
DULL PLODDING FELLOW, the SCHO-
LAR for a PEDANT, and WHATEVER carries
a Face of *Gravity* or *Sober Manners*, become
the Subjeét of our *Scorn* or *Raillery.*

II. PREJUDICE is very apt to infeét the
Minds of *Young People*, and miſlead them in the
Judgments they form of *Others*. The *Warmth*
of their CONSTITUTIONS makes them *Eager*,
and *Want* of EXPERIENCE makes them liable
to *Miſtakes*; while, having met with *few Miſ-
fortunes* to mortify the *Pride* of *Heart* that is

Q   natural

natural to *Youth*, their *Inclinations* or *Aversions*, though never fo *ill-founded*, are not *eafily* Removed.

BUT, *Thirdly*, What *blinds young People* the moft is FLATTERY. Befides the *Vanity* that s common to *all Men*, and lays open even the moft *Difcerning* to Attempts of this Kind, the *Franknefs* and *Good Nature*, which are ufual among the *younger Sort*, render them lefs *Sufpicious*, and confequently more *Unguarded*, than Thofe who have lived *longer* in the World, and known more of the *Arts* of it. They therefore receive the *Commendations* of the *Unskilful*, and the *Careffes* of the *Self-interefted*, without calling in Queftion the *Judgment* of the ONE, or the *Sincerity* of the OTHER.

THE *Firft Thing* then I would recommend to You, is, always to carry this *Reflection* in your Mind, That THERE IS EVER SOMEWHAT LIKE PRIDE THAT ACCOMPANIES REAL MERIT. Men of *That Character* make but very *flow Advances*, and never purfue *Strangers* with Offers of *Intimacy*. When therefore you meet with any One, who opens his *Cabinet* to you *at once*, You may almoft venture to conclude,

clude, it contains nothing but *Trifles*. This is not, however, fo eftablifhed a *Maxim*, but that we fee fometimes, tho' very rarely, in Exception to it, *Two Perfons* of *good Underftanding* STRIKE OUT A FRIENDSHIP, as it were, *at a Heat :* Yet then this happens from fome *lucky Agreement* of their *Sentiments* and *Studies*, or from fome *generous Overture* of *real Service*, That fufficiently diftinguifh it from the LUST OF FANCY, or the ARTIFICE OF FALSE PROFESSORS

ANOTHER Confideration that ought to be of Weight with you, to direct you not only in the *Choice* of your COMPANIONS, but to *qualify your felf* for COMPANY, is This, THAT NO CONVERSATION CAN LONG BE PLEASING, THAT IS NOT, IN SOME DE-GREE, PROFITABLE We may be Fond for a while of the *Gay*, the *Giddy*, and the *Frolickfome* ; but we fhall find, in Time, that there muft be a *Sound Head*, as well as a *Chearful Heart*, to make the Entertainment lafting. It is not a Man's *Perfon*, or *Fortune*, or fome *fafhionable Impertinence* in his *Talk*, (which with the unthinking paffes for *Wit*) that will protect him

from

from the *Contempt* that never fails to fall on *Coxcombs* in the End.

LET *Party* in RELIGION never enter into your *Choice* of a COMPANION. The Marks of *Right* and *Wrong* in Matters of *Opinion* are very uncertain, and can never be settled by Men equally Fallible. I would therefore always prefer the *Conversation* of a HERETICK of *good Sense,* to *That* of the moſt ORTHODOX *Blockhead* in *CHRISTENDOM.*

TRUTH is the *Firſt Quality* to be regarded in a Perſon with whom one *Converſeth.* Without *That,* WIT is often *Pernicious,* and PLAISANTRY is always *Forced* and *Unnatural.*

CONVERSATION is no doubt the beſt *Reformer of Manners.* But in order to make it be ſerviceable to *That End,* we ſhould ſtudy the peculiar *Vices* and *Infirmities of our own Natures.* It is not enough we CONVERSE with only ſuch who are of a *Valuable,* the Skill lies in *chuſing* ſuch as are of a *Proper Character.* If the *Complexion* of our TEMPER be *Splenetick* or *Melancholy,* we ſhould enliven it with the *Mirthful* and the *Sprightly.* If we are Apt to run into to indecent *Levities,* we fhould correct That Irregularity by affociating with the *Grave.* If we have a *rougher Caft* of *Mind,* or are confcious of any Thing *fhocking* in our *Humour* or *Addrefs,* we fhould wear off that *Ruft,* and endeavour to *polifh* our felves, by frequenting the Company of fuch, who are diftinguifhed for their *Complaifance* and *Good-Breeding.*

THAT Thing called *Good-Breeding,* is too much neglected among the *Englifh.* Our COUNTRYMEN think it fufficient if they are poffeffed of the more *folid Virtues,* without the Ornaments of *Life.* But this is certainly a *Miftake.* Many an Affair has mifcarried by the neglect only of fome fmall *Circumftance* or *Ceremony.* In fhort, the WORLD is like other *Miftreffes,* and we muft *Drefs at Her,* if we expect to *Gain Her.*

THERE is a bewitching *Softnefs* in fome Men's *Civility,* that is ftrangely *Reconciling.* It difarms one's *Caution* at the firft *Encounter.* And they may be faid to *Look,* rather than to *Reafon* a Man into their *Opinion.*

Forwardnefs

Forwardnefs in CONVERSATION, doth always *Difguft*, but *Affurance* is *Neceffary :* For Want of *This* it hath often been obferved, that Four or Five *Englifhmen* have met together, and not one of them hath dared to break the Ice in half an Hour Befides, the *Sinews* of REASON fhrink, and GOOD-SENSE looks out of *Countenance*, when delivered from the Mouth of a *Bafhful Man.*

A *Numerous Acquaintance* is *inconvenient*, becaufe by that Means you may be drawn into Engagements which you fhall afterwards Repent, though not eafily g t clear of, (for nothing is fo difficult, as to fhake of a *Fool*. or a *Knave*, who hath once crept into ones *Familiarity* ,) nothing but downright declaring War, and that is not always Expedient, can free you from the Incumbrance of fuch *ufelefs* or *defigning Allies*) and as a *numerous* Acquaintance is *inconvenient*, a *numerous* Company is *Unedifying*. It is a Kind of *Chaos*, and nothing *Beautiful* can arife from fuch *Jarring Elements*. But a *General Acquaintance* is always *improving*, and a *General Converfation diverting :* For there we enjoy *Variety* without *Hazard*, or *Confufion*.. To be linked in the
So-

Society of *one particular Order of Men*, muſt *narrow* our VIEWS, and *warp* the UNDERSTANDING. This is very remarkable among the *Students* of our UNIVERSITIES, and INNS OF COURT. THE ONE imagine REASON to have no *Authority*, but in the *Chair* of ARISTOTLE, while the others think SHE is never ſo well employed, as when ſhe is *Putting of Caſes*. In like manner, to be perpetually inſiſting upon the *ſame Topic* of *Diſcourſe* is tireſome to *a liberal Mind*, that is ſtill impatient after *new Diſcoveries*. We ſhould, in this, imitate the *Prudence* of *thoſe Merchants*, who having but a *ſmall Stock of their own* to ſet out with, make a *Trading Voyage* from *Port* to *Port*, and by exchanging the *Commodities* of one PROVINCE, or COUNTRY, for *thoſe* of *Another*, bring back at laſt *vaſt Returns* for THEMSELVES. Thus we too may make our Advantage by converſing *Promiſcuouſly*, with Men of *Ability* in their ſeveral *Profeſſions*, We ſhall learn from every one ſomewhat that is either *Uſeful* to our ſelves, or *Acceptable* to Others If any Thing I have here ſuggeſted can be ſo to YOU, I ſhall think the little Time I have beſtowed on *Theſe Reflections* very well ſpent. I have forborn to enlarge them, becauſe I know the *Preſent Turn* of AFFAIRS entertains you

much

much better, than any Thing could do that my SOLITUDE can produce. Believe me upon *all Occasions*, and in *all Places*, MY DEAR *CAMPBELL*,

Your *Affectionate*

Humble Servant,

R. P.

EPITAPH

For my dear Friend David Campbell, *Esq;*

SPrung from an Ancient, and Illuftrious Line,
    (O may it to *Eternal Ages* fhine!)
Here * lies Interr'd a much lamented YOUTH,
For *Senfe* Diftinguifh'd, and Efteem'd for *Truth:*
Whom Heav'n had fafhion'd with *peculiar Care,*
And form'd the *Darling* of the BRAVE and FAIR.
To the *rich Talents* NATURE did impart,
He joyn'd the *fine Embellifhments* of ART :
Yet liv'd as much *Unenvy'd,* as *Admir'd.*
But ah! how foon alas his LIFE expir'd.
The *Noble Plant* was drefs'd in *Beauty*'s Pride ;
Gaily it *Bloom'd,* but in the *Blooming dy'd*
Ie VIRTUES mourn! ye LOVES and GRACES weep!
And round Your VOT'RY's Urn ftrict VIGILS keep!
And you, SWEET MAIDS, who lately *Blefs'd* his
                        (*Charms,*
Tho' he no more muft *fold you in his Arms,*
Cherifh the *Dear Remembrance* in your HEART,
And let no FOP intrude *where* CAMPBELL had
            R   (a *Part.*

---

* *In* St James's *Church* Weftminfter

FAMILIAR LETTERS.

TO

Colonel WILLIAM STANHOPE.

Dear Sir,

OCTOB 4 1714

THO' after Addressing Two Letters to you just before, it may seem Impertinent to trouble you so soon with a Third, yet I cannot resist the Temptation of giving you Joy upon the *late Promotions*; in which I hope you may find your *Interest*, as well as your *Inclination gratified*. While the rest of the World are *making their Court*, upon *this Occasion*, in *Town*, I am content here in the *Country* to read the *Triumphs* of my FRIENDS twice a Week in the *Gazette*. My *Ambition* at present is turned *quite another Way*, and all *my humble Endeavours* are directed to *Please* the FAIR. There is a little *Papist Villain* in the Neighbourhood, ('tis a Defect in our Language, that the Termination of the *Adjective* doth not mark the *Gender*, but you are to understand

derſtand this in the *Fæminine*) who hath robbed me of my my *Heart* ; and I have ſcarce had an Hour's ſound Sleep, except it was at *Church*, theſe Two Months. I know that all this is *very Ridiculous* , and that an HALF-PAY OF-FICER ought no more to be in *Love* than a COM-MON WHORE. People of ſuch *Precarious Sub-ſiſtence* ſhould give into no *Paſſion* that is not ſup-ported by *Gain*. But when INDISCRETION cheats us in the Shape of PLEASURE, *who can eſcape the Snare?* I have *this Comfort* ſtill in Re-ſerve———— that, as I have an HEART *entirely* ENGLISH, it is odds I ſhall not continue Two Months longer in the *ſame Mind*. There is *one* Inſtance, however, of my *Conſtancy*, that will never, I am ſure, be *impeached :* I wiſh indeed it were not clogged with the *Obligations* you have laid upon me, and then you would know it is as much upon the Account of *your Perſonal Merit*, as any *Favours* you have *conferred* on ME, that I profeſs my ſelf,

S I R,

Your moſt Faithful

and Obedient Servant,

R. P.

To a YOUNG LADY, *who told me,
the Army had no Religion* ; *and chal-
lenged me to ſhew her a* PRAYER,
that had been made by a Soldier.

MADAM,

IT was always with the greateſt Attention that I received the Honour of
your Commands, and it is an equal
Pleaſure to me, when I am employ-
ed to execute them : But the Task you impoſed
upon me laſt Night, was what, I confeſs, ſur-
prized me. In a Viſit where I hoped to have
been entertained as a *Lover*, I little expected to
be conſulted as a *Divine* ; nor did I believe you
would have had the Curioſity, inſtead of hear-
kening to the Faithful *Vows* I was addreſſing to
YOU, to enquire about thoſe I made to HEA-
VEN. As St. *PAUL* became *All Things to All
Men* that he might *gain Some*, ſo I find too (I
ſpeak it under all the Reſtrictions of Modeſty)

tha

that a Man muſt become *All Things to all Wo-men*, if he would pretend to *Succeed* with *Any*. It is an unaccountable Prejudice, that prevails of late againſt our PROFESSION , and particular-ly among the FAIR SEX, who ſeem to judge that *Virtue* and *Vice* conſiſt rather in the *Dreſs* of a TRIBE, than the *Habit* of the MIND. The PRAYER I ſend you incloſed, (which I give you my Word of Honour, was made by a SOLDIER) will, I hope, convince you, there are ſome MI-LITARY MEN who deſerve not to be *Excommu-nicated* from *the chaſteſt* DRAWING-ROOMS. I ſhall ſubmit to your LADY MOTHER, whether the AUTHOR, or her CHAPLAIN be the better CASUIST of the Two : But when the Queſtion ſhall ariſe about a GALLANT, I beg you to believe, you'll never find one, who is with more *Devo-ſion* than my ſelf,

MADAM,

Your moſt Faithful, &c.

A SOLDIER'S PRAYER.

O GOD, thou Searcher of Hearts, and Judge of all Men, before whose Awful Throne we should tremble to Approach, did not thy Mercy make thy Justice less Terrible; look down, I beseech Thee, with Favour and Compassion upon me, miserable Sinner! Pardon my Offences, and pity my Infirmities. Be not extreme to mark my Follies : *For in thy Sight shall no Man living be justified.* Remember, I am but poor Dust and Ashes, the Child of Vanity, and the Sport of Passions. Without thy Aid, O Lord, all our Endeavours after Righteousness are Fruitless, all our Wisdom empty Pride, all our Happiness Delusion. Do thou enlighten therefore my Mind, and sanctify my Heart, that I may Know and Practise the Things that *belong to my Peace.* Redeem me from the Bondage of my Sins, and raise me to the Fellowship of thy Saints. O let not the many and repeated Instances of my Guilt provoke thee to withdraw from me the Assistance of thy Holy Spirit. But accept of my unfeigned Repentance; second my Resolutions of Amendment; and secure me from
the

the Danger of a Relapfe. Particularly, O Lord, guard me from the Temptation of * ⸻ ⸻ which I have fo often committed, even after the clear Conviction, and profeffed Abhorrence of my own Confcience, and thereby merited thy moft heavy Difpleafure. *Set thy Law ever before me*, that the Terror of thy Threats may reftrain me from Vice; and the Encouragement of thy Promifes incite me to Virtue. Make my Obedience to thy Will my Delight, as well as my Duty; that I may ferve Thee with Purity and Truth; not by Starts only, when Afflictions may humble me, or the Eye of the World obferve me; but in a Conftant, Uniform, and Sincere Devotion, without Lukewarmnefs, without Hypocrify.

After thy Spiritual Graces, in the fecond Place, I beg a Bleffing upon my Temporal Concerns. Profper my honeft Endeavours in that Station wherein thy Providence has placed me in this World. Give me the Benefit of Health, and the Quiet of Contentment in all my Fortunes. Protect me from all open Violence or Injuries, and defend me from the *Arrows that fly in the dark*,

the

---

* Here mention thofe Sins to which you are moft fubject by Nature, or evil Cuftom.

the Backbitings of a malicious, and the Flatteries of a deceitful Tongue. Bleſs all my Relations and Friends.   Forgive, and reconcile my Enemies : Teach me to make a right Uſe of Both , that the Malice of the One may awaken my Caution, and the Kindneſs of the Other confirm my Conſtancy. Let me not live wholly Unprofitable in my Generation.   Give me the honeſt Ambition of deſerving well of as many as I am able.   In all my Aims, Deſires, and Hopes, let me conſider the Dignity of my Nature, and ſtudy to promote the Glory of thy Name.

Laſtly, As in Duty bound, I offer up my moſt hearty Praiſe and Thankſgiving for all thy Mercies and Benefits vouchſafed to me, thy unworthy Servant: For my Creation, Preſervation, amidſt all the Dangers with which I have been encompaſs'd, and for all the Comforts and Advantages of this Life : But above all, for the glorious Proſpect of a Better, through the Merits of thy Son, my Redeemer.   To whom with Thee and the Holy Ghoſt be aſcribed, *&c.*

TRANSLATIONS

FROM

Catullus, Tibullus, and *Ovid* :

WITH

An ESSAY upon the ROMAN ELEGIAC POETS.

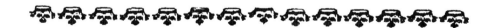

A N

ESSAY

UPON THE

Roman ELEGIAC POETS.

 HAVE Wondered, that among
fo Many who have Bufied or
Diverted Themfelves in *Tran-
flating* the Ancient *Claffick* P O-
E T s, fo Few have thought the
Writers of ELEGY Worthy
their Pains, or Amufement. I cannot but Believe that *Thefe* have fucceeded as happily in
their Way, as the *Others*, and that They may
be Read with no lefs *Advantage* than *Pleafure*.
For my own Part, I can affirm, that when at
any time my Mind hath been ruffled by fome

peevifh

peevish Accident or *Disappointment*, I have always found my Temper sooner Composed by taking a Turn with *TIBULLUS* in my Hand, than by having recourse to the *Lessons* of PHILOSOPHY, or the *Precepts* of DIVINES. Whatever is very *solemn*, carrieth with it, I don't know how, somewhat of *Constraint :* And it frequently happens by an unlucky Disposition either in the *Pupil*, or the *Preacher*, that *Those severer* Kinds of *Discipline* (I speak not This with the least Irreverence) serve rather to *Punish*, than *Reform* Us. It is perhaps no Difficult Matter to *Convince* One of the *Reasonableness* of This or That Action, but the Secret lies in *Engaging* One in the *Practice*. It is a *Memorable Sentence* of a *celebrated* MORALIST This,

Tutus est vitium fugere, & Sapientia prima Stultitiâ caruisse —————— Horat.

" It is the *Beginning* of VIRTUE to *Depart*
" from VICE, and the *First Step* towards
" WISDOM is to *Forsake* our FOLLY."
May it not as justly be said, The *First Step* towards HAPPINESS is to *Forget* our MISERY? The best Method to bring *That* about is not, I presume, by *Alarming* the THINKING FACULTY, but by *Soothing* and *Lulling* to *Rest* our *too Active* and *Unquiet* REFLECTIONS.

Whilst

WHILST *Our poor tottering* BARK continues in This Uncertain *Voyage* of Life, and is so often kept out at *Sea* in *rough* and *stormy Weather*, far from the sight of any *Hospitable Shoar*, the SOUL, its PASSENGER, cannot sure but feel a *mighty Satisfaction* arising within, when she finds Herself afterwards *Stealing*, as it were, away under *smoother Course*, and born *gently* down the *Tide* of TENDERNESS in *soft* and *easie Gales* of PASSION.

THERE is a *Charm* in VERSE that never fails *agreeably* to Affect a *Heart* that is *rightly placed:* and there is, in my Opinion, something *peculiarly moving* in the VERSES of That *Good-natured Class* of POETS *CATULLUS, TIBULLUS, PROPERTIUS,* and *OVID.* There are but *Few Pieces* of *CATULLUS,* it is true, that can strictly be ranked among *Those* of the ELEGIAC ORDER: But whenever HE doth Touch upon the *softer Subjects* of HUMANITY, his *Sentiments* have the utmost *Propriety* and *Delicacy;* and therefore I could not but mention HIM among *His Companions.* They were, *All Four,* Men of *Family* and *Condition* in their Country. Their *Inclinations* led Them naturally to PLEASURE, and

and Their *Good Sense* to a Discovery of the *Knavery* of BUSINESS, and the *Vanity* of AMBITION. The *Three Former* may be said to have Been as *extraordinary* a TRIUMVIRATE, as, perhaps, any Age hath Produced, I mean in an *Idle Way* of Life : *Polite* in their MANNERS, *Easie* in Their FORTUNES; *Successful* in Their A-MOURS; *Happy* in *each Other's* ACQUAINTANCE, *Beloved*, in general, while They LIVED, and universally *Lamented*, when They DIED. As for *OVID*, He was certainly Master of all the *fine Qualities* and *Accomplishments* that could be desired in a GENTLEMAN. But having Offended AUGUSTUS, either by Happening to be an *Un-expected Witness* of that EMPEROR's *Love-Intrigues*, or else by too *lasciviously* Describing *His Own* (which was the *Crime* Pretended) He was *Banished* from *ITALY* in his *Fiftieth* Year, and Languished out the Remainder of His Days at *TA-MOS* (the Modern *TEMESWAER* as some think) There are I believe but two Instances in Story of a *Punishment* like *This* for What, at the worst, could be called *only* an *Indiscretion* : One in the Person of *OVID*, The Other in That of *RA-BUTIN*. Their *Masters* were equally *Absolute*, equally *Wise*, and equally *Jealous*.

F R O M

FROM this Little Draught of *Their Chara-
&ers,* One may judge how *Edifying* any of *Their
Compofitions* muft needs be to an *Elegant Under-
ftanding.* And, indeed, What *Sincerity* in
FRIENDSHIP, What *Fondnefs* in LOVE, What
Kindnefs to RELATIONS, What *Inflances* of *All
the Social* VIRTUES do We not meet with in
Their Writings? Not to mention a thoufand
Ornaments of *Wit,* a wonderful *Sweetnefs,* and
eafy *Cadence* in their *Numbers,* and fo True a
Picture of Life, that one can fcarce Fancy the
Scene to lye at the *Diftance* it is placed

THERE is *One Objection,* which I muft not
pafs over, and that is generally charged upon
Thefe POETS: I mean, Their too great *Li-
cence,* and *Obfcenity* in Their *Ideas* and *Language.*

To This I would Reply, That if upon fome
Occafions, They feem not to have been very
Scrupulous about the *Terms* They made ufe
of in Communicating their *Amorous Adven-
tures,* it ought not to be imputed to a *Scandalous Singularity* in THEM, but to the *Common Indulgence* of the AGE in which They
Flourifhed. *HORACE* muft Plead *Guilty* to the
fame

same Indictment. Nay, *VIRGIL* Himself, as Applauded as HE is for His *Modesty,* hath left many *Expressions* in His ECLOGUES that might be Argued of *Wantonness.* After All, the whole Matter will turn upon this Single Point. A Person whose *Principles* are *Uncorrupted* may freely Converse with *These* AUTHORS without Danger of *Infection :* And for Such who have more *Wickedness* than *Wit* (the Greatest *Curse* that can befal a F O O L) their *senseless Vice* will tempt Them to Pervert even the most *Sacred Things* to the *vilest Purposes.* However, though *All* their P O E M S may be *Read* in the *Originals* with *Safety,* I do not pretend to say They can *All* be *Translated* with *Decency.* But since Many of Them may, it is Pity, I think, We have not More of Them in ENGLISH, to Enrich our Language with a Variety of *Pleasing Images,* that are as *Innocent,* as they are *Delightful.*

T H E R E is *One Difficulty* that will still lye upon the Hands of Any who shall Undertake this Work, and *This* ariseth from their frequent *Allusions* to the *Ceremonies* and *Notions* of Their RELIGION. *Instances* of This abound even in

Those

Those Copies of their Verses that are writ the most in the *Spirit* of LEWDNESS : (as SUPER-STITION hath ever been an *Especial Bawd* to LUST) But for All such as are Proper to be *Translated*, they may be Rendered by a few *Explanatory Notes* not only *Intelligible*, but very *Entertaining*, to a *meer* ENGLISH *Reader*.

WHAT I have here delivered, is not said with Design to Talk into Credit any little Attempts of Mine, (whose Passion for a *Muse* never yet came to be a serious Affair) but to Recommend the Performance to some Body who hath more Leisure, as well as Better Abilities for such a Work.

T   TRAN-

TRANSLATIONS

FROM
CATULLUS, TIBULLUS, &c.

To *LESBIA*.

CATULL. Carmin. XXIX.

Ille mi par esse Deo videtur,
Ille, si fas est, superare Divos.

BLEST as th' *Immortal* GODS, and far more
          (*Blest,*
(Their careful *Providence* disturbs Their Rest)
Is the fond YOUTH, who, gazing on Thy Face,
Adores each *dawning Smile,* each *rising Grace;*

          And

And fits and liftens to thy Charming Tongue,

Whofe *Speech* is Tuneful as the *SYREN's Song* /

Struck with the pow'rful *Magick* You difpenfe,

My *Soul's* difarm'd of ev'ry *Guardian Senfe.*

A *liquid Fire,* piercing as *Light'ning's* Flame,

Darts through my *Veins,* and *loofens* all my Frame

My *languid Eyes,* and *fault'ring Voice* confefs

That *NATURE faints* beneath the *fweet Excefs.*

Wrapt in *Amaze, Confus'd, Intranc'd* I lye,

Loft in *foft Tranfports* of *Extatick* Joy.

Wanton *CATULLUS !* idly doft Thou Rave !

Art THOU then funk to be a WOMAN's Slave ?

Sloth and *Luxurious Eafe* are Dang'rous Things.

Beware —— they oft have ruin'd *mighty* KINGS,

Thofe *Suns* (when *Love* does once th' *Afcendant*

get)

Who Rofe in *Glory,* in *Difhonour* Set.

The Fourth ELEGY of the Second Book of TIBULLUS.

Hic mihi servitium video, dominamque paratam.
Jam mihi libertas illa paterna vale.

I See my Fate—— I Own the *Tyrant* Dame——
Freedom adieu ! That vain Paternal Claim.
But *Hard's* the *Bondage* that the *Slave* constrains,
Whom *LOVE*, like *Me*, for *ever* binds in *Chains.*
Offend, or *Merit*, equal is my Smart.
Cease, cease thy *Tortures* ; spare a *bleeding* Heart.
Better, than thus in sad *Despair* to moan,
Transform'd on some bleak Mountain to a *Stone*,
Or on the naked Beach a *Rock*, sustain
The *Storms* of *Heav'n*, or *Fury* of the *Main* !

My

My Days no *Peace*, My Nights no *Comfort* know,

Each Hour's *imbitter'd* with the *Dew* of *Woe*.

My tender ELEGIES in *tuneful Pray'r*

Have oft *assail'd* the *unrelenting* FAIR :

But *Deaf* to MUSICK's soft *Perswasive* Pow'r,

No *Charm* can *melt* Her but a *Golden Show'r*.

Farewell then PHŒBUS, and the MUSES' *Quire* !

'Twas not to Sing of *Wars* I tun'd my *Lyre* ;

Nor to Describe the *Travails* of the SUN ;

And *swift-revolving Labours* of the MOON.

One *Wish Alone* invok'd your *sacred Aid* ——

To *smooth* my *Passage* to the *scornful* MAID.

But since *Wealth* only can *Admittance* gain,

By Glorious Mischief *Riches* I'll obtain.

Murther —— or *Rob*--- yes *Rifle* ev'ry SHRINE ,

And my *first Violence*, VENUS, be on *Thine* !

THOU ! that *Assign'd* the *mercenary Jilt* ;

Inspir'd —— and *Pleas'd* beheld the *thriving Guilt*.

Curst be the Man (His *Pride* hath *Fatal* been)

Who first *display'd* i' th' EMERALD's *sprightly Green*

The *Tyrian Dye*, or COAN *Bombacine* !

Thes

These are the *Baits* that Tempt the *Fickle* Sex;
And *Lovers Joys* with *Rival Cares* Perplex.
Thus WOMEN Learn't (by *Truth* secur'd Before)
With *Dogs* to Guard, with *Bolts* to Lock the Door
Presents, alas! are *Passports* still o'course;
No *Dogs* then Bark, no *Bolts* resist *their* Force.
The Plagues are endless that afflict Mankind,
When HEAV'N trusts *Beauty* to a *Venal Mind*.
Hence *Broils* ensue; Hence slighted Youths *Blaf-*
(*pheme:*
Hence CUPID's grown so *Infamous* a Name.
But may the *Wretch* who *meanly* can *Despise*
For sordid *Pelf* True *Love* (the *noblest Prize*)
See in fierce vengeful *Flames* her *Treasures* blaze;
Or *Winds* disperse the *Heaps* her *Treach'ries* raise.
And when she *Dies*, neglected will she Fall;
By None *Regretted*, who had *Cheated* All.
Far diff'rent Fate the gen'rous Nymph attends,
Whom *Kindness*, and whom *Constancy* commends.

Belov'.l

Belov'd while YOUNG ; *Esteem'd* when past her
                             (BLOOM ;

In AGE *Rever'd*; and *Worshipp'd* in the TOMB.

Some *Good old* MAN, Remindful of the *Charms*

That once had made Him *Happy* in *Her Arms*,

Yearly shall *Visit* her Distinguish'd URN,

Fresh *Garlands* strow, or Grateful *Odours* burn.

Just is the *Cause----* but ah how *Vain* to *Plead!*

For *LOVE*, at last, will have *His Laws* obey'd.

With all my *Spleen* (should *NEMESIS* Command)

Content I'd sell th' old *Mansion Seat*, and *Land*.

Nay more, could All the *Drugs* THESSALIA bore,

Or wild *MÆDEA* brew'd on *PONTUS'* Shore,

Be *Mix'd* together in one *baneful Cup*,

To gain a *Smile* from HER, I'd *Drink it up*.

The

The Thirteenth *ELEGY* of the Fourth Book of TIBULLUS.

To His MISTRESS.

Nulla tuum nobis subducet femina lectum.
Hoc primùm juncta est fœdere nostra Venus.

THink me not *False* to the *First Vows* I made;
    Nor that some *Fairer She* may wrong Thy
                           (Bed.

The *Boasted Arts* of All the *Sex* are Vain :
Their *Smiles* no *Pleasure* give, their *Frowns* no
                                  (Pain.

Alone

Alone YOU *Charm* ME. But, beholding THEE,

A *Thousand more*, perhaps, are *Charm'd*, like ME:

And O! I *wish* (let *Love* the *Wish* attone)

That THOU wer't *Charming* in *my Eyes* Alone!

Vain-glorious Fops, of *Envy'd Blessings Proud*,

Expose their *Treasure* to the *Rival Crowd*,

Delight in *idle Show*, and *empty Noise* :

The *Wife in Silence* brood upon their *Joys*.

To *Forest Wilds* I cou'd with THEE retreat,

Where never *Path* was worn by *Human Feet*.

No CLIME can *low'r*, where your *Bright Look.*

(appear ,

No *Place* seem DESART, when my LOVE is *there*.

Nay, I attest Thy *JUNO*'s sacred Pow'r,

(*JUNO* the *Guardian* of the NUPTIAL *Bow'r*,)

Tho' Tempted by some BEAUTY of the *Skies*,

The *Heav'n* that BEAUTY profer'd I'd *Despise*.

What have I said ? *Fool* that I was to *Swear*,

Or *fondly satisfy* thy *Jealous Fear* !

Safe

Safe from Alarms, You *now* will urge your Sway,

(Ah Babling Tongue that did my Heart betray !)

No Hopes of *Liberty* to Me remain :

But I, a *Slave Profess'd,* must *Drag* your *Chain.*

Lo *VENUS !* at thy *Altar* Bound I lye.

O *Gentle* GODDESS *Guard* Thy VOTARY !

THE
NOONING.

From OVID, Book I. Elegy V.

Æstus erat, mediamque dies exegerat horam:
Apposui medio membra levando toro.

'TWAS *Summer*, and, with *sultry Heat* opprest,
    At *Noon* I laid me down in Bed to *Rest*.
The *Curtains* of my *Window*, *slightly drawn*,
Let in a *doubtful Beam*, that look'd like *Dawn*;

Or

Or the faint *Glimm'rings* that through *Forests* play ;

Or *Twilight twinkling* at the *Close* of *Day.*

Such *pretty Masquerades* of *Light* and *Shade*

Suit with the *Blushes* of a *Wishing Maid* ;

And serve, with *Decency*, to usher in

Ladies who dread the *Shame*, but love the *Sin.*

CORINNA lo ! appear'd, in *loose Array*,

Adown Her *Neck* her *comely Tresses* stray :

Like *Great SEMIRIMIS Her Figure* shew'd,

Like *LAIS smiled*, as *Lovely* and as *Lewd.*

I *seiz'd* Her *Gown*, and broke thro' *that Defense* ;

(The *slender Outwork of Unguarded Sense*)

At first she *struggled*, but 'twas plain to see,

She *Fought* for *Honour*, not for *Victory.*

Stript of Her *Robe*, and *Naked* to *my View*,

How *Faultless* was Her *Make !* Her *Shape* how
(*True !*

What *Arms* I *saw* and *felt !* What *Plump round*
(*Breasts !*

And how they *Heav'd !* ---- as *Longing* to be *Prest.*

How

How *firm* Her *Thighs!* How *smooth* Her *Belly* rose
Beneath Her *slender Waste!* The *Rest----suppose.*
Beauty and *Youth* in their *full Vigour* shone;
And close I *Clasp'd Her Body* to *my Own.*
Spent with *Excess* of *Joy Intranc'd We Lay:*
Give me *such* N o o n s, ye Gods, to *ev'ry Day.*

The

The LOVER Militant.

From OVID, Book I Elegy IX. Ending at
the 32d Verse.

Militat omnis amans, & habet sua castra Cupido:
Attice, crede mihi; militat omnis amans.

CUPID and *MARS* are GENERALS *Wise* and
                                  (Bold:
Truſt me, Dear Friend, the *Parallel* will hold.

In *Both* their CAMPS alike ſucceed the YOUNG:

Love Courts the *Gay,* and VICT'RY Crowns
                                  (the *Strong.*

The OLD in vain their *Uſeleſs Weapons* weild,

Fumblers in *Bed,* and *Cripples* in the *Field.*

                                         Re-

Recruits for *Each* are *Chose* with equal *Care*,

And None fhould dare to *Woo*, who cannot *War*.

With *Frequent Duty*, and with *Watching* fpent,

(The LOVER at the *Door*, the SOLDIER at the *Tent*)

On their *cold Pofts* Both lie whole whole Nights
(*Awake*,

And often, *long* and *toilfome Marches* make.

O'er *Hills*, through *Floods*, in *Cruel Froft* and
(*Snow*,

They feek a MISTRESS, or Purfue a FOE.

No *Diftance* tires, no *Hazard* can Affright ;

The *Danger* ferves but to *Provoke* the *Fight*.

In *hoftile* CAMPs the CHIEFS employ their *Spies*·

And LOVERS *watch* their *Rival* LOVERS Eyes.

FORTS are Approach'd by *Mine*, or Took by *Storm* :

LADIES Won--- *Sword in Hand*, or elfe in *Form*.

Your *active* PARTISANS, in *Ambufh* laid,

Surpriz'd in *Sleep* their Enemies *invade* :

(As by *Finefse* the GREEKS did once *Deftroy*

The Troops that RHESUS brought to Succour
(TROY.

Th'

Th' *Alert Gallant* does thus with *kinder Rage*,

While the dull *Husband snores*, the *Wife engage*.

Yet sometimes *Both* Defeated of their *Aim*,

Repuls'd by *Guards*, Retire with *Loss*, and *Shame*.

Doubtful alike's the Fate of *Arms* and *Love* :

The *Vanquish'd* oft, at last, the *Victors* prove.

Disgrace befalls as well the *Great* as *Small* ;

And *Those* scarce *Rise*, you'd swear could never *Fall*.

Let None then Think that *Love*'s a Sport for *Boys*,

He must *Drudge* hard, Who *gains* its utmost

(*Joys.*

X   THE

THE
RING.

A PRESENT *to His* MISTRESS.

From OVID, BOOK II ELEGY XV

Annule, formosæ digitum vincture puellæ,
In quo censendum nil, mihi dantis amor.

GO little RING, and may'st Thou *Welcome*
(prove,
Not for *Thy Value*, but the *Donor's Love.*
Go little RING, and while the wanton MAID
Well-pleas'd surveys Thee on *Her Joint* display'd,
Tell Her, *Thy Circle* was contriv'd with Art,
The *Type* of *One* That *fits* a *Better Part*

Happy

Happy who now Her *Lilly Hand* ſhalt Grace!

O how I wiſh *my---- Perſon* in *Thy Place!*

Then I ſhould oft Her *pretty Bubbies* feel;

And ſometimes too, perhaps, might *lower ſteal,*

Slide off *her Finger* down *her glowing Breaſt,*

An *Unſuſpected,* but a *Buſie Gueſt.*

Or when She *ſeal'd* ſome tender *Billet-doux,*

And *wet* the *Gem* to make th' *Impreſſion true,*

Admitted to *thoſe Charming Lips* of *Bliſs*

In *roſie Dew*-I'd *ſnatch* a *Luſcious Kiſs.*

A Part in *any Office* let me ſhare:

But to be *laid aſide* ——— I could not bear:

My *Orb contracted* to a *narrow'r Space*

Would *cloſer Cling,* nor *quit* its *ſtrict Embrace.*

You need, *Dear Life,* no Scruples entertain:

My *Figure's* no *Diſgrace,* my *Weight* no *Pain.*

Dreſt, or *Undreſt,* You ſtill may keep Me on;

And ev'n in *Bed,* or *Bathing* wear *This Stone.*

But yet, methinks, if *Naked* You appear'd,

The R I N G wou'd ſoon into a M A N be *rear'd,*

Stretch'd in full *Vigour* ev'ry *Member* rise,

And the *Bold* LOVER act without *Disguise.*

Come, *This is Trifling* —-- Little GIFT Depart,

And tell HER that THOU bear'st with Thee My

(HEART

ON

ON THE
DEATH of *TIBULLUS*.

From **OVID**, Book III. Elegy IX.

Memnona fi mater, mater ploravit Achillem,
Et tangunt magnas triftia fata Deas,

IF *THETIS* Wept, Her Son *ACHILLES* Slain,
And HUMAN *Ills* can give IMMORTALS *Pain*;
O Sable * ELEGY ! Thy Treffes loofe ——
Too juftly now *That Name* becomes the MUSE.

Thy

---

* The Name of One of the MUSES as well as of *That Kind* of POESY over which She Prefided, and in which *TIBULLUS* excelled.

Thy *Glory* loft, Thy *Harmony* Deplore——

The *Gentle Soft* TIBULLUS is no more.

See ! the poor *Boy*, the *Child* of VENUS Mourns !

His Smother'd *Torch* no longer *Blazing* Burns.

His Empty *Quiver* hangs *Revers'd*——and, lo !

He droops His *Wings*, and breaks His *ufelefs Bow*,

And beats his *naked Breaft*, in rage of Woe.

Bedew'd with *Tears* his *Locks* o'erfpread his *Eyes*,

And his *Dear little Heart* e'en *burfts* with *Sighs*.

In fuch *fad Plight*, with fuch a *Piteous Moan*

He *Wail'd* the TROJAN *Chief* his Mother's Son.

Nor does the GODDESS lefs *Her Grief* exprefs,

ADONIS' *Fate* fcarce gave her more *Diftrefs*.

WHY do They *Flatter* Us with *Mighty Words* ?

Stile Us *Divine* ? Of *Fame* the *Sov'reign Lords* ?

Frail DEITIES, alas ! but of *a Day*,

Whom DEATH's cold Hand foon turns to *Common*

(*Clay.*

Say,

Say, what Avail'd it to the || B⸱⸱⸱D of *THRACE*

His *Boasted Skill?* or His *Cœlestial Race?*

That HE and *LINUS* own'd One *Heav'nly* SIRE?

That *Beasts* grew *Tame* Admonish'd by His LYRE?

¡ Ah *LINUS! LINUS!* in *Condoling Strains*

The *Lofty* PINES *Reply,* the SIRE *Complains.*

Add We to *His* the Great ⃰ MÆONIAN Name,

Whose *Fruitful Fount,* feeds each *Poetick Stream,*

Ev'n HE could not the least *Exemption* have.

His *Works* indeed still *Triumph* o'er the *Grave.*

In *Them,* tho' long since *ruin'd,* TROY *survives* ;

And Chaste *PENELOPE*'s *Example lives.*

Thy Name too ⃰⃰ *DELIA,* ⃰⃰ *NEMESIS* and

(Thine,

Alike *Recorded* shall alike too *Shine.*

Thou

---

§ *ORPHEUS*

† Instead of Æ*linon,* as it is usually Printed, it should be αἲ λίνον, i e ah *Linon* *LINUS* was Son of *APOLLO,* and Instructed *ORPHEUS* in Musick But notwithstanding His high Descent and extraordinary Talents, Perish'd like a Common Mortal

⃰ *HOMER.*

⃰⃰ Fictitious Names under which *TIBULLUS* celebrated Two ROMAN Ladies who were His *Mistresses*

Thou *DELIA* who his *earlieſt Love* didſt ſhare,

And Thou ſweet *NEMESIS* his *lateſt Care.*

But, what's the *Fruit* now of Our *Pious Fears?*

Our *Daily Sacrifice ?* Our *Nightly Prayers ?*

If *Good Men* ſuffer thus (Forgive me *JOVE*)

Who can Believe a *Providence* Above ?

Nor FAITH, nor PURITY can ſtop Our *Doom :*

DEATH *drags* Us from the *Altar* to the *Tomb.*

Is VERSE *Thy Pride ?* See ! where *TIBULLUS*

(lyes——

How ſmall an *Urn* will *Thoſe Remains* ſuffice.

And have then *Fun'ral Flames* without controul

Laid Waſte the *Temple* of that *Tuneful* SOUL ?

O *Periſh*, *Periſh* the Rever'd Abodes,

The *Glitt'ring Temples* of the *Faithleſs* GODS,

Who *Patient* could Behold the *Guilty Scene,*

That drew ev'n *Tears* from BEAUTY's *Tyrant*

Queen.

YET

YET thus 'twas Better, in his *Native Land*
To meet his Fate, than on a *Foreign Strand*,
Huddled in Dirt by some † *Phæacian* Hand.
His MOTHER here Her *kind Concern* could shew;
Close his *Dim Eyes*, and Give a last *Adieu:*
His SISTER Testifie Her *tender Care*
With *Hands Uplifted*, and *Dishevel'd Hair:*
And the *Fair* PARTNERS in *His* HEART too prove
Rivals in *Sorrow* as before in *Love*.
DÆLIA, Departing from the *Mournful Train*,
Cry'd, " *Hapless Object* of my *Present Pain!*
" I *Charm'd* THEE once, nor *Charm'd* THEE
(then *in vain*;
" *Vigour* and *Joy Danc'd sparkling in thy Eyes*. "
Stung with the Thought, Proud *NEMESIS* Re-
(plies:

Y   " Boast

" Boaſt not the *Sallies* of his *roving Youth :*

" * *His Laſt Faint Dying Graſp Confirm'd His*

(*Truth*"

If, when the BODY's Dead, the SPIRIT flies

To ſeek *new Seats,* and more *Indulgent Skies,*

TIBULLUS ſure will *That* ELYSIUM find

Where Dwell the *Brave,* the *Virtuous,* and th

Ki

There *Learn'd* † CATULLUS ſhall Salute H

(*Gue*

And *Gen'rous* || *CALVUS* meet Him on the Coaſt

T

---

* *TIBULLUS* in his Laſt Elegy   the Latter Part of which
Addreſſed to *DELIA* makes her a very fond Inſinuation of [...]
Conſtancy in theſe Two Beautiful Lines

   Te Spectem Suprema mihi cum venerit hora,
   Te teneam moriens deficiente manu

O, 'tis artfully introduceth *NEMESIS* repeating the Laſt of Them
in a kind of Triumph over Her *Rival,* who had, 'tis probable, been
Neglected for ſome time by Her Lover, while the other Enjoyed
thoſe very Marks of his Endearment which ſhe had been flattered
with the Hopes of
  † *CATULLUS,* although He Died very Young, had the Reputation not only of Great *Wit,* but of Excellent *Learning,* and
that in the Opinion of the moſt *Learned,* and which may ſtill
ſeem more *Extraordinary,* in That of the moſt *Witty* of the Age
in which He lived
  || *CALVUS* was an Eminent POET, and the Common
FRIEND of *CATULLUS* and *TIBULLUS*

There *GALLUS* too (if * *Violated Fame*

Compell'd the *Heroe* to that *sad Extream*)

Well-pleas'd shall entertain the *Gentle Guest*

Who now augments the Number of the *Blest*.

And *here* may no *rude Hand* disturb His BONES.

Light fall the *Cov'ring* EARTH, and *Decent* lye

(the STONES.

Y 2

---

* *Violated Fame*, &c. To make this Passage Familiar to
the ENGLISH *Reader*, it will be necessary to enter a little into
the History of GALLUS. He was a Person whom *AUGUSTUS*
raised from a *Private Condition* to the highest Degree of *Trust*
and *Power*. He was afterwards Accused of having Abused his
Master's *Favour*, not only by an *Arbitrary Administration*, and
great *Oppression* in *ÆGYPT*, over which a Kingdom He had been
set to Preside, when it was reduced into a *Province*, but also
by an *Insolent* and *Neglectful Behaviour* towards the EMPEROR
himself, especially if He happened to be Heated with Wine.
The Malice of his *Enemies*, and his own imprudent Conduct at
length Disgraced Him. And (as the *Ingratitude* of One Man
is generally Punished by the *Treachery* of Another) his *Bosom-
Friend* and most *Intimate Companion VALERIUS LARGUS*, was
the Chief Instrument in his *Prosecution* and *Ruin*. His *Re-
sentment* of the severe *Proceedings* in the SENATE against him,
(They having Condemned HIM to *Banishment* and his ESTATE
to *Confiscation*) and the *Indignation* he conceived at the *Base
Treatment* he met with from ONE he had so much *Caress'd* and
Obliged, tempted him to lay *violent Hands* upon Himself. AU-
GUSTUS expressed His *Concern* for his *Death* in a *Style* worthy
so Great and so *Gracious* a PRINCE, and, in a sort of *Rebuke*
to the SENATE for their *Harsh Sentence*, Complained of *His
hard Fate*, who Alone said He, was not Allowed to *Chastise
the*

the *Failings* of *His* FRIENDS *after his own Manner* GALLUS
was a moſt Accompliſhed R O M A N, and is Celebrated by
VIRGIL and all the Beſt POETS of his Age   The *Judicious*
will obſerve, that though O *VID* touches upon this Subject
with great *Delicacy*, yet in *thoſe Days* it was thought no *Crime*
to do Honour to the Memory of a *Fallen* COURTIER, who
had many *Shining* and *Valuable Qualities*

T O

TO HIS

Grace the Duke of *ARGYLL*;

WITH THE

Life of POMPONIUS ATTICUS.

THE MUSE, that Scorns to *Flatter*, or De-
(*fame*,
In ev'ry *Change* of FORTUNE *still* the SAME ;
That, Careless how the *Factious Crowd* Divide,
Courts not their *Folly*, nor their Leader's *Pride* ;
To Thee, *ARGYLL!* who wer't Her earliest
(Praise,
Aspires once more Her Faithful Voice to raise :

Not

Nor Fears the *Strain* can *Unharmonious* be,

That Sings of *ATTICUS*, and Sings to THEE.

Viewing *This Image* of *ROME*'s Fav'rite *Son*,

Pleas'd She Beheld *Some Features* Like *Your Own*.

Like THEE HE Liv'd *Untainted* in an Age

Deform'd with *Crimes*, and Mad with *Civil Rage*.

Like THEE HE *firmly* to the LAWS *Adher'd*,

Yet more by PRUDENCE than by PARTY *Steer'd*

Like THEE HE Learn'd AMBITION to Defpife,

Yet Gaz'd on GLORY with a *Lover's* Eyes.

Like THEE when Rais'd by *Favour*, or *Succefs*,

Defert He Cherifh'd ; and Reliev'd *Diftrefs*.

Like THEE *Difdaining* each low Vulgar End,

Confefs'd the PATRIOT, and Avow'd the

(FRIEND.

Like THEE HE met —— ah *Worft* of Human

(Wrongs !

Ungrateful *Hearts*, and falfe Invidious *Tongues*.

But pafs We That *Severe Remembrance* by.

The Palms Oppref's'd fhoot fafter to the Sky.

O Fam'd

O Fam'd in in *Council !* as Renown'd in *Fight !*
Contemplate here this Old *Illuſtrious* KNIGHT ;
In all Events *Superior* to His *Fate* ;
Divinely *Good,* as Eminently *Great :*
Whoſe Gen'rous *Exit* ſhew'd Him to Excell
No leſs in *Dying* than in *Living* well.
How FEW in *Thoſe laſt Conflicts* do We find
But *Sink* beneath the *Burthen* of their *Mind ?*
Tho' VALOUR Guards the *Tent,* or STATE the
(*Door,*
The *Scene* ſoon changes in *That Dreadful Hour.*
Each *Guilty Thought* will *then* preſs *rudely* in,
Like CÆSAR *Stab'd* by our own *Darling* Sin.
But HE knew Nothing to *Alarm* His Soul :
No *Clouds* of *Vice* His *Sunſhine* did Controul :
With undiminiſh'd *Luſtre* HE Retreats,
And as HE *mildly* Roſe, as *calmly* Sets.

SHALL

SHALL then some *Pedant Scribe*, or *Rev'rend*
                                        (*Drone*
That dully Nods upon a *Pulpit-Throne*,
Who meanly *Merit* by *Profession* Scan,
Exclude from HEAVEN this *Just*, this *Pious* Man-
Sure FAITH Alone is but a *Weak Pretence* ;
And Want of CHARITY is Want of *Sense*.
The *Barren Fig-tree* was of right *Accurst*,
But the Fair *Fruitful Vine* for Use was *Nurst*.

    GIVE Me THOU POWER *Immortal!* and
                                        (*Unchang'd!*
Whose *Care Paternal* has through *Ages* rang'd ,
(CHRISTIAN or PAGAN, *Both* Thy *Influence* felt,
Whose *Bounty* is to All Thy *Creatures* dealt)
Give Me to Travel o'er those *Realms* of *Light*,
Where *EPICTETUS* shines *serenely* Bright ,
Where *VARRO* and *POMPONIUS* lead the Way;
Who Follow VIRTUE ne'er can *Go astray*.

PROLOGUE

PROLOGUE

To the TRAGEDY of

Sir WALTER RALEIGH.

STruck with each Ancient GREEK or ROMAN
(Name,
Blindly We Pay *Devotion* to Their *Fame.*
Their Boasted CHIEFS in *Partial Lights* are shown:
Neglect, or *Envy,* still Attends *Our Own.*
POETS and PRIESTS, the People to Deceive,
Form GODS and HEROES *Neither do Believe.*

Our

Our AUTHOR ſcorns All *Worſhip* but the *True* :

He brings *Unqueſtion'd Wonders* to Your VIEW.

An ENGLISH MARTYR ſhall Aſcend the Stage,

To *Shame* the *Laſt*, and *Warn* the *Preſent Age*.

The TRAGIC *Scene* with moving Art will tell

How *Brave* He *Fought* ———— how *Wrong'd* the

SOLDIER Fell.

AMBITION is a *Miſtreſs* Few enjoy !

Falſe to Our Hopes, and to Our Wiſhes *Coy* ;

The *Bold* She *Baffles*, and *Defeats* the *Strong* ;

And *All* are *Ruin'd* Who *Purſue* Her long.

Yet ſo *Bewitching* are Her *Fatal Charms*,

We think it *Heav'n* to *Dye within Her Arms*.

Thus *RALEIGH* Thought—— and in the *Glorious*

(*Strife*

Immortal *Honour* gain'd—--- but loſt His *Life*.

Jealous of *Virtue* that was ſo *Sublime*,

His COUNTRY Damn'd His *Merit* as a *Crime*.

The TRAYTOR's Doom did on the PATRIOT Wait :

He Sav'd---- and then He *Periſh'd* by the STATE.

A Pa-

A Patient MONARCH, too *securely* Wife,

(*Unhappy* KINGS! They See with Others Eyes)

Weakly Confented to the Guilty Deed,

And made *Three* KINGDOMS in their CHAM-

(PION *Bleed.*

BRITONS, by *This Example* Taught, *Unite!*

Wound not the PUBLICK out of *Private Spight.*

To Great *Atchievements* Juft *Rewards* allow ;

Nor tear the *Lawrel* from the VICTOR's *Brow.*

Exert Your *Vigour* in the NATION's Caufe ;

But *Grudge* no RIVAL His *Deferv'd Applaufe.*

Safely We may Defy *MADRID* or *ROME*,

If no Sly *GUNDAMOR Prevails* at HOME.

SOME

MEMOIRS

OF

William Wycherley, Esq;

SOME

MEMOIRS

OF

William Wycherley, Efq;

 HIS GENTLEMAN was Son
of ...... *WYCHERLEY*, Efq;
of *CLEVE* in *SHROPSHIRE*,
five Miles diftant from *SHREWS-
BURY*, who was Poffeffed of
an ESTATE of about *Six Hundred Pounds* a
Year. It is faid He did not ftand much *Indebted*
to the *Tendernefs* of His FATHER, when his
Misfortunes gave Him moft reafon to *Demand*,
and *Expeĉt* His *Affiftance* ; namely after the
Death of King *CHARLES*, and the *Abdication*
of King *JAMES* the Second, with BOTH WHICH
PRINCES

PRINCES He had been in a great Degree of *Favour.* However That may be, He was certainly *Obliged* to HIS CARE for a *Liberal Education,* as well as to NATURE for *His Extraordinary Talents,* which He *Improved,* and *Embellished* with the utmost *Refinements.* After some Time spent at the UNIVERSITY, He was removed to the INNS of COURT, and *Entered* of the MIDDLE TEMPLE But making His *First Appearance* in Town in a *Reign* when WIT and GAIETY were the *Favourite Distinctions,* He soon left the *Dry Study* of the LAW, and gave into *Pursuits* more *Agreeable* to *His own* GENIUS, as well as to the *Taste* of the AGE. It was not long before He Became universally *Known,* and as generally *Caressed* by whatever there were of Persons *Eminent* for their *Quality,* or *Politeness* ; and, among Others of *that Character,* and *Rank,* the Famous Duke of *BUCKINGHAM* honoured Him with His *Familiarity,* and *Esteem.* But whether He received any *more Profitable Marks* of His FRIENDSHIP than *Publick Professions,* and *Outward Civilities,* I am not Able to Declare. A *Story* that Mr. *WYCHERLEY* related to Me, upon another Occasion, makes Me inclined to Believe, that *That Careless,* though *Ingenious,* NOBLEMAN might possibly *Neglect* to *Reward* MERIT

MERIT in HIM, as well as in the PERSON I am going to Mention.

Mr. *WYCHERLEY* had always laid hold of any Opportunity which offered, to Represent to HIS GRACE how well Mr. *BUTLER* had *Deserved* of the ROYAL FAMILY by Writing HIS *Inimitable* HUDIBRAS, and that it was a *Reproach* to the COURT, that a Person of His *Loyalty* and *Wit* should suffer in the *Obscurity*, and under the *Wants* HE did. The DUKE seemed always to *Hearken* to Him with *Attention* enough : and, after some time, undertook to *Recommend His Pretentions* to HIS MAJESTY. Mr. *WYCHERLEY*, in hopes to keep Him *Steady* to *His Word*, Obtained of HIS GRACE to *Name a* DAY, when He might Introduce *That Modest* and *Unfortunate* POET to *His New* PATRON. At last an *Appointment* was made, and the *Place of Meeting* was agreed to be THE ROE-BUCK. Mr. *BUTLER* and HIS FRIEND Attended accordingly : THE DUKE too joyned Them But, as the DEVIL would have it, The *Door* of the *Room* where They sat was *Open*, and HIS GRACE, who had seated Himself near it, Observing a PIMP of His Acquaintance (*the Creature* too was a KNIGHT) trip by with a *Brace* of LADIES, immediately *Quitted* His

A a

Engage-

Engagement to *follow* Another kind of *Bufinefs*, at which He was more *Ready* than in doing *Good Offices* to MEN OF DESERT; though No One was better *Qualified*, than HE was, both in regard of His FORTUNE and UNDERSTANDING, to *Protect* THEM: And from *That Hour* to the *Day* of his DEATH, Poor *BUTLER* never found the *leaft Effect* of HIS PROMISE.

BUT to Return to Mr. *WYCHERLEY*——— HIS COMPANY was not only Courted by The MEN, but HIS PERSON was as well Received by the LADIES; and as K *CHARLES* was extremely *Fond* of HIM upon account of His *Wit*, fome of the ROYAL MISTRESSES, I have been credibly Informed, fet *no lefs Value* upon *Thofe Parts* in Him, of which They were more *Proper Judges*. Thus the *Circle* of His LIFE was filled with All the *Delightful Variety* That FREEDOM, FAVOUR, and EASIE FORTUNE could adminifter to an *Elegant* MIND, and *Vigorous* CONSTITUTION. It is Known to Every One who hath Converfed in the World, that the AMOURS of *BRITAIN* in the *Firft Years* of *That* MONARCH might Furnifh as *Diverting* MEMOIRS, if well Related, as *Thofe* of *FRANCE* Publifhed by *RABUTIN*, or *Thofe* of *NERO's* COURT Writ by *PETRONIUS*. And it would
then

then perhaps, upon a nearer Inquiry, be found, that *Many* of the *Boafted Patterns* in MODESTY in the FAIR SEX, and of WISDOM in OUR OWN, That are fo *Edifying* to THIS PRESENT AGE, were the *Fortuitous Iffue* of PA-RENTS *remarkable* for Nothing in the FORMER but Their LUXURY and LEWDNESS. I cannot forbear to Mention (juft for the *Oddnefs* of the Thing) one Piece of *Gallantry*, among many others, that Mr. *WYCHERLEY* was once telling me They had in *Thofe Days.* It was THIS: There was an HOUSE at the BRIDGE-FOOT, where *Perfons* of *Better Condition* ufed to *Refort* (You fee how diftant the *Scene* then laid to what it doth Now) for PLEASURE and PRIVACY. The *Liquor* the LADIES and their LOVERS ufed to Drink at *Thofe Meetings* was CANARY; and, among *Other Compliments* the GENTLEMEN paid their MISTRESSES, *This* it feems was always *One,* to *take hold of the Bottom of their* SMOCKS, and, *pouring* the WINE *through That Filtre,* feaft their *Ima-ginations* with the Thought of *What* give the *Zefto,* and fo *Drink a Health* to the TOAST.

HE is juftly *Celebrated* among the *Beft* of Our ENGLISH COMICK POETS. His PLAYS are an Excellent *Satire* upon the *Vices* and *Fol-*

lies

lies of the AGE in which He lived. *His* STYLE is *Masculine*, and *His* WIT is *Pointed :* And yet with All that *Severity* and *Sharpness* with which HE appears on the STAGE, They who were of his *Familiar Acquaintance* Applauded him for the *Generosity* and *Gentleness* of *His* MAN-NERS. HE was certainly a GOOD-NATURED MAN : And I reckon it as ONE *Great Mark* of *such a* DISPOSITION, that HE was as *Impatient* to hear HIS FRIEND *Calumniated*, as some other People would be to find THEMSELVES *Defamed.* I have more than once been a Witness of that *Honourable Tenderness* in HIS TEMPER. But the present Lord *LANS-DOWN* hath in so handsome a Manner *Vindicated* Him upon THIS HEAD, that I refer the READER to HIS APOLOGY, which hath long since been made PUBLICK.

HE was *twice* MARRIED : In the *Younger Part of His Life* to the *Countess* of DROGHE DA, who settled her *Whole Fortune* upon Him. But, his TITLE being *Disputed* after *her Death,* the *Expences* of the *Law,* and other *Incumbrances* so far *Reduced* him, that He was not able to satisfie the *Impatience* of his CREDITORS, and they flung him at last into PRISON.

I have

I have been affured, that the BOOKSELLER who Printed his *PLAIN-DEALER*, by which he got almoft as much *Money* as the AUTHOR gained *Reputation*, was fo *Ungrateful* to his BE-NEFACTOR, as to refufe to Lend him *Twenty Pounds* in his *extreme Neceffities.*

In *That* CONFINEMENT He Languifhed SEVEN YEARS : Nor was He *Releafed* from *Thofe Bonds*, 'till King *JAMES* going to fee the PLAY I juft mentioned, was fo Charmed with the *Entertainment*, that He gave immediate Orders for the *Payment* of HIS DEBTS, adding to *That* Grace a PENSION alfo of 200 *l* per *Annum*, while HE Continued in *ENGLAND*. But the *Bountiful Intentions* of *That* PRINCE towards him had not the *Defigned Effect*; purely, as I have been told by the late Lord *DUN-BAR*, through the *Modefty* of this Poor Gentleman, who was afhamed to Confefs to the Earl of *MULGRAVE* (whom the King had fent to Demand it) the full *Account* of fo *large* a *Sum* as he knew to be *Owing* by him. Mr. *WYCHER-LEY* hath acknowledged to Me, that *That* NOBLEMAN juft named, lent him likewife once 500*l.* upon his Bond. HE laboured under the Weight of *Thefe Difficulties*, 'till *His* FATHER *Dyed :*

Dyed: and *then* too the ESTATE that Defcended to him, was left him under very *Uneafie
Limitations,* He being only made TENANT for
LIFE. Befides,, he was at that Time HIMSELF
of a very *Advanced Age* ; *Weak* in *his* BODY,
and *Broken* in *his* SPIRIT ; Drawing towards
the *Cloudy* EVENING of a LIFE, that had fcarce
the *faint Glimmerings* remaining of *That* LUS-
TRE which made HIM fo *Gazed* at in *his* ME-
RIDIAN. How fully now ought it to *Convince*
US of the *Vanity* of all HUMAN PRETENTIONS,
and of the *little Reafon* we have to *Pride* OUR-
SELVES in the *Falfe Glitter,* and *Fading Orna-
naments* of FORTUNE, or the *fhort-liv'd Perfe-
Étions* of OUR NATURE, when we *Reflect* up-
on the *Example* of *This* PERSON, in whom
were Beheld fo many *Cruel Reverfes* of BOTH !
HE, who had been *Indulged* in the *Sweets* of
PLENTY, even to *Excefs* ; Who had *wantonly
Roved* through all the *inchanting Mazes* of
PLEASURE ; Who was *Admired* for his WIT,
and *Valued* for his WORTH ; This MAN, alas !
lived to fee HIMSELF, in a fhort time, *Neglected*
by HIS FRIENDS, *Forfaken* by HIS RELA-
TIONS, and, in the end, *Condemned,* by the
Iniquity of his FATE, to *Suffer* under a *Clofe*
and *Long* IMPRISONMENT And when, after
many Years, he was, at laft, *fet at Liberty* from
That

That RESTRAINT, and might feem, by the DEATH of his FATHER, to be lifted up into higher Expectations, and an *Eafier Seat* in Life, HE not only found HIMSELF ftill *Fettered* in his FORTUNE by the *Narrow Settlement* his FATHER had made of *His* ESTATE, but, what was Worfe, *Afflicted* with SICKNESS, and *Decaying* apace in his INTELLECTS. HE was fo CONSCIOUS of this his *Declining Condition*, that upon PUBLISHING, Ten or Eleven Years before he DYED, a BOOK of VERSES to *Which* he Prefixed a PRINT that had been taken from the PICTURE SIR *P. LELY* had formerly *Drawn* for him, HE ordered *This Motto* to be placed underneath it,

Quantum Mutatus ab illo !

a MELANCHOLY EJACULATION ! if HE had not the HOPES of ANOTHER WORLD to COMFORT him after the *Difappointment* and *ill Ufage* he had met with in THIS. Under thefe Circumftances, *Confined* as they were, he took care to *leffen* every Year, *confiderably*, the DEBT he had Contracted. But feeing no likelihood that he fhould be Able *intirely* to *Difcharge* IT by what he might, with *Convenience*, fpare out of his ANNUAL RENTS ; and not being allowed by his FATHER's WILL to *raife any Money* by MORTGAGE, or SALE of his Land, HE took

a Mea *Method* of doing it, that was in his *Power*, tho' Few fufpected it to be in his *Choice*, at *Thofe Years.* This was by making a JOIN-TURE. HE had often indeed told a GENTLE-MAN of my *Acquaintance* (but it was underftood to be faid by HIM rather IN *Terrorem* to his NEPHEW, than what was meant as his *Real* INTENTIONS) " That He was Refolved to " *Dye* MARRIED, though He could not bear the " Thoughts of *Living* MARRIED." Accordingly, juft at the *Eve* of *His* DEATH, he was joyned in WEDLOCK to a *Young Gentlewoman,* and *Eleven Days* after the *Celebration* of *thefe His Second* NUPTIALS, in the Year 1715, and about the EIGHTIETH of his AGE, he DYED, with fo *little Reluctance,* that HE might be faid to *Drop* off the TREE of LIFE, like FRUIT that had *hung* long *Expecting* to be *Gathered* HE lyes *Interred* in the VAULT of *COVENT-GARDEN* CHURCH.

F I N I S.

THE
LIFE
OF
T. P. ATTICUS.
WITH
REMARKS.

By RICHARDSON PACK Esq;

FORTUNA *fævo* læta *Negotio,*
Et ludum *infolentem* ludere PERTINAX,
   Tranfmutat *incertos Honores,*
    Nunc *Mihi,* nunc *alii* BENIGNA.
Laudo *Manentem.* Si *celeres* quatit
Pennas, *refigno* quæ dedit, *et mea*
   Virtute me involvo------

                           Horat.

LONDON:
Printed for E. CURLL in *Fleetftreet,*
MDCCXIX.

PREFACE.

I Remember to have been once Told in Conversation by the Ingenious Father Van Eckt, *formerly* Agent *at the Court of* Barcelona *from That of* Dusseldorp, *of a Friend of* His, *an* Italian, *Who had so* Perfect *a* Mastery, *both of the* Latin *and* His Mother Tongue, *that*

in

in a Translation *He made of the* Whole Volume *of* Lives *Writ by* CORNELIUS NEPOS, *He was so far from Committing any Confiderable* Miftake, *that He did not find Occafion, upon Revifing it afterwards, to Alter any one* Line, *or* Expreffion *from What it was When it* firft *fell from his* Pen. My Abilities *are, I confefs, fo very much* Inferiour *to the happy* Skill *of* That Learned Gentleman, *that I freely declare it hath been a great deal longer before I could in* any Degree *Satisfy my Self in the* Verfion *I Attempted of* This Single Life *of* ATTICUS: *And,*

And, *after Perusing it several Times*, *and Correcting* many Faults *That had Escaped my Observation in the* Rough Draught; *I must, I fear, stand Indebted to the* Candour *of the* Reader *for* Pardoning many more *That may still Deserve His* Censure. *However, I am not without Hope that This* Copy, *Imperfect as it is, may not be Thought a* Disgrace *to the* Original. *If I have not done all the* Justice *I desired to my* Author, *I may venture, I believe, without Vanity to say, I have been less* Injurious *to Him than the* * Three Others Who Pre-*

---

* Sir M. Halt, Mr. Morgan, and a late *Anonymous* Translator.

Pretended Before, to make Him Speak ENGLISH *in* Publick.

There is one Objection *Which I Foresee will be made to This Performance by some* Verbal CRITICKS *That I am so far from being in* Pain *about, that I Value My Self for having taken a Method* They *will* Condemn: *I mean, that in Some Places I have rather* PARAPHRASED *than* TRANSLATED. *Not to Mention the Difference of the* Idioms; *and What Mr.* LOCKE *hath somewhere Remarked, That,* There is Scarce a Word in any one Language That is *the* Sign of

PREFACE.

of a COMPLEX IDEA, Which can be rendered by a SINGLE TERM in Another That shall exactly Correspond to It: *There are* Many Things *in* Antient Authors *of Which there needed only a* Hint *to be Given to make Them Understood by Their* Contemporaries, *That will require a* Comment *to Convey Them* Intelligibly *to a* Modern Reader. *This might be Proved by several Instances Which I could Produce out of This Little Book that lies before Me.* But without Offering any Thing else in my Defense, it is Sufficient I have the Authority of the Celebrated

lebrated Names of COWLEY, SPRAT, *and* DRYDEN *to Plead for my* Practice; *with Whom I had much rather be Thought to* Err, *than receive the senseless* Applause *of a Thousand* Stiff Conceited SCIOLISTS.

ERRATA.

Page 22, Line 1 Read, *of His.* Ditto, Line 11, for *General,* read *Generals.* Page 36, Line 7, for *or,* read *of.* Page 47, Line 1, for *And,* read *But.* Page 51, Line 9, for *then,* read *than.*

TO HIS
GRACE

THE

Duke of *ARGYLL*.

WITH THE

LIFE of *ATTICUS*.

Printed in the Year MDCCXIX.

To His GRACE

THE

Duke of *ARGYLL*.

HE MUSE, That Scorns to *Flatter*, or

Defame,

In ev'ry *Change* of FORTUNE *still*

The SAME;

That, Carelefs how The *Factious Crowd* Divide,

Courts not Their *Folly*, nor Their Leaders' *Pride* ;

A   To

To Thee, ARGYLL! Who wer't Her earlieſt
   Praiſe,

Aſpires once more Her Faithful Voice to raiſe :

Nor Fears the *Strain* can *Unharmonious* be,

That Sings of ATTICUS, and Sings to THEE.

Viewing *This Image* of ROME's Fav'rite *Son*,

Pleas'd She Beheld *Some Features* Like *Your Own.*

Like THEE HE Liv'd *Untainted* in an Age

Deform'd with *Crimes*, and Mad with *Civil Rage.*

Like THEE HE *firmly* to the LAWS *Adher'd,*

Yet more by PRUDENCE than by PARTY
   Steer'd.

Like THEE HE Learn'd AMBITION to
   Deſpiſe,

Yet Gaz'd on GLORY with a *Lover*'s Eyes.

Like THEE when Rais'd by *Favour*, or *Succeſs,*

Deſert He Cheriſh'd ; and Reliev'd *Diſtreſs.*
                                                  Like

To his Grace the Duke of ARGYLL. ❦

Like THEE *Disdaining* each low Vulgar End,

Confess'd the PATRIOT, and Avow'd the

FRIEND.

Like THEE HE met------ah *Worst* of Human

Wrongs !

Ungrateful *Hearts*, and false Invidious *Tongues.*

But pass We That Severe Remembrance by.

The Palms Oppress'd shoot faster to the Sky.

O Fam'd in *Council !* as Renown'd in *Fight !*

Contemplate here This old *Illustrious* Knight ;

In all Events *Superior* to His *Fate* ;

Divinely *Good*, as Eminently *Great :*

Whose Gen'rous *Exit* shew'd Him to Excell

No less in *Dying* than in *Living* well.

How

How FEW in *Those laſt Conflicts* do We find

But *Sink* beneath the *Burthen* of their *Mind ?*

Tho' VALOUR Guards the *Tent,* or STATE
   the *Door,*

The *Scene* ſoon changes in *That Dreadful Hour.*

Each *Guilty Thought* will *then* preſs *rudely* in,

Like CÆSAR *Stab'd* by our own *Darling* Sin.

But H-E knew Nothing to *Alarm* His Soul.

No *Clouds* of *Vice* His *Sunſhine* did Controul:

With undiminiſh'd *Luſtre* HE Retreats,

And as HE *mildly* Roſe, as *calmly* Sets.

  Shall then ſome *Pedant Scribe,* or *Rev'rend*
   Drone

That dully Nods upon a *Pulpit-Throne,*

          Who

Who meanly *Merit* by *Profeſſion* Scan,

Exclude from H E A V E N This *Juſt,* This *Pious*
    Man ?

Sure F A I T H Alone is but a *Weak Pretence ;*

And Want of C H A R I T Y is Want of *Senſe.*

The *Barren Figtree* was of right *Accurſt,*

But the Fair *Fruitful Vine* for Uſe was *Nurſt.*

    Give Me T H O U P O W E R *Immortal!* and
    Unchang'd !

Whoſe *Care Paternal* has through *Ages* rang'd ;

(CHRISTIAN, or PAGAN, *Both* Thy
    Influence felt,

Whoſe *Bounty* is to All Thy *Creatures* dealt)

Give Me to Travel o'er Thoſe *Realms* of *Light,*

Where E P I C T E T U S ſhines *ſerenely* Bright ;

                    Where

§ *To his Grace the Duke of* ARGYLL.

Where VARRO and POMPONIUS lead the
  Way;

Who Follow VIRTUE ne'er can *Go astray.*

O D E,

To Major *PACK*,

U P O N

Reading His Excellent T R A N S L A T I O N, and R E M A R K S on the

LIFE of POMPONIUS ATTICUS.

WHILST We in vain our ISLE Inflame,

To *Vertue*'s fair Persuit, You Give

To warm each Breast a ROMAN *Name*,

And teach us *better* how to Live.

Who can thy ATTICUS Explore,

Nor feel his Soul with *Pity* Glow;

Who read The God-like PATRIOT o'er

And longer live his Country's *Foe?*

b   Your

ODE, *to Major* PACK.

Your bosom panting after *Fame*

    Disdains the *Censures* of your ISLE;

Where to Record a *Virtuous* Name

    Is not to *Praise*, but to *Revile*.

Cou'd we Thy ROMAN's Love repeat

    Inspir'd to *Pity* Human Woe,

The aking Heart would *Seldom* beat,

    The Mournful Eye would *Never* flow.

No Stream the *Wretch's* Sorrows fed,

    But Gave His Bosom equal Pain,

And each despairing *Drop* He shed,

    Was answer'd with a *Tear* again.

Their adverse Fate the *Virtuous* Bless,

    Sure, from His Love, *Relief* to find;

Which, in *His* view, to give *Distress*,

    Was *almost* deem'd to be more *Kind*.

ODE, to Major PACR.

So much each *Foe* His VIRTUES Charm,

    So sure each Wond'ring Breast subdue;

His *Goodness* blunts each *Rival's* Arm,

    And leaves The SWORD *no more* to do;

Tho' oft with Thoughts of Vengeance prest,

    The Guilty Weapon to distain;

HE bravely bares His naked Breast,

    And Urges ROME to strike----IN VAIN.

In vain the Steel Her Sons Unsheath,

    To *Bribe* His FRIENDSHIP, or *Remove*;

Which Boasting *Power* to stop his *Breath*,

    Yet wanted *Force* to Shake His *Love*!

What Ease Thy *Pity* must Supply,

    To EXIL'D worth What Succour Give;

Prompted by FATE, to Sink and Die,

    Inspir'd by THEE to Rise and Live!

        b 2   Thy

ODE, *to Major* PACK.

Thy *Triumphs*, CÆSAR, wanted Charms,
    Thy *Lawrels*, POMPEY, ceas'd to Bloom
Since from each WARRIOUR's *Guilty* Arms,
    His ROME was sure to meet her *Doom*.

With Pious Grief those *Wreaths* HE Views,
    Which round each *Victor's* Temples Grow,
Assur'd THAT Arm which *most* Subdues,
    Was *But* his COUNTRY's *Greater* FOE.

Tho' Full to ROME, Her *Ensigns* Wave,
    And Flame Ador'd along the Skies,
HE Thinks *whose* Blood them *Triumue* Gave,
    And calls away his *Aking Eyes*.

Then, (most His *Brav'ry* to Commend.)
    He bids His Gen'rous *Bounty* Flow,
When to Relieve a wretched *Friend*,
    Was *But* to gain a certain *Foe*.

What

O D E, *to Major* P A C K.

What Glory to Your MONARCH's Name,

    Are You ordain'd by Heaven to bring;

Whose SWORD *so well* can Guard his *Fame,*

    Whose VOICE so well that *Fame* can Sing?

With Both MINERVAS doubly *Bleſt,*

    A doubtful *Tranſport* YOU Inſpire;

Concealing in one happy Breaſt

    The WARRIOUR's *flame,* the POET's *fire.*

O ſtill FAM'D YOUTH your Self Exceed,

    Your Country Smiling to peruſe

Her Vanquiſh'd Rivals doubly Bleed,

    Both by your *Sword,* and in your *Muſe!*

While to Your happy ſhaded Brow

    Each *Power* a diff'rent Wreath conveys;

The God of WAR His *Lawrel Bough,*

    The God of VERSE his *Peaceful* Bays.

                                What

O D E, *to Major* P A C K.

What *Tranſport* does Your ARM Inſpire,

    Your VOICE what ſofter *Paſſion* move,

One, to *Awake* the WARRIOUR's Fire

    And One to *Sooth* the VIRGIN's Love!

With Joy, thy ROMAN's ſmiling Shade

    Forgets His *Bliſs*; well pleas'd to ſee

His *Fame* and *Worth* ſo greatly *Paid*,

    By ALBION *Read*, and *Sung* by THEE.

O! did Each Breaſt Thoſe *Vertues* feel

    Thy HERO's *Life*, or *Death* diſplay;

What MONARCH then cou'd draw his *Steel*,

    What pious SUBJECT not *Obey*?

No *Art* thy ALBION then wou'd Try,

    No *Other Force* Her SOVERAIGN prove,

To tell How Each on Each Rely,

    But WE our *Smiles*, and HE his *Love*.

O

ODE, *to Major* PACK.

O may this *Soft*, this *Laſt* DEBATE,

    At length compleat BRITANNIA's *Reſt*;

And *Facb* lament His *kindeſt Fate*,

    Unlcſs the *Otl er* is as *Bleſt*.

                           T. NEWCOMB.

THE
LIFE
OF
POMPONIUS ATTICUS.

POMPONIUS ATTICUS, Defcended from One of the moft * Ancient Families among the ROMANS, was of the *Equeftrian* Order, which Dignity His Anceftors had all along Enjoyed. He was Happy in a

B   Father

---

* *He deived his Pedigree from* NUMA POMPI-LIUS, *the fecond* ROMAN *King, One of Whofe Sons was called* POMPO *from whence his Pofterity were Styled* POMPONII.

Father equally Careful and Indulgent; and One who, in the Account of Thofe Times, paffed for Rich, but above all Things Remarkable for his Love of Letters : Who, as He had *Himfelf* a true Relifh of *Learning*, was very Diligent to have His *Son* Inftructed in all kinds of *Knowledge* that were Proper for His Years. The *Boy*, befides a Natural *Docility*, had a wonderful *Sweetnefs* in his *Voice*, and in his *Mien* That rendered his *Pronunciation* and *Delivery* as *Graceful*, as the *Quicknefs* of his *Parts* was *Surprizing*. Thefe Promifes of a Shining *Genius* made Him looked upon even at *School* with a *Diftinction*, that gave no fmall Uneafinefs to the Generous Youths Who were his *Fellow-Pupils :* Tho' their *Emulation* no way leffened their *Affection* towards Him. Of That Number were L u c i u s T o r-q u a t u s, C a i u s M a r i u s the Son, and M a r c u s C i c e r o :
All

All Whom He so far Engaged by his Agreeable Manners in those earlier Acquaintances of Life, that No One was ever after Dearer to Them in the Whole Course of their Fortunes.

HE lost His Father betimes: And soon after, in the Civil Dissentions in which PUBLIUS SULPITIUS the *Tribune* of the People was put to Death, He *Himself* was in danger, tho' then very Young, to have shared the same Fate by Reason of his Relation to Him; ANICIA a Cousin-German to POMPONIUS having Married MARCUS SERVIUS the Brother of SULPITIUS. Alarmed therefore with What Befell his *Kinsman*, and Observing afterwards the Confusions in which CINNA'*s Faction* had involved the City ; and finding He could not Hope, during such Commotions, to Live with Dignity and Ease at *Home*, but

that,

that, while C I N N A's and S Y L A's
different Interests divided the Common
wealth, He muſt unavoidably Offend
either the One Party or the Other; He
judged it to be a Fit Seaſon for Him to
Proſecute His Former *Studies*, and to that
end removed Himſelf to A T H E N S.
Not that in thoſe *Doubtful Times* He denied His Help to any of His *Friends* Who
were under the Diſpleaſure of the Go-
vernment, of Which M A R I U S was
an Inſtance : Whom He Supported with
Money in his Flight, after He had been
Declared an *Enemy to His Country* by
Thoſe in Power. However, that His
own *Domeſtick Concerns* might receive no
Detriment by His Reſidence *Abroad*, He
Tranſported the Greateſt Part of His Effects with Him. Here His Generous Way
of Living deſervedly gained Him an Univ-
verſal Eſteem among the A T H E N I A N S.
For, not to mention the Service His *Per-*
ſonal

fonal Credit, which was already grown very Confiderable in the World, might do Them, He more *immediately* Obliged Them by frequently Relieving the Poverty of their *Publick Stock* out of His Wealthier *Private One.* Thus whenever any Sudden Demand was made upon Them for Money they Owed, and They could not raife the Sum but upon unequal Conditions, He never failed to interpofe his Afliftance : However, it was upon thefe *Exprefs terms* ; that as He would Require no *Intereft* for What He *Lent* Them, fo They fhould Oblige Themfelves to be Punctual in the *Payment.* In *Loth Which* He really Confulted Their *Advantage :* As He neither Encouraged Them in a *Negligence* of Their Affairs by fuffering Them to run in *Arrear*; nor Plunged Them ftill deeper in *Debt* by loading Them with *Ufury.* To thefe kind Offices He added another piece of Liberality

rality by giving to Each Citizen a Bounty of *Wheat* of Six Bushels, which Measure They call a *Medimnus* in their Language.

HIS Deportment in This Place was with That *easie Grandeur*, that He seemed at once upon a *level* with the *Lowest*, and yet an *Equal* with the *Highest*. In return, *They* studied every Way to do *Him* all imaginable *Publick Honours*; and, among other marks of their Respect, Addressed Him to Accept of his FREEDOM. But He Declined That Favour, because He knew it was the Opinion of Some People, that a ROMAN *Citizen* forfeited the Privileges of That Title, upon his being Admitted a *Denizen* in any FOREIGN *Town*. He perpetually Opposed, so long as He Continued Here, the Setting up His *Statue* ; but could not Prevent it, after His Departure : And there were some Erected in Memory of HIM,

HIM, and of * PILIA, in the Places of their moſt Solemn Worſhip. For They had in a manner Revered Him as *Their Oracle*; had Conſulted *his Advice*, and Relied chiefly upon *his Management* in the Adminiſtration of all Their *Publick Buſineſs*. It may certainly be reckoned among the Principal *Bleſſings* of FORTUNE to *Him*, that he was *Born* in THAT CITY Which was The MISTRESS of the *World*; that The SEAT of *Univerſal Empire* was His MOTHER EARTH: And it is as Great a *Mark* of His PRUDENCE that When He Became an *Inhabitant* in That UNIVERSITY and COMMON-WEALTH, Which for *Antiquity*, *Politeneſs*, and *Learning* Excelled all Others, He

was

---

* *The Learned are very much at Variance in determining Who this Perſon was, but as the Wife of* ATTICUS *was Named* PILIA; *many Interpreters have Thought it was to Her the* ATHENIANS *paid This Compliment.*

was no lefs Eminent in Their *Affecti-on*, and in Their *Efteem*.

WHEN SYLLA Arrived here, in His Return from ASIA, He conftantly during His Stay made the Young POMPONIUS His Gueft, Charmed with the *Sweetnefs* of his *Temper*, and his *Accomplifhments* in *Learning*. For He had the GREEK *Language* fo *Familiar* to Him, that One would have almoft Thought ATHENS to have been the Place of his *Birth*: But yet when he Spoke the ROMAN, there was a *Propriety* and *Beauty* in his *Expreffion* that was not to be *Acquired*, and plainly Difcovered it felf to be *Natural*. His *Rehearfals* too in *Poetry* either LATIN or GREEK were with a juftnefs of *Cadence*, and an Elegance of *Pronunciation* That Nothing could Exceed. Upon thefe Accounts His *Perfon* grew fo Admired, and His

Con-

Conversation so Coveted by SYLLA, that He would scarce ever suffer Him to be out of His Company; and He Endeavoured by all the Arguments He could use to Engage Him in His *Expedition.* But to All his Persuasions and Offers POMPONIUS made Him no Other than This Modest Reply; " Do not, Sir, I " Beseech You, Urge Me to take up " Arms against *Those,* whom I *Abandon-* " *ed,* and I T A L Y too, only, that I " might not be Obliged to serve with " *Them* against *You*". SYLLA accepting His *Excuse,* and acknowledging His *Compliment,* gave Order, upon His Departure, that All the Presents the *City* had made Him should be sent to ATTI-cus.

H E Continued in This *Voluntary Ex-ile* Here for many Years; and though He was no *Indiligent Manager* of His *Fortune,* and what Time He could spare from His Application to *That* was generally Given to the Pleasures of *Study*, or Taken up in Consultations and Business relating to the ATHENIAN *State*, yet He found many Opportunities to perform very Important Services to His Friends on the *Suffering Side*. He frequently Assisted at Their *Private Rendesvouz*, and was never Wanting to Them in any *Exigence*, as was seen in the Case of CICERO, to Whom He shewed an inviolable Fidelity in all his Misfortunes ; and sent Him at one Time, upon his being Obliged to fly His Country, Two hundred and fifty thousand * *Sesterces.* The Affairs of ITALY being at last Composed, and *Peace* restored, He Returned to ROME in the Consulship, as I remember, of

L u-

---

* *A Thousand S sterces is Computed to be* 7 l. 16 s 2 d *of our Mony*

LUCIUS COTTA and LUCIUS TORQUATUS. But He was so *Regretted* at ATHENS, that The Day He Left It looked like a Day of *General Mourning* There, *the Whole City* Witnessing by Their *Tears* the Sense They had of Their *Future Loss*.

HE had an *Uncle*, one QUINTUS CECILIUS, a ROMAN Knight, a mighty Friend of LUCIUS LUCULLUS, *Rich*, but of a *Nature* the hardest in the World to be *Pleased*. The *Moroseness* of This Old Man, which scarce any one else could Bear, He submitted to with That Deference and Observance, as to keep himself in his good Graces, without having once Disobliged him, to the Last: And accordingly He reaped the Fruit of his *Piety*. For CÆCILIUS on his Death-Bed appointed him by his Will, *Heir* to *Three Fourths* of his Estate, by which

Suc-

Succession he Gained ten Millions of *Sesterces.*

THE Sister of ATTICUS was Married to QUINTUS TULLIUS CICERO. This Match had been brought about by MARCUS CICERO, with Whom ATTICUS had lived, from the time of their being *Schoolfellows,* in the strictest *Union,* and with much more *Familiarity* than with QUINTUS: By which it may appear, that *Similitude* of *Manners* is of Greater Force, than *Affinity,* in FRIENDSHIP. There was likewise That *Intimacy* between Him and HORTENSIUS, the most Celebrated *Orator* of That Age, that it was Doubtful Which of the Two, CICERO or HORTENSIUS, loved Him best: And, What was very Extraordinary, *He* by His Good Offices effected that in *Them,* between Whom there was so Great an

Emula-

Emulation of PRAISE, there was not the leaft *Envy* of SUCCESS, but a Perfect *Agreement* between the *Illuftrious Rivals.*

WITH Regard to the COMMON-WEALTH his *Conduct* was fuch, as Gave Him the Reputation of *Adhering*, as He really did, always to the *Right Side:* Not that He would ever *Embark in any Party-Adventures Whatfoever* ; Declaring, that he Thought a Man to be as little His own *Mafter*, Who had once Launched out on the *Waves of* AMBITION, as He was, Who lay Beating on *Thofe* at SEA. And for This Reafon he never flood *Candidate* for any *Publick* POST or EMPLOYMENT, though He might very well have Pretended to Them upon account Both of His *Intereft*, and of His *Birth*. But the CONSTITUTION had been *Broken*, and BRIBERY was grown fo *Barefaced*, that Thofe *Offices* could not be *Obtained* without *Violation* of the L A W S, nor *Exercifed* with *Integrity* (fo depraved were the *Morals* of the *Party*) without *Danger* to the P E R S O N. To the *Publick Sales* He came not. The *Publick Revenues* He neither *Farmed* himfelf; nor would He be *Bound* for Any Who did. He never *Openly* or *Privately Accufed* Any Man. *Contention* was What He Hated; and He was never Known either to be *Plaintiff* in a *Caufe* of his Own, or *Defendant* at the *Suit* of Another. Though He Accepted the *Lieutenancies* That had been Offered Him by feveral C O N S U L S, and P R Æ T O R S, He would Follow None of Them into Their P R O V I N C E S: Content with the *Honour* of the *Commiffion*, He Defpifed the *Profit* o it: Nor would He even Accompany His Relation Q U I N T U S C I C E R O, when he went P R Æ T O R

into

into ASIA, though He might have Obtained the Rank of a LEGATE or GENERAL OFFICER There; Thinking it Below *Him*, Who could not be Tempted with *the Vanity* of Commanding in CHIEF, to ACT under the *Direction* of ANOTHER. And in This He not only Confulted His *Dignity*, but His *Quiet*, Avoiding thereby all Sufpicions of *Guilt*, or *Corruption:* While, at the fame Time, *The Court he made to Any One was the better Received*, fince it was known, *His Profeffions* of fervice were *Sincere*, and not owing either to His *Hopes*, or to His *Fears*.

HE was about *Sixty*, when CÆSAR's *Civil War* firft broke out. He had therefore the Exemption of *Old Age* to Plead, and did not Stir at all from the *City*. Such however, of His Friends who left the Town to Follow POMPEY's Fortune,

He

He furnished with Whatever they Wanted at his *own Expence* ; and THAT GENERAL was not in the least Offended that *He* did not *Perfonally* Attend Him. For he had laid no *Obligations* upon ATTICUS, as He had on many Others, whom He Advanced to *Riches* and *Honours* in the COMMONWEALTH, fome of Whom Followed Him into the Field very *unwillingly*, while the Reft incurred his *Difpleafure* by remaining *Neuters* at home. On the Other fide This his *Inaction* was fo Acceptable to CÆSAR, that when, after his *Victory*, He levied by his *Mandatory Letters* certain Sums from feveral particular Perfons, He not only gave ATTICUS no Trouble of That Kind ; but Releafed, in Compliment to him, His NEPHEW, and QUINTUS CICERO, Whom He had Taken *Prifoners* in POMPEY's Camp. Thus *by Keeping Steady to his*

OLD

OLD MAXIMS, *He freed Himself* from NEW DIFFICULTIES, *and* NEW DANGERS.

IN the REVOLUTION That Succeeded CÆSAR's *Death*, when the Government was in the Hands of BRUTUS, and CASSIUS, and the Whole City seemed to turn their Eyes upon his Conduct, He was in such Favour with BRUTUS, as That Young Nobleman lived not more familiarly with Any of his Equals in Years than with This Old Gentleman, and not only used him as his *Counsellour* on *Serious* and *Weighty Occasions,* but always made him a *Party* in his more *Pleasurable Conversations.* There had been a *Project* set on foot at That time by some People to raise a *Private Bank* among the ROMAN *Knights* as a Reward to the ASSINATORS of CÆSAR.   This They

D   Thought

thought might be eafily Brought about, if the *Principal* Members of *That Order* gave into the *Scheme*: Accordingly AT-TICUS was Clofetted by CAIUS FLA-VIUS the Confidant of BRUTUS, and told, it would much Encourage the *Contribution*, if he would Begin the *Subfcription*. HE, Who always Thought the *Services One did one's Friends fhould be Done without any View* to FACTION, and *Abhorred* all fuch *Counfels*, Replied, that if BRUTUS wanted any *Supply* that He could Afford Him, He might freely ufe his Purfe : But for the *Other Demand*, He would neither *Confent* to it *Himfelf*, nor would He endeavour to *Perfuade Any One* elfe to *Comply* with it. Thus *by the Breath of This Single Man That Whole Confederacy was Diffolved at once*. Nor was it long before the *Scene Changed*, and ANTHONY became *Superior* ; fo that BRUTUS and CASSIUS finding Their

Affair-

Affairs in the *Provinces* (which for Form fake the C O N S U L S had Committed to Them,) in a Defperate Condition, Betook Themfelves to *Flight*. A T T I C U S Who would never enter into an Affociation as many Others did to provide an *Iftablifhment* for T H A T   P A R T Y while it was *Flourifhing*; now B R U T U S was in *Difgrace*, and Obliged to *Quit* I T A L Y, fent Him a Prefent of one hundred thoufand *Sefterces:* And at another time made Him a Remittance to *Epirus* of three hundred Thoufand more. Nor did He pay his Adoration to the *Rifing*, any more than He turned his Back upon the *Setting Sun*.

A F T E R This followed the Battle of M U T I N A. And Here if I barely Style Him P R U D E N T, I fhould give Him too mean a Character, Who might feem rather I N S P I R E D: (if

a Per-

a Perpetual Natural Goodnefs, which no
Accidents could Increafe, or Diminifh,
may Deferve *That Appellation*.) ANTHO-
NY is *now* Adjudged *an Enemy to his
Country*; He Abandons all ITALY,
there appear not the leaft Hopes of his
Reftoration.   Not only His *Enemies*, Who
were very *Numerous*, and They very
Powerful, but even His *Friends* (fuch I
mean who lately had been fo) Confpired
in His *Ruin*, Every One making a kind
of *Merit* of Their *Hatred to Him*. All Who
were known to have been in any Degree
of *Confidence* with Him are *Profecuted* · His
Wife is in Danger of being *Defpoiled* of
Her *Eftate* ; His *Children* are *Threatned* with
Deftruction. Well! how doth ATTICUS
behave on This Occafion?   HE had always lived in the moft *intimate Familiarity* with CICERO, and had the *higheft
Efteem*, and *Kindnefs* for BRUTUS;
yet was He fo far from *Indulging* Their
Revenge

Revenge againſt ANTHONY, that, on the contrary, He *concealed* many of *His Partiſans*, till They could make Their Eſcape; and *Aſſiſted* Them in all Their Neceſſities: In particular, PUBLIUS VOLUMNIUS met with ſuch Uſage at his hands, that He could not have Expected, or Deſired more from a *Father.* And for FULVIA, the Wife of ANTHONY, Who was Detained in Town by ſome *Law-Buſineſs* She had Depending, the Doubtful Iſſue of which made Her extremely Anxious, He was very Active on her Behalf, and performed many Signal Services to Her. He appeared for Her frequently at the Courts of *Judicature,* and was Her *Bail* in every *Action* that was Commenced againſt Her. Nor was *This* All. *She* had, in her more Proſperous Circumſtances, Agreed for the *Purchaſe* of certain Lands, and entered into *Articles* for Payment of the Money

at

at a *Day Appointed*; but, after the Calamity That befell her Family, She was in no Condition to Raise it: Upon This, ATTICUS Interposed, and Advanced Her the Necessary Sums without *Interest*, or any *Consideration* Whatever: Esteeming it *The Greatest Gain, to Enjoy the Reputation of a* GRATEFUL MIND, *and* to convince the World it was the MAN and *not* His FORTUNE, *to Whom He was a* FRIEND. Nor could Any One Imagine that he had any Other View at *That Juncture.* For there was not the least Colour to Believe that ANTHONY would once more be at the Head of Affairs. However, This His *Universal Tenderness* was Reprehended by some *Warm Patriots* as a *Remissness* in his Country's Cause, and a Want of *Zeal* rather than an Excess of *Charity.* But it was a *Rule* He had laid down to *Himself,* to Consider less the *Popularity* than the *Principle*

ple of *Actions*; and while They were Confiftent with his own *Honour*, He little Valued the *Cenfure* or *Applaufe* of Other Men.

ON a fudden there was a *Reverfe* of *Fortune*. Upon ANTHONY's Return into ITALY, Every One believed ATTICUS to be in *Imminent Danger*, becaufe of his Known *Inclinations* to CICERO and BRUTUS. Accordingly, upon the Arrival of the GENERAL, He left the *Forum*, and, not Doubting but He fhould be in the Number of the *Profcribed*, He privately Withdrew to the Houfe of PUBLIUS VOLUMNIUS, whofe Obligations to *Him* I mentioned a little Above, (for fo *Various* and *Sudden* were the *Changes* in thofe Times, that the fame Perfons who were juft before in the *Height* of *Power*, fhould foon after perhaps be in *Danger* of Their *Lives*) and

and carried with Him Q U I N T U S
G E L L I U S C A N I U S, One his E-
qual in Years, and the Likeſt to Him in
Character. This too may ſerve as a Proof
of the *well natured* and *even Diſpoſition* of
A T T I C U S, that the *ſame Perſon,* Who
had been His *Companion* at *School,* was
the *Friend* of his *Riper Age,* Their *Affection* ſtill Increaſing with their *Years.* But
although A N T H O N Y had ſuch an *Im-
placable Reſentment* againſt C I C E R O,
that He was not only an *Enemy* to HIM,
but to *Every one* elſe Who had been *His
Friend,* and ſeemed Reſolved to Include Them All in the ſame P R O-
SCRIPTION; yet upon the many Repre-
ſentations that were made to Him in behalf of A T T I C U S, He was not Unmind-
ful of *His late Good Offices*; and, In-
quiring where He might Direct to Him,
Writ Him upon the Spot a *Letter* with
his own hand, requiring his Immediate
Attend-

Attendance, and Assuring Him of His *Protection* to HIM and GEILIUS CANIUS, Both whom he ftruck out of the *Fatal Lift*; and, to prevent any *Miftake*, or *Infult*, it being *then* Night, He Ordered a *Guard* for their *Safe-Conduct*. Thus was ATTICUS Delivered from a very Terrible Apprehenfion; and HIS VIRTUE was not only a *Defence* to *Himfelf*, but to *His Friend* likewife, Whofe *Safety* he had as much *at Heart*. Nor did He ever indeed in any of the *Sad* CATASTROPHES That were fo Frequent in Thofe Days, feek out a *Shelter* from the *Storm* for *Himfelf Alone*: As if He had Judged, The GOOD *Fortune* That is *Solitary* to be but *Happinefs at Halves*. If then The PILOT deferves Commendation, Who through *Wintry Weather*, and *Rocky Seas* Conveys His *Veffel* INTIRE into *Port*; *What Singular* PRUDENCE *muft* HIS *be Thought, Who*

E

in Thofe Tempeftuous Seafons of the STATE, *When Dangers Threatned the* wary POLITICIAN *from every Side*, could yet *Steer* through fuch *jarring Interefts*, and make the Voyage of Life not only without *Shipwreck*, but with *Succefs !*

HAVING thus Extricated *Himfelf* out of thefe *Difficulties*, He made it His Only Study to be Ufeful to Thofe who were ftill *Labouring* under the *Like*. And, as The GOVERNMENT had fet a Price upon the Heads of the *Profcribed*, the more to Encourage the Common People to a Difcovery of Thofe Unhappy Perfons; Such of Them who had Taken Refuge in EPIRUS were by His Direction Supplied with All neceffary Provifion, and were at full Liberty to remain there while it fhould be with Their Convenience. His Procedure was the fame after

ter the Battle of PHILIPPI, and the Death of CAIUS CASSIUS and MARCUS BRUTUS, When He took under His Protection LUCIUS JULIUS MOCILLA and his Son, with AULUS TORQUATUS, and several Others of the *Unfortunate Side*, giving Orders for Transporting to SAMOTHRACE from EPIRUS Whatever they Wanted for Their *Subfistance*. It would be Endless to Enumerate the Particular Benefits He did of this Kind. Let it suffice to take Notice in General, that His *Liberality* was neither *Lukewarm*, nor *Temporizing*. The very Occasions on Which He Exercised it plainly Evince that He had no *Pride in Boasting His Services* to the GREAT ; but *His Pleasure lay in Succouring* the DISTRESSED. Among many Other Examples SERVILIA the Mother of BRUTUS is a Remarkable One : Whom He Treated with the *same*

b 2   *Regard*

Regard after the *Death* of Her SON, &c. When He was in the midst of His *Triumphs*. Thus *Bountiful* and *Generous* it was Impossible He should live long at *Variance* with any Man : Who never *Injured* any One *Himself*, and When *Others* had *Wronged* Him, Studied rather to *Forget* than *Revenge* it. The Beauty of His *Character* will appear the same, if We Behold it in an *Opposite Light* : Where We shall find, that the *Civilities*, or *Favours* He at any time met with were laid up in *Everlasting Remembrance* ; while Those he had *Bestowed* were no longer Thought on by *Him*, than the *Gratitude* of the *Receiver* put Him in Mind of His *Benefactions*. It is an *Old* and a *True Saying*, that OUR MANNERS MAKE OUR FORTUNE. And indeed HE must have taken much more *Pains* about HIMSELF than His FORUTNE, who was so *Finished* and so *Faultless* in all Respects.

IT

IT was in Confideration of thefe No-
ble Qualities that MARCUS VIPSANI-
US AGRIPPA, the *Favourite* of Young
CESAR, Who by His *Own Pretenfions*,
as well as the *Powerful Recommendation*
of OCTAVIUS, might have Matched
Himfelf into any the *Richeft*, or the
Greateft Family in ROME, preferred the
Alliance of ATTICUS to *Them All*, and
Chofe a *Private Gentlewoman*, the Daugh-
ter of a ROMAN *Knight* to make *His
Wife*. The Perfon who Concerted This
Marriage (for I think That ought by no
means to be paffed over in Silence) was
MARK ANTHONY, One of the *Tri-
umvirate* for Modelling the COMMON-
WEALTH; in *Whom* though He had
Then gained fuch an *Intereft*, as that He
might have Enlarged His Fortune to
What Degree He could Wifh, Yet was
He fo far from entertaining any Mercena-
ry

ry Thoughts, that He made no Other Use of it, than to Screen *His Friends* from the *Dangers*, and *Inconveniencies* to Which They had Expofed Themfelves. This was very Notorious in That PRO-SCRIPTION. The TRIUMVIRATE had *Confifcated*, and *Condemned* to *Sale*, after the ufual Way Things were Then Managed, the *Eftate* of LUCIUS SAUFEIUS an old ROMAN Knight, Who was Poffeffed of Lands of Great Value in ITALY, but, led by the Study of *Philofophy*, had for many Years lived at ATHENS. ATTI-CUS by His Diligence and Addrefs Sol-licited That Affair fo happily, that The Same Meffenger, Who was fent to In-form SAUFEIUS with the *Lofs*, Carried Him the News of the *Recovery* of His *Pa-trimony*. It was alike Owing to His Of-ficious Induftry that LUCIUS JULIUS CALIDIUS, (Who, I may fay without Flattery, was the *Beft Poet* our Age could

Boaft

Boaſt after the Death of LUCRETIUS and CATULLUS, and no leſs deſervedly Eſteemed for His *Integrity*, and every other *valuable Quality*) was Reſtored to the Enjoyment of a Large Eſtate in AFRICA that had been Taken from Him in His Abſence, When, after the PROSCRIPTION had run through the *Equeſtrian* Order, *His Name* too was Carried in by PUBLIUS VOLUMNIUS General of the *Engineers* to ANTHONY. Whether *This Attempt* was more *Difficult*, or more *Glorious* in ATTICUS is Hard to Determine : But This is Certain, He was *The* SAME *in all Places* ; and ABSENT, or PRESENT His Friends might ſecurely rely upon *His Care* whenever *They ſtood in need of it.*

NOR was His PRUDENCE leſs Worthy to be *Imitated* in His DOMESTICK, than His VIRTUES to be *Admired* in His CIVIL

CIVIL *Life.* Though he was Known always to be a Vaft *Moneyed* Man, yet no One was more *Cautious* in *Purchasing,* or lefs *Expenfive* in *Building.* It is True, He was as well *Lodged* as moft People were, and had every Thing about him Befitting a *Perfon* of his *Rank.* For he Lived in the *Seat* on the *Quirinal* Hill That His Uncle had left Him : A *Seat* the Pleafure of Which indeed confifted not fo much in the *A-partments* within Doors, as in the *Beauty* of a *Wood* which lay Adjoining to it. (For the Houfe it felf, it was Old, and the *Architecture* difcovered more of *Contrivance* than *Coft* ; and He contented Himfelf barely with keeping it up as He found it, adding Nothing but the Neceffary *Reparations*) As to His *Attendants,* if we fhould judge of *Servants* by Their *Ufefulnefs,* His were the beft Chofen That could Be ; but to regard the *Show* only, His *Equipage* made but a very *Slen-*

der

der *Appearance*. It Confifted chiefly of *Youths* Who had been All Inftructed in *Letters*, and were either Excellent *Readers*, or Skillful *Amanuenfes*, infomuch that He had fcarce a *Footman*, Who could not Perform Either of Thofe Duties tolerably well. He was no lefs Curious in relation to the *Artificers* He employed in His Works ; Who were All *Mafters* in their feveral *Trades*, and, What was more Extraordinary, there was *No One* among Them Who had not been *Born in His Houfe*, and *Trained up there* to His refpective *Handicraft*. This Kind of *Management* fhewed Him to be alike an Enemy to *Vanity*, and *Idlenefs* For as His *Indifference* about Thofe *Ornaments* of Life in Which Others place Their Greateft *Diftinction* was an Inftance of His *Philofophy* ; fo This *OEconomy* in Providing at *Home* Thofe Things for Which He muft have Paid a far Greater Price *Abroad*, was

F an

an Argument of His *Diligence*. Upon the Whole, He Appeared in His Way of Living, *Elegant* rather than *Magnificent*; *Splendid* but not *Gaudy* ; *Neat* to a Degree of *Niceness*, and yet carefully avoiding all manner of *superfluity*. His *Furniture* was Such as was *Decent* : Nothing *Wanting*, nor any Thing That looked *Crowded*. I must not omit upon this Occasion to Acquaint the Reader (though to some perhaps it may seem Trifling to mention it) that notwithstanding He kept at least as Good a House as any Man of His Quality in ROME, and Invited to His Table Persons of All Conditions with a very Liberal Hospitality, yet His Expence upon That Head did not amount to above three thousand * *Asses per* Month. I can Affirm This with Assurance, because I have seen the *Diary* that He kept, and

was

---

* 10. *l* 18. *s. d.* in our Money.

was thoroughly Acquainted, by reason of our Intimacy, with all His Family Concerns.

HIS GUESTS were, during their *Meals,* Entertained, instead of *Interludes* or Conforts, with some Agreeable *Lecture* by One of Those *Youths,* Whom He kept in His Service for That Purpose. And We were wont to Think it no small Addition to our *Welcome* to have our *Minds* thus Feasted as well as our *Palates.* For in *This* too He shewed His *Skill,* that the Company He chose at Those Hours were of a *Taste* not different from his *Own.* When He received so Great an Addition to His Circumstances by the *Death* of His UNCLE, there was not the least Alteration in His *Ordinary Method of Living.* The Figure He made was far from being *Obscure,* When He had only the * *Two Millions*

lions

---

* *Sesterces.*

lions left Him by His Father : Nor did He appear with Greater *Affluence,* after He was Mafter, by That Other Succeffion, of *Ten Millions* more. He *ftood up-on an Equal Height in Both Fortunes.* He had no Fine *Gardens,* no Sumptuous *Villas* in the Neighbourhood or the Town, nor *Houfes* of *Pleafure* adjoyning to the Sea, nor any Land at all in ITALY but Two *Farms,* One at ARDEA, the O-ther at NOMENTUM. His *Revenue* con-fifted wholly of His Rents in EPIRUS, and His Houfes in the *City.* By Which We may See, He Valued an Eftate more by the *Fruit* it Produced, than by the *Number,* or *Largenefs* of it's *Branches.*

HE had a mighty *Veneration* for TRUTH. And as He was never *Guilty* of telling a LYE Himfelf, fo He *Detefted* That *Vice* in Any Body elfe. His *Mirth* therefore was not without a mixture of *Severity;*

as

as His *Gravity* on the other side was always Tempered with *Good-Breeding*. So that One could hardly say whether He was more *Beloved*, or *Revered* by His Friends. His *Word* might always be Depended upon as *Sacred* : For He never *Gave it*, but When He might be sure *religiously* to Observe it : Looking upon it as a Sign of a *Light* rather then a *Liberal* Mind to *Promise* What One was not Able to *Perform*. He was of *Indefatigable Industry*, in Solliciting Any Matter That was Recommended to *His Care* ; And When once He *Undertook it*, from That Moment He looked upon it as His *Own Business* ; and, as if His *Reputation*, (than Which Nothing could be Dearer to Him,) *lay at Stake* in the Affair, He could not Rest till He had *Accomplished it*. For This reason The Two CICEROS, MARIUS, CATO, QUINTUS HORTENSIUS, AULUS TORQUATUS, and

seve-

feveral Other ROMAN Knights Intru-
fted Him as Their *General Agent*. By This
too We may Obferve, that it was not
out of *Sloth*, or *Incapacity*, but from
CAUTION, and JUDGMENT that He
Declined all *Publick Employments*.

OF His HUMANITY and POLITE-
NESS, no Greater Teftimony can be
Brought than *This*, That He rendered
Himfelf *Agreeable* to All *Ages*, and All
Tempers; alike *Acceptable* to SYLLA,
and to BRUTUS: Though He was but
a *Youth* when The Firft was an *Old Man*,
and an *Old Man* Himfelf, when The Other
was in the *Pride* and *Bloom* of His Life.
It is no Wonder then, that He was the
Delight and *Darling* of Thofe Friends
Who were His *Equals* in Years, and Bred
up in a long *Acquaintance* with Him, as
QUINTUS HORTENSIUS, and MAR-
CUS CICERO were; The Laft of
Whom

Whom had fo *intire an Affection* for Him, that His Own Brother QUINTUS TULLIUS CICERO was fcarce *Dearer* to Him, or had a *freer Admittance* to his *inmoft Thoughts*. Of This, befides Thofe Other Books that are Publifhed, in which He makes fuch frequent Mention of Him, His LETTERS are a *Proof*; Whereof there are *Sixteen Volumes* all Addreffed to ATTICUS, containing an Account of the moft confiderable *Tranfactions* and *Occurrences* from His *Confulfhip* to His *Death*. In *Thefe* He hath fo fully fet forth the *Aims* of the LEADERS of the different *Parties*, the *Corruptions* and *Faults* of the GENERALS and COMMANDERS, the *True Springs* fiom whence the feveral REVOLUTIONS in the COMMON-WEALTH took their *Firft Motion*, that whoever Reads *Them* will not be much at a lofs for any Other *Hiftory* of Thofe Times; and muft Acknowledge the

the Vaſt *Penetration*, nay, *Foreſight* of
the AUTHOR. For CICERO hath not
only with great Exactneſs Gueſſed at *E-
vents* that might be ſaid to be in Train
during His *Life*, but with a kind
of *Prophetick Spirit* Foretold *Events*
that but very *lately* came to Paſs, and
lay *Then* hid in the Diſtant Scenes of *Fu-
turity.*

OF His PIETY to His *Relations* I need
ſay no more, than What I Heard Him ve-
ry juſtly Valuing Himſelf upon at the
Funeral of His MOTHER (Whom He
Buried in Her Ninetieth Year when He
Himſelf was in His Sixty-Seventh) "That
" *He never was once* in *Diſgrace* with
" HER, *or in Diſpleaſure againſt His*
" SISTER " (Who was of very near the
ſame Age with Himſelf) This is a Sign,
that Either no Cauſe of *Complaint* had e-
ver fell out between *Them*, or elſe that
He

He was fo *Indulgent* towards them, as to Think it a kind of *Crime* to be *Angry* with Thofe Whom NATURE had Taught Him to *Love*. Nor was This the Effect of NATURE only in Him (though SHE Goveins in a Great Meafure Our *Wills*) but of REFLECTION. For He had fo thoioughly Digefted the PRECEPTS of the Beft PHILOSOPHERS, that they became the Conftant *Rule* of His *Practice*, and were much more the *Ornament* of His *Life*, than of His *Difcourfe*.

HE was a Great *Obferver* of the Manners of Our ANCESTORS, and very *Studious* of ANTIQUITY, of Which He made Himfelf perfectly Mafter, as may be feen by Thofe Exact *Chronological Tables* He hath left Us in His * TITLES of

---

' In eo Volumine, quo MAGISTRATUS ornavit. *A verbal Tranflation would appear very Stiff, and The Title I have given His Book feems fully to take in the Defign of it.* G

of HONOUR. For there is not any *Law*, or *Peace*, or *War*, or remarkable *Tran-saction* Whatever of the ROMAN People that is not there taken notice of, and ranged in its Proper Order of Time, and, What was very difficult, He hath fo interwoven the *Genealogies* of *Families* that one may there fee the *Lineage* of Every GREAT MAN He mentions. He did This likewfe apart in other Books for the ufe of Particular Friends ; as the *Pedigree* of the JUNIAN *Family* at the Requeft of MARCUS BRUTUS : Noting from Whom Each Perfon, from its Firft Origin to This Prefent Age, was Defcended ; What *Employments* He had been ho-noured with in the COMMONWEALTH, and the *Year* in which He had Born *Them*. In the fame Manner He went through the *Races* of the MARCELLI, The CORNE-LII, The FABII, and The ÆMILII. No-thing can be more Entertaining than Thefe

little

little MEMOIRS to Any Who are Cu-
rious in Their Inquiries after Great Men.
He hath Touched too a little upon POE-
TRY, juft fo far as that He might not,
I fuppofe be a Stranger to its Harmony.
For He hath given us in *Verfe* the *Chara-
cters* of fuch of our COUNTRYMEN
Who had eminently Diftinguifhed Them-
felves by their *Civil,* or *Military Virtues*;
and This in the compafs only of Four or
Five Verfes placed under Their Images :
So that it feems fcarce Credible fuch a
Variety could be Contained in fo fmall a
Space. He was the Author of another
Book Writ in the GREEK *Tongue,* Be-
ing an Account of the CONSULSHIP
of CICERO.

THUS far I had gone in my Relation
While ATTICUS was yet *Alive.* But
fince it hath been my Fate to *Survive*
Him, I fhall add fome Particulars more

to

to What I had already Publifhed, and
Illuftrate ftill farther the Truth of that
Maxim I mentioned above, THAT OUR
MANNERS DO (for the moft Part)
MAKE OUR FORTUNES. Nor can
there be Produced a more *Memorable Example* of *This* than in *the very Perfon* of
Whom We now Write. For Though
He never did Afpire to *any Higher Title*
than That of *Knighthood* to which He was
Born, Yet He lived to fee Himfelf Honoured with the *Alliance* of OCTAVIUS
CÆSAR Heir to the EMPEROUR JULIUS, to Whofe *Acquaintance* and Familiarity He had before been Recommended
merely by HIS ELEGANCE OF LIFE,
for Which * CÆSAR was fo Confpicuous, as by *That* to have Won to His *Interefts* all the Great Men in ROME, of
equal

---

* *He was not Stiled* AUGUSTUS *till fome Years after.*

equal *Quality*, though lefs Succefsful *Ambition*. (For fuch a *Tide* of Profperity Flowed in upon OCTAVIUS, that FORTUNE Denied Him no *Favours*, That She had ever Granted to Any of Her *Votaries*, and Conferred on *Him* all the Honours That a ROMAN *Citizen* could poffibly *Attain*.) Now there was Born to ATTICUS by His *Daughter*, the *Wife* of AGRIPPA, a *Grand-Child* of the fame Sex. CÆSAR, when *This Little One* was fcaice *a Year* Old, *Affianced* HER to TIBERIUS CLAUDIUS NERO His *Son in Law* by *LIVIA DRUSILLA. And *This Match* gave a Sanction to Their

Amity,

---

* *This Lady was the Wife of* TIBERIUS NERO, *Who yielded Her up to the Entieaties, or Authority of* OCTAVIUS *When She was Big with Child by Himfelf, and within thi ee Months of the time of Her being Delivered of* DRUSUS, *Who was Born afterwards in* OCTAVIUS's *Houfe. The Priefts gave a Difpenfation for This* MARRIAGE, OCTAVIUS *having Divoiced his Wife* SCRIBONIA *for Her Infupportable Temper ; and it appears, that the Good Man* TIBERIUS NERO *was*

well

Amity, and made Their *Intercourse* more *Frequent,* and *Familiar.*

NOT but CÆSAR, before *these* *Espousals*, both in his *Retirements* from the *Town*, constantly Entertained ATTICUS by every Messenger He sent Thither, with a Journal of his *Amusements*, and more particularly of his *Studies*, Describing to Him the Places too of his Residence, and giving him an Account What time he Proposed to Stay in any

or

---

well satisfied too in the Matter For when H. D. which was soon after the New Consummation, He appointed OCTAVIUS *by His Will* GUARDIAN to His Two Sons, namely, TIBERIUS CLAUDIUS NER (*mentioned here by* NEPOS) *And* DRUSUS *the Other, Who was Born three Months after he had Consented to Part with His* WIFE. They were Youths of Extraordinary Natural Endowments, and had, by the Care and Fondness of AUGUSTUS, the Advantage of the most refined Education. Their *Noble Atchievements in the War* they managed against the GRISONS, the SWISSERS, and BAVARIANS, are Celebrated by several Authors, and gave Occasion to those two Sublime Odes of HORACE, *the* 4th *and* 14th *of the Fourth Book.*

of them : And even When he was at
ROME, and, by reason of his infinite
Engagements in *Business*, could not Enjoy, so often as he Wished, the *Conver-*
sation of his FRIEND, He scarce let a
Day Escape in which he did not *Write*
to *Him* ; either to Demand his Resolution of some Point of *Antiquity* ; or perhaps Proposing to Him some Question in
Poetry ; or else by the *Facetious Style* of
his own Letters inviting Him into the lar-
ger Fields of *Humour* and *Wit*. It was
Owing likewise to This *Freedom* of *Com-*
merce in which CÆSAR indulged *Him*,
that the Temple of JUPITER FERE-
TRIUS, founded in the CAPITOL by
ROMULUS, is in the *Good Order* We at
present Behold it, OCTAVIUS having,
upon the *Admonition* of ATTICUS, *Re-*
paired it, after the *Roof* was *Uncovered*,
and the Whole Building through *Age* or
Neglect in a manner *Dilapidated*. Nor
was

was He lefs Favoured with the *Correfpondence* of ANTHONY : Who, in Whatever Part of the World, though never fo remote, He happened to Be, Informed *Him* with the greateft Exactnefs of His *Intentions*, and *Actions*. Now how *Nice* muft the *Conduct* of THAT MAN be, Who could *Thus* not only Keep up the *Acquaintance*, but Preferve the *Good-Will*, nay Enjoy the *Confidence* of TWO PERSONS, between WHOM there was not a *Secret Emulation* only, but the moft *Open Breach*, and *That* of the *Higheft Nature* too, Which every One Knoweth to have been the Cafe of OCTAVIUS and ANTHONY, Who Both *Aimed* alike, at the *Dominion*, not of ROME Alone, but of the WHOLE EARTH!

IN *This Manner* having Compleated the Circle of *Threefcore* and *Seventeen Years*, and, as He Advanced in *Age*, Advancing

vancing ftill in *Dignity*, in *Favour* and in *Fortune*, (for He had acquired feveral *Inheritances* purely by the *Title* of His VIRTUE which recommended *Him* to the *Donors*) and Enjoyed fuch a Felicity of *Conftitution*, as never in Thirty Years time to have requir'd the leaft *Medicine*; He was Seized with a *Diftemper*, which at firft indeed Both *He* and His *Phyficians* Defpifed. They Believed it to be a * TENESMOS, For which there were certain Slight, and fpeedy Remedies Propofed. Having Lingred three Months without any other Pain than was caufed by the Methods of His Cure, on a fudden the *Difeafe* fell with That force upon

H One

---

* *A Violent* Motion *without the* Power *of going to* Stool. *A Difeafe that is faid by the Phyficians to be often the Fore runner of the Difentery or Bloody-Flux; as it proceeds too from the fame Caufe, being Occafioned by a fharp Humour that falls upon the Sphincter, and by Swelling and Inflaming That Mufcle hinders Evacuation.*

One of His *Inteſtines*, that at length it turned to a putrid F I S T U L A which broke through His *Loyns :* But, before it came to This *Criſis*, finding His Pains increaſing every Day, and that the Violence of the *Diſtemper* had alſo brought a *Feaver* upon Him, He ſent for His *Son-in-Law* A G R I P P A, and with Him likewiſe for L U C I U S C O R N E L I U S B A L B U S, and S E X T U S P E D U C E U S: Whom When He ſaw Entering His Room, He reclined his Head upon His Arm, and Addreſſing Himſelf to Them ſaid, " As " You have All been my Witneſſes with " what *Care* and *Diligence* I have applyed " my ſelf to the *Re-eſtabliſhment* of my " H E A L T H during This I L L N E S S, " it were needleſs for me to trouble You " with many Words upon That Subject. " I have hitherto ſubmitted to the *Ad-* " *vice* of my F R I E N D S ; and left No- " thing Untried That had been *Preſcribed*

" for

" for my R E L I E F: But it is now
" high Time that I should at last *Consult*
" *My Self.* And of *This* I was Willing
" to Inform Y O U: I am Determined
" then no longer to *Nourish* my D I S-
' E A S E. For in Truth, Whatever *Food*
" I have Taken these several Days, hath
" no Otherwise *Lengthened* my L I F E,
" then by Keeping Me *Awake* to *Those*
" P A I N S of which there remain not the
" least *Hopes* of a C U R E. First there-
" fore let me *Intreat* You to *Approve* my
" R E S O I U T I O N; and, in the next
" Place, I must *Conjure* You, however,
" not to Attempt to *Dissuade* me from
" *It*; for *That* would prove but V A I N.

H A V I N G Ended *This Speech,* (which
He delivered with a *Voice,* and *Counte-*
nance, That shewed as little *Concern,* as
if He had been Removing only from
One *House* to *Another,* and not out of *This*

Life

Life into *Eternity* ;) A G R I P P A *Weeping*, and *Embracing* Him, Prayed and Begged, that H E *would not Haslen to Pay* THAT DEBT which NATURE *would too soon Exact from* H I M ; *and that, as there was still a Possibility of his Recovery*, H E *would not Rob Himself and the World of so* PRECIOUS *a* LIFE ; He made not the least Reply ; but by an *Obstinate Silence* discouraged Their farther Endeavours.   After He had Abstained for two Days from all kind of *Nutriment*, His F E A V E R left Him, and His Other DISTEMPER too seemed Abated.   Nevertheless He persisted in His *Purpose* ; and the fifth Day after taking That *Resolution*, Dyed, on the last of *March*, in the *Consulship* of C N Æ U S DOMITIUS and C A I U S S O S I U S.   He was Carried to the Grave on a little

* *Fu-*

* *Funeral Bed*, and (as He had exprefly directed) without any manner of *Pomp*; but Attended by all the *Good* and the *Virtuous*, and an infinite Concourfe of the *Common People*. He lyes Buried in the Monument of His UNCLE QUINTUS CÆCILIUS, adjoyning to the APPIAN *Way*, Five Miles diftant from ROME.

This Way of Burial is ftill Cuftomary in fome Roman *Catholick Countries, as in* S P A I N, *where they carry their Dead on an open kind of Couch or Litter, expof'd to the Publick View. And as it was a Cuftom among the* Ancients, *for Thofe Who had Born any Great Office in the* S T A T E, *or Acquired fome Diftinguifhing Honour in* W A R, *to be Buried in the Robe of their* Magiftracy, *or* Triumph, *The* Modern *Superftitious commonly give Direction that Their Friends fhall, after their Deceafe, Cloath them in the Habit of fome* Religious Order *for which They had Profeff'd the greateft* Reverence, *or* Devotion, *When They were Living.*

REMARKS

UPON THE

LIFE of ATTICUS.

THERE can scarce, I Believe, be Found in All *Ancient*, or *Modern* Story, a CHARACTER That may Furnish us with Matter for more *Delightful,* or more *Profitable*

fitable Reflection than THIS of ATTICUS. FOR He was *Endowed* with such Extraordinary *Gifts* of NATURE, and *Adorned* with such Peculiar *Graces* of ART, as could not fail to Gain Him the *Love*, the *Esteem*, and the *Veneration* of All who *Knew* Him; and to render Him alike the *Wonder* of *Posterity*. When I Consider His Noble *Birth*; and Liberal *Education*; and Superiour *Genius*; and Accomplished *Manners*; and Exalted *Charity* (a *Charity* That Succoured the *Poor*; and Protected the *Persecuted*; not only in Spite of *Their Enemies*, But, Which

Which was the more *trouble-some Opposition*, in Spite of *His Own Friends*;) I fay, When I Confider All Thefe *Shining Qualities*, That were fo Confpicuous in *Him*, and Call to Mind withal *Thofe Times* of *Confufion* in which He *Exerted* Them; HE Appears, Methinks, Like fome FORTUNATE PLANET Arifing upon a *Tempeft-beaten* World, That by the Power of its Friendly Influence *Repaired*, every Where in its *Glorious Courfe*, the *Ravage* and *Ruin* of the STORM. *Happy* certainly was His COUNTRY in fuch a PATRIOT! More Hap-

I

py still *Those Selected* FEW who Shared the *Pleasures,* and *Advantages* to be Enjoyed in such a FRIEND!

BUT, Although The CONDUCT of This *Excellent Person* is in *All Things* Worthy to be *Admired*; in *Most Things* to be *Imitated*; in *Many Things,* indeed, scarce *Imitable*; Yet the *Motives* of it in some Instances were so *Particular* that they need an *Explanation,* at the Distance between *That Age* and *Ours,* lest His EXAMPLE should be Pretended to Justify
Prin-

Principles, and *Actions* very *Different* from *His Own*.

THE COMMONWEALTH of ROME had in *His Days* received many *Shocks*, and was at length *Overturned* by the *restless Ambition* of *Private Men*. The *Governments* That, in Confequence of *Their Enterprifes*, were Erected upon the *Bafes* of the feveral FACTIONS, which Prevailed by Turns over Each Other, were *Illegal* in Their *Eftablifhments*, and as *Tyranical* in Their *Adminiftration*. For *This Reafon* He Declined (and He fhewed His *Wifdom* in so Doing) to Declare Himself of *Any Party*, since The *Leaders* of Them *All* were alike *Wandering* from the *True Centre* of UNITY, The LAWS of ROME. And as He Beheld with *Grief* Their Unnatural *Projects*, which He well Knew would be *Executed* with *Violence*, and could be *Maintained* only by *Rigour*: So He Beheld with *Horrour* the Cruel *Revenges* That in every REVOLUTION were constantly *Exercised* by the *Side* That had lately been *Oppressed*, When afterwards It Grew to be *Uppermost*. He *Mourned* Their VICTORIES, For it was over Their

Their *Wretched Country* that
They TRIUMPHED; and *Pitied*
Their DISGRACES, becauſe
THESE were as *Barbarouſly
Inflicted*, as THE OTHER had
been *Unjuſtly Obtained.* His
INACTION therefore during
THOSE USURPATIONS (when
the People of *All Factions* were
Struggling not for *Liberty,* but
Chains) was both HONOURA-
BLE, and PRUDENT; and The As-
SISTANCE He gave to the PRO-
SCRIBED (many of Whom had
no Greater *Crime* than Their
WEALTH) was an Argument
of His COURAGE, as well as an
Inſtance of His HUMANITY.

BUT

BUT *This His Procedure* is by no means to be Pleaded in *Defense* of *Such*, Who have Encouraged the *Insolence*, *Promoted* the *Pretensions*, or *Supported* the *Attempts* of FOREIGN INVADERS, and DOMESTICK REBELLS ; nor of *Those*, who *meanly* Sat NEUTERS in the *hazardous Tryal* When Our CIVIL, and RELIGIOUS *Rights* were lately *Both* at *Stake*. To *Relieve* the *Necessities*, and *Comfort* the *Afflictions*, and *Interpose our Good Offices* for the *Pardon* of the Most CRIMINAL may Become

come US as MEN, and as CHRISTIANS : But at the same time We are *strictly* to *take care* that We do not, under the *false Colours* of HUMANITY and CHARITY, Serve the *Treacherous Purposes* of SEDITION, and FACTION. The GOVERNMENT of ENGLAND is not Changed from what was the *Natural, Antient,* and *Legal* CONSTITUTION : And *Whoever* is an *Enemy* to HIS *Present* MAJESTY'S TITLE (a TITLE That hath been Confirmed in many *Free Parliaments* in Two *Former Reigns,* and to which, I Believe, *Eight Parts* in *Ten*

of

of the *Nation* too have *Voluntarily* Sworn ALLEGIANCE) ought no lefs to be Reputed an *Enemy* to the PEACE of the KINGDOM.

IT is *Amazing*, indeed, that Any One who hath been *Born* under the *Equal Diſtribution* of the LAWS, and *Bred* under the *Excellent Diſcipline* of the CHURCH of ENGLAND, fhould be *Diſaffected* to the *Eſtabliſh-ment* of *King* GEORGE, on the *Safety* of Whoſe *Perſon*, and the *Succeſſion* of Whoſe *Family*, The *Other Two* ſeem *entirely*, under G O D, to *De-pend*

pend. And that the *Disaffection* should have been so *General* as to Break out in those *Dismal Effects* that are too Fresh in Our *Memories*, and Which, it were to be Wished, could be Buried in Everlasting *Oblivion*, is still more *Prodigious.* But since GOD was Pleased to Permit This *Raging Pestilence* to Visit our *Land*; since it hath left in several of our *Provinces* many Marks of the *Fury* of its wild *Paroxysms*; and since it is E-vident by a Thousand *Ill Symptoms*, (Notwithstanding the Various *Methods* of *Cure* that have been *Tryed*; The *Severer*

K   Ones

Ones of PHLEBOTOMY and CUPPING; the *Gentler* LENITIVES; and *Golden* ALTERATIVES;) That the FEAVER is not yet quite *Allayed*, but lies Lurking in the *Veins* of our huge LEVIATHAN; it is our Indifpenfible Duty to Obferve the Exacteft *Difcipline*, and the Niceft *Caution*. Let Us not, however, by any *Unreafonable Fears*, Magnify the *Danger*; nor by an *Ignorant Officioufnefs*, and too *Bold* a *Practice*, Inflame the *Difeafe*. Let Us rather under *Thefe Difficulties* That have *Embarraffed* the *Strong*, and *Puzzled* the *Wife*

Wise, Remember to Look up to the GREAT PHYSICIAN A-bove, on whose *Skill,* and in whose *Care* We should place Our *Chief Confidence.* HE Knoweth, and HE *Alone,* the *True Causes,* and the *Proper Remedies,* of All Our *Internal Disorders;* and will, We may humbly Hope, at last, in His *Merciful Providence,* Watch some *lucky Season* of *Address,* to Pour an *Healing Balm* into the *Distempered Blood* of the *Nation,* and Give Us *Ease,* and *Rest,* and *Happiness* after so many Terrible *Convulsions* that have Distressed OUR STATE.

IT is very Difficult to Difcourfe upon a *Topick* fo Delicate as *This* (and I prefume juft only to *Touch* upon it,) without Provoking the *Malice* and Alarming the *Ignorance* of the *Bigots*, and *Incendiaries* of One Side or Other. But This I am fure may be Affirmed with *Truth*, and I hope too without *Offence*, that They have *All* in Their Turns, more or lefs, Contributed to the *Publick Diffentions* and *Difcontents.*

MANY of THOSE, who Called Themfelves TORIES, were Per-

Perſuaded, during ſome *late Councils*, through Their own *Weakneſs*, and the *Inſidious Arts* of *DeceitfulWicked Men*, to Embark in *Deſigns*, of which, it is but *Common Humanity* to Believe, They did not at Firſt Foreſee the *Conſequences*. *Theſe Deluded Perſons*, out of a *vicious Modeſty*, rather than Acknowledge Their *Error*, and take upon Themſelves the *Shame* That was Due to their Senſeleſs CREDULITY, have ſince, I Doubt, Moſt of Them Incurred a *Guilt*, of Which the very *Idea* once would have *Startled* Them.

AGAIN,

AGAIN, There are *Some* among the WHIGS, (more *Fortunate*, 'tis True, in the *Choice* of Their MASTERS, but as *Dully* perhaps in the RIGHT, as Their *Adversaries* have been *Blindly* in the WRONG) Who, *Fierce* of the *Merit* of Their LOYALTY, take all Opportunities to *Triumph* over the *Mistakes* and *Failures* of Their Neighbours; and with a *Zeal* without *Knowledge*, and a *Devotion* without *Charity*, take a *Pride*, nay indulge a kind of *Lust* in *Oppressing* a *Disgraced Party*

Party, Which by their Frequent *Infults* They have driven in a manner to *Defpair*, and from *Inconfiderable* FOOLS have made Them *Dangerous* MAD-MEN.

BUT there is *Another Set*, more Mifchievous than *Either* of the AFORE-MENTIONED, Who Acting from no *Senfe* of HONOUR, *Obligation* of LAW, or *Principle* of RELIGION (Things which neither Their *Education*, or *Commerce* of *Life* could ever bring Them Acquainted with) and Senfible too

that

that Their *Conduct* hath not always been the *Clearest* in the World ; have endeavoured to Wipe out Old *Stains*, and Blot out the very Memory of Their *Former Dependancies*, by being Industrious to Infuse groundless *Jealousies* into their *Superiours*, and render the *Virtue* of Good Men *Suspected*, Who, *Honest* and *Undesigning* Contented Themselves with the *Conscience* of Their *Integrity*, without endeavouring to *Intrude* upon the *Publick* with the *Noise* and *Warmth* of *New Converts*, and *False Professors.*

The

The Aspersions with which several Persons entirely Devoted to HIS MAJESTY have been Traduced by These *mean Informers*, hath done the GoVERNMENT more *Diſſervice* than I fear *ſome Perſons* are Willing, for Their *Own Sakes*, to *Confeſs*.

COURTS are a Sort of CLIMATES extremely Subject to *Change* of *Weather* : The *Warmth* of the SUN in *Thoſe* Higher Regions draws up many *Vapours* That frequently Diſturb the *Calmneſs* of That

HEA-

HEAVEN: And The GREAT are, for the moſt Part, ſo Buſied with Their Fears of being *Eclipſed* by Their RIVALS, that The *Dark* and *Sullen Clouds* That are Hovering Below among the PEOPLE paſs often *Unregarded.* But it cannot ſure be Suppoſed, that Men ſo *Penetrating,* and ſo *Diſintereſted,* as THEY Who *Preſide* over OUR AFFAIRS, will not always have Their POLITICAL BAROMETER under the obſervation of Their Eye: Will not Watch every *Degree* the HUMOUR Mounts

to-

towards STORMY; nor, While They are Gathering in *Their Own Little* HARVEST, will be such *Unfaithful Stewards* to Neglect the COMMON FIELD.

F I N I S.

BOOKS Printed for E. CURLL.

MISCELLANIES in *Verse* and *Prose*. With Two Essays upon Study and Conversation By *Richardson Pack* Esq, 8vo. Price 3 s.

II. POEMS upon Several Occasions. With a Dissertation upon the *Classics*. By Mr. *Addison*. Adorn'd with curious Cuts. 8vo. Price 5 s.

III. The Poetical Works of the Right Honourable *Charles* late Earl of *Halifax:* With his Lordship's Life, including the History of his Times. With A True Copy of his Last Will and Testament, and a Character of his Lordship and his Writings. by Mr. *Addison*. Price 5s.

IV. The Works of the Earls of *Rochester*, *Roscomon*, *Dorset*, &c. adorn'd with Cuts, in 2 Volumes. Price 5 s.

V. The Poetical Works of *Nicholas Rowe* Esq, Price 4s.

VI. Poems by Mr. *John Phillips*. To which is perfix'd his Life, by Mr. *Sewell*, and his Effigies curiously Engraven. 12o. Price 1s.

VII. *Poems* on several Occasions, by the late Reverend Mr. *Pomfret*, viz. 1. The *Choice*. 2. *Love* Triumphant over *Reason*. 3. *Cruelty* and *Lust*, occasion'd by the Barbarity of *Kirke* a Commander in the *Western* Rebellion, who debauch'd a young *Lady*, with a Promise to Save her *Husband*'s Life, but hang'd *him* the next Morning. 4. Instructions to a *Friend* inclin'd to *Marry*. 5. *Strephon*'s Love for *Delia* justify'd 6. A Prospect of *Death*, &c. The Fourth Edition. 12o. Price 2s.

VIII. Mr. *Young*'s Poem on the *Last Day*. The 3d. Edition corrected throughout, and very much Improv'd. Adorn'd with three Curious Cuts. 12o Price 1s.

RELIGION
AND
PHILOSOPHY:
A
TALE.
WITH
Five other PIECES.

By Major PACK.

LONDON,
Printed for E. CURLL in *Fleetstreet.* M.DCC.XX.
(Price 6 d.)

Advertisement.

THE *Epilogue to the* Spartan Dame *having been printed with that* Play, *and the Song being set to* Musick, *I intreated the Favour of the Author to have leave to Print them in the same Size with his other Miscellanies; and to which he has been pleased to add the Four other Pieces hereunto subjoined.*

The Reader is desired to correct an Oversight committed in the Title of the second Copy of Verses, thus; instead of Earl, *read* Duke of Greenwich.

RELIGION

AND

PHILOSOPHY.

A TALE.

IRIS, a tender soft believing Maid,

By too much Eafineſs to *Vice* betray'd,

Lamenting now the fleeting Pleaſure loſt,

Her Beauty faded, and her Wiſhes croſt;

With

With Shame reflects on all her Wand'rings paft,
And fain would fix in *Virtue's* Seat at laft:
Abjures the WORLD ; and, in her fable Veil,
Learns to look folemn, and devoutly rail:
But, finding ftill ftrong Conflicts in her Heart,
From Nature ftruggling with the Pow'r of Art,
Lives an odd Mixture of *Coquet* and *Prude*,
Awkardly Pious, and Demurely Lewd.

HER perjur'd Rover, whom *Ambition* fir'd,
(*Glory* the Swain, and *Love* the Nymph infpir'd)
The Gay PHILAUTUS, had forfook the Plain,
Seduc'd by Hopes of *Honour* and of *Gain*;
Proud to be thought a Wretched Tool of State,
Indulg'd his Vanity, and urg'd his Fate;

Till

Till feeing *Chance*, not *Worth*, decide the Prize,

Juft *Patriots* fall, and artful *Villains* rife,

He flies the C O U R T, and all its gilded Snares;

And feeks fome *humble Spot*, remote from *Cares*:

Yet, whilft he meditates this wife *Retreat*,

Envies, I know not how, thofe Fools *The Great*;

And, under all his felf-denying Grace,

Still feels a fecret Paffion for a *Place*.

Dull are our *Maxims*! Falfe our grave *Pretence*!

R E A S O N, at laft, will prove the *Dupe* of S E N S E.

Our *Age* is influenc'd as our *Youth* inclin'd,

And the fame *Byafs* always rules the Mind.

To His GRACE the

Earl of GREENWICH,

UPON

Reading the following Lines in his PATENT.

CUM Viri illius, cui novos hisce Literis Patentibus Titulos decernimus, & egregia in Nos Patriamque suam merita, & illustre Genus, & Majorum res gestæ, *Historia-*
rum

rum monumentis celebratæ, *fatis incla-*
ruerint, (quibus rationibus adducti fu-
mus eum fummo inter Proceres honore
dignari) *nil opus eft pluribus recenfere :*
ergo, &c.

M Indlefs of Fate in thefe low vile Abodes,

MADMEN have oft ufurp'd the *Style* of GODS.

But, that the MORTAL might be thought DIVINE,

The HERALD ftrait new-modell'd all the LINE;

Or venal PRIEST, with well-diffembled Lye,

Præambled to the Croud the *Mimick* DEITY.

Not fo Great SATURN's Son, Imperial JOVE,

HE reigns *unqueftion'd* in the Realms above.

No Title from *Defcent* HE need infer;

HIS *Red Right-Arm* proclaims the THUNDERER.

Such,

Such juftly be thy Pride, Illuftrious Peer!

Alike, You fhine *unrival'd* in your Sphere:

All *Merit* but your *own* You may difdain;

And KINGS have been YOUR ANCESTORS *in vain*.

S O N G:

Set to MUSICK

By Mr. Rofengraefe.

I.

TELL me, ténder Youths, who languifh

For fome Fair Difdainful She,

If you feel the cruel Anguifh,

That afflicts and tortures Me.

II.

II.

Are your Sighs in Tempests rising?

 Do your Tears in Torrents flow?

Doth the Nymph, your Grief despising,

 Falsely smile, to mock your Woe?

III.

Lo on raging Billows tossing,

 Just in Prospect of the Coast,

Hidden Rocks my Passage crossing,

 Me poor shipwreck'd Lover lost!

FRAGMENT

O F A

LETTER.

WHEN GLORY doth the HERO's Bosom fire,
How *sweet* is HOPE! how *gay* is young DESIRE!
Of all those INSTINCTS which to MAN are given,
AMBITION seems the *loudest Call* of HEAVEN:
Indulge then, FRIEND, thy noble *Thirst* of FAME,
Nor let vain *Fears* thy gen'rous *Ardour* tame.

Who

Who would live always *dully* on the SHORE,

That might the *Wonders* of the DEEP explore?

Down the *strong Current* let us *swiftly* glide,

Spread all our *Sails*, and *aid* the swelling *Tide* !

If *Rocks* appear, or sudden *Tempests* rise,

With *Pilot* REASON gravely we'll advise ;

By *her Directions* steer the doubtful *Course*,

Here use our *Skill*, or there employ our *Force*.

Yet ne'er *Despair*, though every *Planet lour*,

But trust to FORTUNE for some *smiling Hour*.

Each bold ADVENT'RER will a *Season* find

When that *Coy* MISTRESS of the World is *Kind*.

The *faint Addresses* of the *Bashful* fail,

But the *Home-pusher* always will prevail.

Thus, oft repuls'd, a YOUTH who long had born

With *humble Awe* his haughty FAIR-ONE's *Scorn,*

At length with *Luft* and *Indignation* fir'd,

Refolv'd to gain by *Force* what He defir'd ;

And *rufhing* on with *Fury* to her Arms,

In wild Diforder *rifled* all her Charms.

The NYMPH was *pleas'd*; the LOVER was *reftor'd*;

And from her SLAVE in time became her LORD.

EPILOGUE

TO

Mr. *Southern*'s Spartan Dame:

Spoken by Mr. WILKS.

Our Author's *Muse* a numerous Issue boasts,
And many of the Daughters have been *Toasts*.
She who now last appears upon the Stage,
(The Hopes and Joy of his declining Age)

With

With modeſt Fears, a cens'ring World to ſhun,

Retir'd a while, and liv'd conceal'd a *Nun* :

At length, releas'd from that Reſtraint, the *Dame*

Truſts to the Town her Fortune and her Fame.

Abſence and Time have loſt her many Friends,

But *this bright Circle* makes her large Amends.

To You, *Fair Judges*, She ſubmits her Cauſe;

Nor doubts, if *You* approve, the *Mens* Applauſe.

Some *ſullen formal Rogue* perhaps may lour,

(REBEL to *Female*, as to *Royal* Power)

But all the *Gay*, the *Gallant*, and the *Great*,

On *Beauty*'s Standard with *Ambition* wait.

Glory is vain, where *Love* has had no part :

The *Poſt* of *Honour* is a *Woman's Heart*.

Ev'n *Chains* are *Ornaments*, that You beſtow;

The more your *Slaves*, the *Prouder* ſtill we grow.

MAN,

MAN, a rough Creatuie, *savage-form'd* and *rude*,

By You to *gentler Manners* is subdu'd :

In the *sweet Habitude* we grow *refin'd*,

And polish *Strength* with *Elegance* of *Mind.*

OUR SEX may represent the *bolder Powers* ;

The *Graces*, *Muses*, and the *Virtues*, YOURS.

BUT ah ! 'tis pity, that for want of Care,

Madmen and *Fops* your *Bounty* sometimes share,

Wretches in *Wit's* despight and *Nature's* born,

Beneath your *Favour*, nay, below your *Scorn.*

May poor CELONA's Wrongs a Warning prove,

And teach the FAIR with *Dignity* to *Love.*

Let *Wealth* ne'er tempt you to abandon *Sense* ;

Nor *Knaves* seduce you with their *grave Pretence.*

Be

Be vile *Profaneness* ever in difgrace ;

And *Vice* abhor'd, as *Treacherous* and *Base.*

Revere Yourselves; and, confcious of your Charms,

Receive no *Dæmon* to an *Angel's* Arms.

Succefs can then alone your *Vows* attend,

When *Worth's* the *Motive, Conflancy* the *End.*

AN
EXPOSTULATION
WITH AN
ACQUAINTANCE,

Who was going to Marry an Old Rich PARSON.

AND hath my Lovely Perjur'd CLOE fwore,

That I muft never, never meet her more?

Is there no kind *Propenfion* in your Heart,

That ftirs to take your injur'd STREPHON's part?

Yes,

Yes, yes, Methinks, thro' all This forc'd Difguife
I fee your Soul *debating* in your Eyes.

Prudence in vain would Inclination hide :
When Love lies *Panting* underneath your Pride.

Wedlock, you fay, will all This *Conflict* end——
And, for a Husband could You quit a Friend ?

Cold are the *Comforts* of That Marriage-Bed
Where *Intereft* only Tempts the Bride to *Wed.*

Canft Thou, now Youth doth every *Senfe* invite
To *Flow'ry Paths* of *daily-new Delight*;

Renounce at once the *Court,* the *Park,* and *Play* ;
The *Pleafures* of the *Night,* and *Scandal* of the *Day* ?

With tedious *Sermons* have thy *Patience* vext,
While *your Head* rambles on another *Text* ?

Or, when *foft Harmony* might Charm thy Ear,
Sternhold's *vile Pfalms* in *viler Conforts* hear ?

D   Live

Live thus *Unknown* to Moſt, *Deſpis'd* by Some,

Abroad *Unpity'd*, and *Diſtreſs'd* at Home?

No, no, You'd ſoon Lament your *alter'd State*,

Wiſh a *freſh Change*, but *Wiſh* perhaps *too late*.

Think then *Betimes*, e'er yet You are *Undone*,

Nor put theſe *Matrimonial Fetters* on.

But if, howe'er, Your Parents have Decreed,

To join You with this Rev'rend Invalid,

Nature may ſtill *Co-operate* with Grace,

And ſome *ſound* Curate fill the Rector's Place.

F I N I S.

CONTENTS.

Lately Printed for E. CURLL, the following Books:
viz.

I. MAjor PACK's Miſcellanies in *Verſe* and *Proſe.* With two ESSAYS upon STUDY and CONVERSATION. The ſecond Edition. Price 3 *s.* 6 *d.*

II. ————His Tranſlation of the Life of POMPONIUS ATTICUS. With Remarks. Price 1 *s.* 6 *d.*

III. ————His Select Tranſlations from CATULLUS, TIBULLUS, and OVID. With an Eſſay upon the *Roman* ELEGIAC POETS. Price 1 *s.*

A

New Collection

OF

MISCELLANIES

IN

PROSE and *VERSE.*

Quod fi non hic tantus fructus oftenderetur, & fi ex his ftudiis delectatio fola peteretur, tamen, ut opinor, hanc animi remiffionem, humaniffimam, ac liberaliffimam judicaretis. Nam cetera neque temporum funt, neque ætatum omnium, neque locorum. Hæc ftudia adolefcentiam alunt, fene ctutem oblectant, fecundas res ornant, adverfis perfugium, ac folatium præbent; delectant domi, non impediunt foris, pernoctant nobifcum, peregrinantur, rufticantur,*
Cicero *Orat pro Archia Poeta.*

Multa fatis lufi   Non eft Dea nefcia noftri,
Quæ dulcem curis mifcet amaritiem.   Catull.

L O N D O N:

Printed for E. CURLL, in the *Strand.*   MDCCXXV.

To his GRACE

JOHN

Duke of Argyll *and* Greenwich. *Lord High Steward of his Majefty's Houfhold, and Knight of the moft Noble Order of the Garter.*

MY LORD,

I Have fometimes wondered how, between the Bufinefs and Pleafures of Life, of Both which

　　　every

every Man has a Share, People could really have so little Good ‑ Husbandry of their Time, as to spend much of it in Compliments: I am sure I will not take up any of your GRACE's in so impertinent an Entertainment. The World is not *now* to be made acquainted with your Great Abilities, and Noble Qualities, and the Eminent Services you have done your Country; nor am I to begin to tell your GRACE with what Sentiments of Gratitude and Respect I have received the many Instances of your Favour, and the Continuance of that Friendship with which

your

your G<small>RACE</small> has long honoured me. At prefent, my Lord,
I fhall only beg leave to make
an humble Offering to your
G<small>RACE</small> of this little Volume
of M<small>ISCELLANIES</small>. They were
the Fruits of my Idlenefs,
but may laft, perhaps, longer than thofe of my Indu-
ftry.   The V<small>ERSES</small> (it may
be thought vain if I called
them P<small>OEMS</small>) were many of
them compofed as I have
been riding, or rather faun-
tering about in a beloved
Angle of the World, (for
*ille terrarum mihi præter
omnes Angulus ridet)* the
Scene on which I have paf-

fed fome of my fofteft Hours; where I was wont to fteal away from the Cares and In-quietudes of Life, and in-dulge myfelf in all the vir-tuous Luxury that calm Sea-fons, delightful Profpects, chearful Ideas, and innocent Paffions could adminifter to the Mind : And where, my LORD, after fo many Wan-derings and Labours, I wifh with Impatience to fpend the *Sabbath* of my *Days.* But my Fortunes, alas! and my Wifhes do not often ac-cord——elfe I could not have wanted a much better Op-portunity than this, of ma-nifefting nifeſting that Attachment and Zeal, with which I have been ever, MY LORD,

Your Grace's

moſt Obliged,

moſt Faithful, and moſt

affectionately Devoted

Humble Servant,

EXON, April
19, 1725.

RICHARDSON PACK.

THE
PREFACE
TO THE
READER.

*I*T *was once my Intention to*
have translated most of the
Lives, if not all, writ-
ten by Cornelius Nepos;
but Laziness, the Love of
Pleasure, and the Want of
Health have, *each in their Turn, diver-*
ted

The PREFACE

ted me from that Undertaking. However, I could not but impose this short Task upon myself of rendering into English the Lives of MILTIADES and CIMON, because I found somewhat both Noble and Amiable in the Character of each, as well as somewhat very extraordinary in the Account given of the latter. For there we are informed, that as virtuous a Man as he was (and certainly he was a Man of Virtue) he did not in the least startle at INCEST; and his Wife, good Woman, committed ADULTERY, purely out of Love to her Husband. My Bookseller acquainting me, that he was going to Reprint my Translation of ATTICUS, I was willing that PHILOSOPHER and these GENERALS should be seen in Company together.

As for the few Copies of Verses that have their Place in the Rear of this small Volume, they were some of them the Result of my Pleasurable Hours, others the Relief of Anxious ones. I writ THEM,

to the READER.

THEM, *in short, as People* beget CHIL-DREN, *in the* Gratification, *or* Dif-charge *of a* PRESENT PASSION, *with-out any Concern at that Time what Fi-gure they might make, when they should come into the World. And as* AUTHORS *are, like* PARENTS, *improper Judges of their* own Productions, *I shall leave them intirely to the Cenfure of the* REA-DER, Courteous, *or* Uncourteous. *The* Good-natured *may, perhaps, be inclined to fpare them, becaufe they are* Little *ones; and tho' none of them should be allowed to pafs for* Beauties, *yet all of them will at leaft, I hope, be thought* Innocent.

POST-

POSTSCRIPT.

IN *too haftily tranfcribing thefe Papers,* two *Omiffions have happened, of which it may be proper to advife the* READER *here.* One *is of the Word* Popular *to be placed before* Governments, *page* 14. *line* 7. The *other is the following* Note *referring to the Word* GALLERY, *mentioned in the laft Line but one of the fame Page.*

   " *In this* GALLERY *the* Stoick Phi-
" lofophers *held their Publick Difputations.*
" *It was called* POECILE *from the Greek*
" *Word* ποικίλον, *various, becaufe of the*
" *Variety of* PAINTINGS *with which it*
" *was adorned.*

ADVER-

AD

LIBELLUM.

O, Little Book, and to the Fair
impart
This *gentle Meſſage* from a *tender*
Heart;

Say, She my *Thought*'s eternal *Darling Theme*,
My *Morning Viſion*, and my *Nightly Dream*.
That when, far Diſtant from That happy Place
Which Her *bright Preſence*, and *ſweet Converſe*
Grace,

Theſe

Ad LIBELLUM.

These Ears no more Her tuneful Speech shall Hear,

Those Eyes no more my languid Soul shall Chear,

Where'er, by FATE compell'd, my Feet may
  Roam,

Her Image in my Breast shall Keep its Home

And Tell the MAID, If She Vouchsafe to Look,

With curious Search, in THEE, my Little Book.

No Guileful Arts, no Venal Praise She'll find,

But the Plain Image of an Honest Mind,

Warm Gen'rous Truths, which from His Bosom
  flow,

Who ne'er Forgot a FRIEND, and can Forgive
  a FOE.

EXON, May
25, 1725

THE

The MUSE's Choice;

OR,

The Progress of WIT.

An Elegiac Epiftle to Major PACK;
occafioned by his MISSCELLANIES
in Verfe and Profe.

Sume fuperbiam quæfitam Meritis.

ERE I fome happy Spirit, free to chufe
Of what bleft Bard I pleas'd, the
pow'rful Mufe.
I'd pafs by Names much prais'd, and
mark the Man,
In whom Dame Nature to plant Wit began;

That

That Wit right studies should improve by Art,

Time to all these ripe Judgment should impart.

Quick should, as *Lynceus'* Eyes, his Fancy be,

His Tongue drop Honey, like the *Hybla* Bee,

Happy his Humour, suiting sev'ral Wills,

As Wine the Shapes of Vessels, that it fills;

His Head a Magazine of Classic Sense,

His Heart a Hoard of Country Innocence,

His Acts sincere, his Manners of that Sort

As might adorn the Pattern of a Court

Next trav'ling, thro' the World, my Bard must go,

Each Court, each Camp, must visit and must know

By him should States of various Realms be seen,

Till Things he, throughly, learnt, and, throughly,

    Men.

'Tis thus illustrious Spirits ought to roam,

And bring the World's collected Wisdom home.

Then, in each Art, each Strain, he would excel,

Since Wisdom is the Source of Writing well.

Were I to have my Choice, and should I aim

To give great Pleasure, and to get great Fame,

Such

Such PACK, and, ſuch alone, ſhould be the Muſe,
I'd, for my Fame, and Reader's Pleaſure chuſe,
Nor wrong my Choice, nor chide, if I ſubjoin,
That, for thoſe Reaſons, PACK, it ſhould be Thine.

Aſſume the decent Pride to Merit due,
Weak is his Worth, whom Praiſe offends, when true:
Where Men are conſcious, 'tis a vain Pretence,
Where Men want Conſciouſneſs, they muſt want Senſe.

Oft have I thought Thee born inſpir'd to ſhow,
What Wit was many hundred Years ago ;
When *Rome* moſt glorious was, *Athens* moſt fam'd,
And each, in Arts and Arms, Earth's Miſtreſs nam'd ;
Wit did, o'er all, triumphant Cenſor ſit,
And the World's Lords, obey'd the Lore of Wit.
Then *Phocion* only to *young Ammon* ſpoke,
That ſingle Speech ſav'd *Athens* from his Yoke.
Phocion, her Friend, made *Ammon* not her Foe ;
Wiſdom prevail'd, and Pow'r repreſs'd the Blow.
If *Ammon* thus that Orator obeyed,
Not leſs by Poets were his Paſſions ſway'd.

     For

For this World's Victor, when *Sichæum* stood,
Envious, the Tomb of fam'd *Achilles* view'd.
" And blest, he cry'd, above the greatest Kings!
" Since Thee the greatest Poet, *Homer* sings
Not with less Envy, future Chiefs shall see
Greenwich thy Hero, and his Poet Thee
All Verses, but thine Own, he may defpise,
Homer, in vain, bids proud *Achilles* rife,
To Thine muft *Homer's* Hero yield the Prize.
Impatient, fierce, of Birth celeftial proud,
Paflions unconquer'd that *Greek* Hero cloud.
Vain was his Birth, if not to Fiction ow'd,
Whofe Acts *mere* Man refemble, not a God.
Not Birth, *pure* Merit makes thy Hero fhine,
His Birth is *Human,* but his Acts *Divine,*
Of which thou form'ft an Iliad in a Line.

– *He may all Merit, but his own, difdain,*
*And Kings have been his Anceftors in vain.**

* See, *The Verfes occafioned by the* Preamble *to the* Duke of Greenwich's Patent, *in Major* Pack's former Volume of Mifcellanies

Oh thou, who can'ft, compar'd with *Greece*, excel,
Bear, as thou may'ft, the *Roman* Parallel
Tully, like *Phocion*, fav'd the States he taught;
And, while *Rome's* Poets Prais'd, *Rome's* Champions
Thus *Julius* and *Augustus*, both, become   [fought.
The firft of *Cæfars* in Imperial *Rome*
The firft of Poets made them thirft for Praife,
And gave them Laurels in Exchange for Bays.
No fmall Exchange! fince, in *Horatian* Odes,
Fix'd, fhines the *Julian* Star, among the Gods.
As highly fung, as far, as bright, appears
The *Britifh* Star, that Garter'd *Campbell* wears.
Campbell, with *Cæfar*, Deed might count for Deed,
But modeft might His Commentary need.
Bays, Laurels, *Cæfar* won, by Wit, and War;
Argyll and You thofe *twofold* Trophies fhare:
He, learn'd like *Cæfar*, can, like *Cæfar*, fight,
You, Brave like *Cæfar*, can, like *Cæfar*, write.
As thy Poetic Lays like *Homer's* rofe,
Or as thy Verfe, fublime, like *Virgil's*, flows,
Like *Cæfar's* fo, or *Tully's*, runs thy Profe.

Oh! How thy *Atticus* refines Delight!
Thy Paintings, more than *Cic'ro's*, pleafe the Sight
Drawn at full Length, and drawn divinely true,
He liv'd *with Tully*, but He lives *by* You
Unfteer'd by Party, obftinately Good,
Pomponius, not, as Factions ebb'd or flow'd,
E'er let dependent Paffions rife or fall
Siding with none, He liv'd belov'd by all.
Him *Cæfar* lov'd, while *Pompey* call'd him Friend,
And *Cato* prais'd, while *Cæfar* did commend
May each Great Man, ye Gods, whom moft I love,
Like *Pack's* two *Attici,* unbiafs'd move!
May they no Strife, but this, in Factions raife,
Which Faction is the moft provok'd to praife!

One Labour more   I Wit's beft Age purfue,
And find it follow'd ftill, and reach'd by you
Next good *Octavius* mounts the happy Throne,
Blufh Chriftian Pow'rs! the Heathen Pattern own!
The Age, *Auguftus* liv'd in, ftill fhall laft,
Till Time's great Period fhall itfelf be paft.

With

With that good Prince, the good *Mæcenas* rose,
Wit finding Them her Friends could fear no Foes.
The growing Language daily Graces gain'd,
And its full strength in Sense and Sound obtain'd
No Fancy could its Phrases wish more rich,
No Voice could lift it to a higher pitch
Then *Virgil* sung —— of Wit the Sov'raign Lord,
Near Eighteen Ages, crown'd, with one Accord,
And, still, the longer read, the more ador'd.
Historians, Orators, and Poets rose,
These polish'd Verse, and those adorn'd the Prose.
Catullus Learn'd, and *Ovid* was the Wit,
And *Courts* grew polish'd, as *Tibullus* writ.
Like Him, does *Gallus*, with each Sex, succeed,
The Ladies languish, and their Lovers read.
In Wit's large Field, now open'd fresh by you,
These Ancients march, and marching we review
Muster'd by Thee are all their Forces shwon,
Ye Moderns, by these Models, mend your own.

The *Learning* of *Catullus*, *Ovid*'s *Wit*,
What *Gallus* and *Tibullus Courtly* writ,

All

All their fine Thoughts, our Panting Beauties prove,

And *British* Bosoms beat with *Roman* Love.

By you convey'd, they feel the Passion whole,

For, in your Versions, you transfuse the Soul.

In Nature, Fortune, Honour, Wit, and Fame,

There's such Similitude, you seem the same.

But, ah! how Nature still o'erpow'rs all Art!

How is thy Head indebted to thy Heart!

O'er thy Translations, how thy Verse are fir'd,

Which are by *Celia*'s brighter Eyes inspir'd.

Had *Celia*, sooner, smote thee with Surprize,

Had her Charms earlier met thy wond'ring Eyes,

To *Celia*, only, had thy Lyre been strung,

And *Latian-Belles* in *British* Lines unsung.

Well, those Translations had, tho' fine, been lost,

Since we more bright Originals might boast

Such were the Tunes, with which you charm'd the

On *Buria*'s, equal to *Arcadia*'s, Plains;   [Swains

With such the *Hyde*, a Grove adjacent, rung,

Nor sweeter those, which once *Catullus* sung

When He, repairing to *Dione*'s Grove,

Describ'd the Vigils of the Queen of Love.

Fair

Fair *Hengrave*'s Woods, fhall Nymphs *Napæan* own,
Deferve, o'er all the Sylvan Gods, Renown,
The Seat of *Venus* and *Apollo* grown.
" Venus *no more fhall be Mount* Ida's *Pride,*
' *The Queen of Beauty, now, frequents the* Hyde :
No more fhall *Tempe* with her *Bay-Tree-Row,*
Where, Grafs perfum'd, and Flow'rs eternal grow,
Pofft *Phœbus* there ; but to the *Hyde* fubmit :
For, here, while finging in their Shade you fit,
The confcious Trees confefs the God of Wit.

Sing on, — like *Orpheus,* charm th'inchanted Place,
See! how frefh *Ivy* wreaths ! how fprout the *Bays !*
See! *Myrtles* fpring at ev'ry Magick Sound!
The *Soldier, Bard,* and *Lover* fhall be crown'd.
Sing on,——He fings,——Thofe Songs, grav'd Barks
   rehearfe,
Each Tree its Head immortal lifts in Verfe.
Thofe Verfe, in Tunes, the Birds repeat, above ;
And warbling Nations fhake the dancing Grove.
Sweet, over all, is *Philomela* heard,
To *Juno*'s Peacocks, *Venus*' Doves preferr'd,
For *Pack*'s fweet *Philomel* is *Cælia*'s Bird.

The

The chirping wanton Sparrow fhe difdains,

Charm'd with what chaunts fuch chaft and dying
>   Strains

As wife, o'er *Lefbia*'s, is fair *Calia*'s Choice,

As fweet, beyond *Catullus*, is *Pack*'s Voice.

Hence fam'd o'er all the Sons of Wit is He,

Fam'd o'er the Daughters of bright Beauty She

As Fires their Radiance, Flames uniting, raife;

She makes His Genius, He Her Glories blaze.

Songs, on fuch Eyes, muft, fparkling more, excel,

And Eyes muft fparkle more, when fung fo well

His Verfe took Flame from her infpiring Eye;

'Tis Flame celeftial,——— and they ne'er can dye

So fure, thofe Eyes, that there recorded ftand,

Shall, Ages hence, admiring Worlds command.

So fure, that Face fhall, in *Pack*'s deathlefs Song,

Bright in eternal Bloom, be ever young.

To raife Her Charms, or lift His Genius higher,

What could the Beauty or the Bard defire?

> Say, what fhall draw me from this darling Theme?

Thy Converfation?——— That repeats the fame.

There

There *Cælia* you, and there I *Cælia* Toaft,

While Youths and Maids ftrive, who fhall praife her

　　　　moft .

Cælia from all the Sex the Palm will bear,

By Men ador'd, yet honour'd by the Fair.

But tho' the Ladies give a lovely Force,

And add fweet Flavours to the beft Difcourfe.

Yet yours to no one Pleafure is confin'd,

All Pow'rs comprizing, that can charm Mankind.

Far, as each Science, It extends, or Art ;

Rules or refines all Paffions of the Heart ;

And, while it elegant the Paffions moves,

Folly reclaims and Wifdom's felf improves.

The *Scholar*, while your Dictates you difpenfe,

Learns *Men*, like *Books*, and *Files* his *College-Senfe*.

The lift'ning Soldier s taught to feek renown,

And his Breaft beats with Courage not his own :

Raw Squires, Polite, as Courtiers, do appear ;

Fops grow lefs Fools, and Wits grow lefs fevere,

And Courtiers, as the Country-Hind, fincere :

Thee, not lefs Women, than the Men obey,

Coquettes grow graver, Prudes themfelves more gay.

　　　　　　　　　　　　　Thus

Thus doſt thou, breeding Honour, Wit, diſpenſe

With univerſal boundleſs Influence.

Well may'ſt thou Converſation make thy Theme,

Whoſe each new Speech adds Vot'ries to thy Fame.

Now let thy *Brudenel,* or thy *Stanhope* ſay,

(Companions of thy Eloquence are they,

Brudenel, whoſe Tongue can charm each beauteous

     Fair,

Stanhope, in Councils, fam'd, of Peace and War)

How rightly I have choſe, were I to chuſe,

To pleaſe the World, *Pack*'s various tuneful Muſe,

How happy the converſing World would be,

Could thy Inſtructions make Men talk like thee

   With thee converſing, we all Time forget,

On Days ſo ſpent, How ſoon the Suns ſeem ſet;

On Nights ſo ſpent, How ſoon thoſe Suns ariſe?

No Reſt ſeems loſt to our unwearied Eyes.

Clocks are dull Monitors we moſtly fear,

That rudely interrupt the raviſh'd Ear,

And cruel cry, 'tis time to ceaſe to hear.

Peace, Death-like Knell! — that Sound untunes the

     Heart,

'Tis Life to hear him, and 'tis Death to part.

Cry

Cry they 'tis Time?—— 'Tis never time to ceafe

Hearing that Tongue, that wou'd for ever pleafe.

Too fhort the Day alone, too fhort the Night;

No Time, that ends, can meafure Heav'ns Delight.

Time, while thou talk'ft like thofe *above*, does fhow,

That we are Mortals dreaming here *below*,

Where our beft Hours of Blifs are dafh'd with Woe

Such, fuch the Hour, that ftole thy Martial Mufe,

When we the Bard did in the Soldier lofe,

When, laft, the Army call'd thee, Friend, away,

We mourn'd, that Virtue fhou'd fo well obey.

Leave, quick, leave *Exeter*, that barren Place

Yields no fine Objects to excite thy Lays.

Here Toafts, by hundreds, wait thy Praife,—return;

Nor let thy Soldiers make the Mufes mourn.

As *Britain*, o'er the World, may Beauties boaft,

So *Bury* breeds, of *Britifh* Towns, the moft.

Had fome old Druid but at *Bury* been,

And Charmers, fuch, as You and I, had feen,

Rapt had he cry'd, This Town all Towns excels,

And, where he counted Women, counted *Belles*.

How

How fair is *Calia* then! —— How Heavenly fair!
Who reigns chief Beauty, where all, Beauties, arc
Hafte, hafte, from *Exeter* to *Bury* flye,
The Mufe can't fing, remote from *Calia*'s Eye.

You on *Our Toafts*, on *You They* vainly look,
By Fancy's Eyes, prefented in your Book
E'en I, that love thy Verfe, now fee, with Pain,
What makes me long to fee thyfelf in vain.
To *Worlds* thy *Books*, to *me* thy *Converfe* give,
In *thofe* my *Name,* near *this Myfelf* would *Live*

Bury St Edmonds,
1725

W. BOND.

VERSES
TO THE
AUTHOR.

OO long, to mercenary Views confin'd,
Has the *Mufe* feem'd to traffick with
Mankind;
Have venal Bards undignify'd the *Bays,*
And for Returns of Bread retail'd their Lays.
At length *fair Science* does with Rapture fee
A generous Prop of her Renown in THEE;
Your Verfe directs a Road fecure to Fame,
And refcues from Neglect the *Poet*'s Name.

C

Let

Let others with pedantick Drudg'ry toil,
And the beft Art by Rules Mechanick fpoil,
Or *Poefy* employ, as fome a *Wife*,
To anfwer all the Houfhold Calls of Life;
You, SIR, your *Genius* as your *Miftrefs* ufe,
And with an Air Polite, gallant the Mufe;
Whene'er you lead her thro' the Court or Grove,
We're taught how *Men of Senfe* fhou'd *Think*, or *Love*,
Or when to bid th'attentive World receive
The boldeft Touches that the Lyre can give,
Greatly felected from the daz'ling Throng,
One CHIEF illuftrates thy immortal Song;
He's fuch as Empire can with Pride behold,
And leaves us lefs attach'd to NAMES of old;
Tho' thro' thy Labours, e'en *thofe Names* furvive,
And, in the *Britifh* Tongue tranfplanted, thrive.
But why fhould *others* feeble Praifes bring,
And with vain Fondnefs leffen whom they fing?
Merit, like *thine,* defies *affiftant Strains,*
And *any Heralds,* but *itfelf,* difdains.

London, May 29.
1725

Ch. Beckingham.

To the AUTHOR.

ON Thee the Mufes All indulgent fhine,
   Their Force, their Sweetnefs, and their
      Mufic Thine
   A tranfient Smile to other Bards is fhown,
But their whole Souls, Bleft Poet, are thy own.
  In Thee the foft *Tibullus* wakes again,
He warbles in thy Heart-diffolving-Strain.
Attending *Love*, confeffes all its Charms,
Arrefts his Wings and folds Thee in His Arms,
Happy the MAID, thy Harmony has fung,
Thy SPRING will Bloom and in the Grave be Young.

Inner-Temple, June 4,
    1725

                         CLIO.

To the AUTHOR.

 ONG the Poctick World a Defart feem'd,
To Monfters, Pedantry, and Dullnefs
damn'd;
'Twas fav'd by PACK, *Apollo*'s Darling Son :
The Mufes made their total Pow'r his own,
VENUS t'infpire Him form'd a COLLETON.

Gray's-Inn, June 7
1725

J. H.

THE

THE
LIVES
OF
MILTIADES,
AND
CIMON.

WITH

PÓEMS *on several Occasions.*

Printed in the Year M. DCC. XXV.

THE

LIFE

OF

MILTIADES.

MILTIADES, the Son of CIMON, was Born at *Athens.* The Antiquity of his Family, the Glory of his Anceftors, and the Modefty of his own Deportment had rendered Him the Darling of his *Country*; and He was now Arrived at an Age, that the *Publick* might, not only

B   Hope,

Hope, but Confide, his Future Conduct would Confirm the Judgment They had made concerning Him; when a Scene of Action opened, which brought Him upon the Stage. It happened, The ATHENIANS had then taken a Resolution to Plant a Colony in the * *Cherfonefe*. And, as Great Numbers were Engaged, and more feemed fond of That Expedition, a Deputation was fent from Them to *Delphos*, to Confult on Whom They fhould confer the chief Command: For, the *Thracians* being in Poffeffion of the Country, it was certain their Intended Settlement would meet with fome Oppofition. The *Prieftefs* of APOLLO directed Them by Name to Appoint MILTIADES to be their General, Affuring Them of Succefs in their Enterprife, if They fhould Place Him

at

* *Hodie*. Morea

at the Head of It. Encouraged by This Declaration of the *Oracle*, MIL-TIADES embarked with a select Body of Troops for the *Cherfonefe*. He touched at ⸆ *Lemnos* in his Way, with a View of reducing *That Ifland* to the Obedience of *Athens*; and accordingly fent the Inhabitants Word, that He expected Them to Acknowledge their Dependance by a Voluntary Submiffion. To This Meffage They gave no Other than This Delufory Anfwer; " That *They would* " *not fail to Comply with the Summons,* " *whenever He fhould Sail from* HOME " *to* LEMNOS *with the Wind at* " *North* "; as knowing while it Blew from That Quarter, it was directly in the Teeth of All who were fteering their Courfe thither from *Athens.* However, MILTIADES not being at leifure to Profecute His

B 2

Defign

---

* *Hodie*, Stalimene-Ifland *in the* Archipelago

Defign on That People, defifted
for the Prefent from any farther
Attempt, and proceeded on his
Voyage.

After his Arrival, having in a
fhort Time Defeated the Forces of
the *Barbarians*, He made Himfelf
Mafter of all the Country he had
propofed; and, the better to fecure
it, Erected *Forts* in fuch Places as
He found Convenient. The Lands
He divided among the *Adventurers*,
Whom He likewife Enriched by frequent Excurfions: Managing the
Whole Affair with a Prudence equal
to his Good Fortune. For, as He
owed his Conqueft to the Valour of
his Soldiers, fo He diftributed the
Fruits of it among Them with great
Equity; and Refolved to fix his Refi-
dence there, having the *Authority*, tho'
not the *Style* of KING among Them;
which He had Acquired as much by
his *Juftice*, as his *Power*. Nor was
He

He the more Negligent on this Account in Paying all due Regards to his *Principals* at *Athens*. By these Means He was continued in That *High Station*, no less to the Satisfaction of Those Who first Employed Him, than of Those He then Governed. And thus having settled all Matters on a firm Footing in his *New Establishment*, He Returns to Lemnos, and peremptorily demands the Surrender of their City in virtue of their *own Stipulation*; Telling Them, " His Home was now in " the Chersonese, *from whence He* " *had Sailed thither with a Northerly* " *Wind.* " The *Carians* (for They were then the Proprietors of Lemnos) seeing Things had taken a Turn they did not Expect, tho' not out of a scrupulous Attention to their Promise, yet Awed by the Success of their Invaders, did not think fit to Dispute his Claim, and

B 3   very

very peaceably Evacuated the Island.
He was no lefs Fortunate in Sub-
duing All the reft of the * CY-
CLADES.

About That Time the King of
Perfia, having Determined to make
War upon the *Scythians*, entered
Europe with an Army from *Afia*, and
laid a Bridge over the *Danube* to
maintain a Communication. He
Committed the Guard of That *Bridge*,
in his Abfence, to certain Great
Lords Who had attended Him from
Æolis and *Ionia*, and Whom He had
Invefted with the Sovereignty of
their refpective Cities, (Judging that
the moft likely Scheme to keep the
Greeks, who were fettled in *Afia*, in
Subjection to Him, was to give the
Abfolute Government of their Towns
to fuch of the *Natives* Who were *his*
Creatures, and Whofe Power and
Safety

---

* *Iflands in the* Archipelago

Safety depended intirely on his Own.)
MILTIADES was one of the Number to Whom the Cuſtody of *That Bridge* was Intruſted. He, having received repeated Intelligence, that the *King*'s Affairs were in an ill Poſture, and that He was hard preſſed by the *Scythians*, Addreſſed Himſelf to the *Other Chiefs* Who were joined in the ſame Commiſſion with Him, and Admoniſhed Them not to let Slip an Occaſion, Fortune had put into their Hands, of Reſtoring *Freedom* to All GREECE. For, ſaid He, if DARIUS were cut off with the Forces He has tranſported with Him, not *Europe* only, but That Part of *Aſia* too, Whoſe Inhabitants are of *Greek* Extraction, would be ſet at Liberty from the Chains, and Inſults of the *Perſians* This, continued He, might be Effected with Eaſe by Demoliſhing the Bridge, in Conſequence of Which Action, the

King and his Whole Army muſt of
Neceſſity either fall by the Sword,
or Periſh in a few Days for Want
of Subſiſtance.   When the *Majority*
ſeemed Inclinable to This Advice,
HISTIÆUS of * *Miletos* Oppoſed it,
repreſenting to Them, that Their
Intereſt, Who were *Princes,* was very
Different from Thoſe of the *Common
People*;   their Authority being founded on That of DARIUS, his De-
ſtruction would put an End to Their
Rule, and probably expoſe Them
to the Revenge of their Countrymen, over Whom He had placed
Them to Govern.   For this Reaſon,
He was ſo far from Agreeing to the
Expedient propoſed, that he thought
their *true Policy* was to Strengthen,
as much as in Them lay, the Dominion of the *Perſians*.   When MIL-
TIADES obſerved this laſt Argument
to

* *Hodʼe,* Melaſſo

to prevail, not doubting but a Debate, to which fo Many had been Privy, would at length be carried to the *King*'s Ear, He withdrew from the *Cherfonefe*, and Retired to *Athens*. The Counfel he gave, though it proved Unfuccefsful, ought neverthelefs to be Applauded, as it was a Mark of his *Publick Spirit*, in Preferring the *General Liberty* to his *Perfonal Command*.

DARIUS, after his Return into *Afia* from *Europe* was Advifed by his Favourites to Attempt the Reduction of *Greece*. In hopes to Accomplifh This Defign, He gave Orders for the Equipment of Five hundred Sail of Ships, aboard Which He embarked Two hundred Thoufand Foot and Ten Thoufand Horfe, The Whole under the Command of DATIS and ANTIPHERNIS. The Reafon he Alledged for This Great Armament, was an Affront offered to Him by the

the *Athenians,* in Affifting the *Ioni-ans,* in Their Affault of *Sardis,* and putting the Garrifon He had placed there to the Sword. The Generals arriving with the Royal Navy before * *Eubæa,* attackt *Eretria* the Capital of That Ifland; Took it, and fent the Inhabitants into *Afia* Prifoners to the King. After which, failing from Thence, They made a Defcent on the Country of *Attica,* and In-camped in the Plain of *Marathon,* about Ten Miles diftant from *Athens.* The City alarmed with fo Nume-rous and Formidable an Enemy juft in their Neighbourhood, did not however Apply for Troops to any of their Allies, except the *Lacedæmo-nians.* To *Thefe* They fent PHI-LIPPIDES, One of Thofe Couriers they call *Day-Pofts,* to inform Them of the Neceffity they had of fpeedy Succours.

---

* *Ho hie,* Negropont

Succours. At the fame time They created Ten *General Officers* among Themfelves: but Thefe Difagreed in their *Schemes*, fome Declaring for an *Offenfive War*, Others thinking it more Advifable to Act upon the *Defenfive* only. MILTIADES laboured all He could to bring Them to a Refolution forthwith to *Incamp*, as the beft Means to keep up the *Hearts* of the *People*, by fhewing Them their *Courage* was not *Diftrufted*; at the fame time that it muft abate the *Confidence* of the *Enemy* to find Themfelves *Faced* in the *Field* by fuch *inferior Numbers*.

Not one City in All *Greece* fent Affiftance to the *Athenians* in This Diftrefs, except the *Plataenfes*. From *Thefe* they received a Reinforcement of a Thoufand Men. With This Addition their Compliment was juft Ten Thoufand. A fmall, but a Refolute, Body, who longed with

incredible

incredible Impatience to come to Action. MILTIADES had therefore much more Sway with Them than his *Colleagues*, whom They looked upon as too *Cautious*. Induced by his Authority the *Athenians* marched their Troops without the Walls of the City to a Convenient Camp that had been marked out for Them : and the next Day, having been drawn up by Him firſt in order of Battle, at the Foot of a Mountain, and in a Line with it, after a new and uſeful Method, This little Army Engaged the Enemy with great Fury. MILTIADES, to prevent their being ſurrounded by the Horſe, had made ſuch a Diſpoſition, that his People were Covered in the Rear by the Steepneſs of the Hills, and Defended on the Flanks by Trees which he had cauſed to be laid up and down, and which would Intangle the Cavalry as often as They Advanced.

DATIS

DATIS, although He was sensible of the Disadvantage He had in the Ground, relying on his odds in Number, was Eager for Attacking the *Athenians*, and the more so, because the *Lacedæmonians* had not as yet Joyned Them. Accordingly, having formed a Grand Detachment of One hundred Thousand Foot, and Ten Thousand Horse from All his Forces, He began the Onset. But the *Athenians* were so Superior in Courage to his Troops, that They intirely routed Them, tho' ten times their Number, and struck such a *Panick* into the *Persians*, that not thinking Themselves sufficiently secured by retiring within their Intrenchments, They fled to their Ships. Never was Any Thing more Glorious than *This Battle*, as certainly never One was gained by such a *Handful of Men* against so *Mighty an Host*.

It

It may not feem an Impertinent Remark to take notice here, What Kind of Reward was conferred on MILTIADES after this *Important Victory* And, by reflecting on That, We fhall more plainly fee, that *The Nature of all Governments is Alike.* For as in Former times the *Publick Honours* among the *Romans* were but Slender, and Thofe too very fparingly Beftowed, (Which made Them held in great Account, whereas now that They are given with Profufion, and without Merit, they grow Cheap and Contemptible,) fo We find it was juft the fame in the *Athenian* Commonwealth. This GREAT MAN Who had in one Day refcued *Athens* and all *Greece* from Slavery, received no other Mark of *Diftinction*, or *Recompence* for his *Services*, than What They call the HONOUR OF THE GALLERY, Where, in The *Picture* which was fet up of the *Battle* of

MARA-

MARATHON, *His Figure* was Placed the *Foremost* of the *Ten Generals*, drawn in the *Act of Exhorting* the Soldiers, and Giving the *Signal* to Engage.   Yet This very People, when their Dominions were Enlarged, and They, by the Bribery and Intrigues of the *Magistrates*, fell afterwards into Corruption, erected no less than *Three hundred Statues* to DEMETRIUS PHALEREUS.

Upon the Success of This Battle, the *Athenians* fitted out a Fleet of Seventy Sail under the Command of MILTIADES, Whose Orders were to Chastise Those Islands That had aided the * *Barbarians* in the late War. The Greater Part returned to their Duty, but some obliged Him to have recourse to Arms.   Among these last was *Paros*, an Island grown Wealthy

---

* *The* Greeks *called all Foreigners, in general,* Barbarous

Wealthy and Proud. When He found He was not likely to fucceed there by Treaty, He landed his Men; drew a Line round the City to cut off their Provifions; and then carried on his Approaches in Form. The Town was upon the Point of Surrendering, When a Grove, at fome diftance on the Continent, but within View of the Ifland, by What Accident I know not, took Fire. The Befiegers and Befieged Both imagined, as foon as They faw the Flames, it was a *Signal* given of the *King's Fleet* coming to the Relief of the Place. This Encouraged the Citizens in Holding out; and MILTIADES too, being unwilling to run the hazard of Encountring a Royal Navy, burnt all the Works he had erected, and drawing off his Forces, Returned home with the fame Number of Ships He brought out; but to the great Offence of the *Commonwealth.*

wealth. Accordingly He was Accufed of Treafon, in *raifing the Siege,* when He might, as They Alledged, have *Taken the Town,* had he not been corrupted by the King of *Perfia*'s Gold. He lay ill at that time of the Wounds He had received before the Place, and being incapable of Pleading for Himfelf, his Brother Tisagoras undertook to Manage his Defence. The Tryal being Ended, He was Acquitted as to his Life, but Sentenced to Defray the Whole Expence of That *Expedition,* the Eftimate of Which amounted to *Fifty* * *Talents.* As He was in no Condition to Pay fo large a Sum, They flung Him into the Publick Jayl, Where He Ended his Days.

But tho' This Pretended Treachery at *Paros* was the Crime laid to his Charge, the real Caufe of his Condemnation

C

demnation

---

* *Each* Attick *Talent,* 48 l 7 s 10 d.

demnation was quite Different. The *Athenians*, in fhort, after the Tyranny of PISISTRATUS, which was frefh in their Memories, grew Jealous of Any *Rifing Man* among Themfelves. And MILTIADES had fo long, and fo often held the Reins of Empire, either as a *General*, or a *Magiftrate*, that He feemed by a kind of *Habit* inured to AMBITION, and incapable of leading a *Private Life*. For during the Whole Time, He refided in the *Cherfonefe*, His Government was Abfolute *there*, and HE Styled a TYRANT, (as All Such are, Who in their *fingle Names* exercife the *Supreme Command* in Cities That were REPUBLICKS before,) tho' His *Sovereignty* was indeed a *Legal One*, as not having been Ufurped by *Force*, but Obtained with the *Confent* of his People, and Supported by his own *Juftice*, and *Bounty*. Behold then the Rock on Which He Split ! HE was in his NATURE fo

Gentle

Gentle and *Humane* in his MANNERS; fo wonderfully *Civil* and *Affable*; (for the meaneft Perfon might have Accefs to Him with Freedom,) He had Eftablifhed fo Great an *Intereft* with the Neighbouring STATES; was fo *Noble* in his EXTRACTION; and fo *Renowned* for his MILITARY CAPACITY; that HIS COUNTRY, confidering all *thefe Circumftances*, looked upon Him as *Dangerous* to *Their Freedom*; and chofe rather to *Ruin* HIM, though *Innocent*, than to live longer in *Fear* of his POPULARITY, and his POWER.

C 2   THE

THE
LIFE
OF
CIMON,
The Younger.

IMON, the Son of MILTIADES, by Birth an *Athenian,* paſſed the firſt Years of his Youth under very great Hardſhips. For as the Father had been laid in Priſon on Account of a *Fine* He was Unable to

Pay

Pay to the *State,* fo the Weight of *That Sentence* fell, after his Death, upon the Son; Who by the Laws of *Athens* was liable to the fame Reftraint, until He fhould Difcharge the Debt. He had taken ELPINICF, His own Sifter, in *Marriage* ; a Marriage made not more *after his Own Heart,* than According to the *Cuftoms of His Country ·* (For The *Son* and *Daughter* of One *Common Father* are not excluded by the ATHENIAN *Ritual* from being *Man* and *Wife.*) Now there was a Perfon named CALLIAS, One Diftinguifhed rather as a *Monied Man,* than a *Gentleman,* having raifed a great Fortune from his Mines, Who was Ambitious of Matching with *That Lady*; and endeavoured to Perfuade CIMON to Refign Her, by offering, upon That Condition, to Satisfy the Whole Demand the *Government* had upon Him. This Propofal HE rejected with Scorn , But

C 3   ELPINICE

ELPINICE declared, she could not bear the Thought that Any of the Offspring of MILTIADES should Perish in a *Jayl*; and since it was in her Power to Prevent it by Consenting to *Marry* This CALLIAS, she would not Refuse Him her Hand, provided He Performed the Engagement He had Entered into on his Part.

CIMON, by *these means* being set at Liberty, soon came to be the *Leading Man* Of That City. His Talents for *Eloquence* were very sufficient; He was Liberal in the highest Degree; and had attained a great Skill in all *Civil*, as well as *Military* Affairs; in which last *Profession* He had been train'd up from a Child by his constant Attendance on his Father in the Wars. *These Qualifications* gave him a mighty Influence over the *People*, and made his Authority likewise much Valued in the *Army*. His First

Firſt Command, as GENERAL, was at the River *Strymon*, where he put to Flight the numerous Troops of the THRACIANS, and afterwards *Founded* AMPHIPOLIS ſettling a Colony there of Ten Thouſand *Athenians.* His next Succeſs was in *Defeating* and *Taking, off* MYCALE, a *Fleet* conſiſting of Two Hundred Sail of *Cypriots* and *Phœnicians.* The very ſame Day of which Engagement at Sea, He had another on Shoar with equal Good Fortune: For as ſoon as He had made Himſelf Maſter of the Enemy's *Shipping,* He landed His Men, and at one Rencounter overthrew the vaſt Forces of the *Barbarians.* As He was Sailing home with great Spoils, after This Victory, having received Intelligence that ſome of the *Iſlands* had revolted from their Obedience, by reaſon of their Preſſures from the Government, He confirmed in their Allegiance ſuch as He

C 4 found

found well Inclined; and Obliged
the Difaffected to Return to their
Duty : Among Thefe the *Dolopes*,
who dwelt in *Scyros*, behaving Themfelves fomewhat Mutinoufly, He
cleared *That Ifland* of its old Inhabitants at once; Dividing their Lands
among his Countrymen. In the fame
manner the *Thafians*, who were grown
Infolent upon their Increafe of Traffick and Riches, were foon Humbled
after his Arrival among Them. And
with the Money arifing from the
Sale of the Plunder He took in thefe
feveral Occafions, He Repaired and
Beautified That Part of the *Citadel*
of *Athens* which lies to the *South.*

When by a continued Series of Profperity He was Arrived to the *Higheft Pitch* of *Glory*, He fell at laft into
the fame *Envy* and *Difgrace*, which
his Father, and All the Great Men
at *Athens* had experienced before
Him.

Him. For, notwithftanding his Merit, He was Condemned, (by a way of *Voting* They call an * *Oftracifm*) to a Banifhment of Ten Years; a Refolution, which the *Athenians* regretted much foonér than He did. For while He with the Conftancy of a *Man* of *Honour* was fupporting Himfelf againft the *Ingratitude* of his *Country*, They were unluckily engaged in a War with the LACEDÆMONIANS, and foon felt the Lofs of his known *Valour* and *Abilities*. Therefore in the Fifth Year of his *Exile* They Recalled Him. And, as He had Entertained a Commerce of Friendfhip with the People of *Lacedæmon*, He voluntarily undertook, upon this Occafion, to make a *Tour* Thither; Where He Negotiated and Eftablifhed a *Peace* between Thofe Two *Commonwealths*, Who

---

* *So called, by their infcribing their Votes on Shells*

Who were fuch Powerful *Rivals*.
Not long after This, He was fent
with a Fleet of Two hundred Sail
of Ships under his Command on an
Expedition to *Cyprus :* But, juft when
He had fubdued the Greateft Part of
That Ifland, He fell into a Diftemper,
That proved Mortal to Him, and Died
in a Town called *Cittum.*

The *Athenians* found a fenfible
Want of this excellent Perfon for
many Years: not only in the Times
of *War,* but during the Seafons of
Peace. For fuch was the *Generofity*
of his NATURE, that though He
had *Mannours,* and *Gardens* in feveral Places, He no where put in a
Steward to reftrain the free Ufe of
What They Produced; to Which
All People in common were Welcome.
He was always Attended, wherever
He Walked, by Servants with *Purfes*
of *Money,* that HE might be Able
to

to Furnish an *immediate Supply* to the *Neceffities* of Such as afked of Him, left by *Delaying* He might feem to *Deny* Them His *Affiftance*. He has often, upon Meeting One in the Streets Who was in *Rags,* or *ill-cloathed,* parted with the *Cloak* from his *own Shoulders,* to *Cover* the *Nakednefs,* or *Poverty* Of his *Fellow-Citizen.* And fo Great was the *Plenty* and *Hofpitality* of his Way of Entertaining at *Home*, that Whomever He met in the *Forum,* That were not præ-engaged, He Invited Them to *Eat* at *his Table,* and This not *occafionally,* but *every Day.* His *Credit,* his *Friendfhip,* or his *Fortune,* was never wanting to Any Man. The *Living,* many of Them, were Enriched by His *Bounty* ; and even the *Dead* were Obliged to His *Charity* : For, Such, Who left not Behind Them wherewithal to *Bury* Them with *Decency,*

cency, had *That Office* of *Humanity* performed to Them at His *Expence*. No Wonder then, if his *Life*, ſpent in the Exerciſe of ſo *many Virtues*, was for the moſt part *Happy* and *Secure*; as his *Death*, which became a General *Misfortune*, was *univerſally* Lamented.

POEMS.

POEMS

ON

SEVERAL OCCASIONS.

BURY TOASTS.

------ *Non alia bibam Mercede.*

Miss MOLLY SPRING.

 N Love's soft Wars She gains a
double Prize,
And Triumphs by her Wit,
as by her Eyes.

En-

Encore *Miss* MOLLY.

AS That Gay Seaſon of the Youthful
       Year,
That bears her Name, for ever Sweet
     and Fair.
But She, like FLORA, ſhou'd improve her
     Charms,
And take an Am'rous ZEPHYR to her
     Arms.

Miss PASTON.

IN PASTON'S Face the *Smiles* and
     Bluſhes meet,
And ſhew her *Heart* both *Tender* and
     Diſcreet.

Miſs

Miss THORNHILL.

BEhold *MINERVA*'s Dignity of Mien,
With all the Sweetness of the *Cyprian*
    Queen!

Mrs. KING.

ETernal *Venus* is around Her Spread!
   May Love, *Luxuriant* Love, attend her Bed!

Lady BETTY HERVEY, *now* Mansel.

SOFT as the Lilly, or the *Provence*
    Rose,
More lasting Fair, and full as Sweet as
    Those.

Countess

Countefs of ROCHFORT.

HER Beauty, like the Sun's impartial
    Light,
Shines forth, and cheers each fond Be-
    holder's Sight :
Secure and Pleas'd, whilft *Honour* is her
    Guide,
She fcorns the dull Reftraints of Fear or
    Pride.

Mifs SUSEY BUNBURY. *now Mrs.* Handerfide.

HER Air, her Voice, each Motion,
    All confpire
To raife in ev'ry Gallant Breaft defire :
Yet fuch nice *Conduct* does the Maid
    adorn,
None Boaft her *Favour*, or Accufe her
    Scorn.

Mifs

Miss MOLLY BUNBURY.

NATURE yet uninform'd by *Art's*
    Difguife,
Sports on her Lips, and fparkles in her
    Eyes :
Unpractis'd in the Mifchiefs of her Sex,
She only knows to *Pleafe*, and not to
    Vex.

Miss HARRIET D'EWES.

HER Value does by long Acquain-
    tance rife,
Always fecure to *Pleafe*, tho' not
    Surprife.

D   *Mifs*

Miſs SMITHSON.

THE CHEVELEY*Graces in the Nymph appear,
A *Rural Innocence,* and *Courtly Air.*

---

* Cheveley, *is the Seat of Lady* Dover, *her Aunt.*

Miſs PEGGY CLAGET.

TRANSPORTING Object of our *Sight* and *Touch!*
Grant *This Senſe* more, or not to *That* ſo much.

Miſs

Miss DILLY SPRING.

HER Youthful Charms a *Gentle*
    Light convey,
Sweet as the *Morning-Star* disclosing
    Day:
Silent She moves, but *Certain* to impart
New *Beauties* to the *Eye*, fresh *Gladness*
    to the *Heart*.

CUPID *not blind.*

NOT far from the * HIDE lives a
    Damsel, so Fair,
I'd Give Her my *Heart* for one Lock of
    her *Hair.*

                    D 2   Her

* *A Celebrated Wood near* Hengrove-Hall *in* Suf-
folk, *the Seat of Sir* William Gage

Her *Cheeks* are like *Roses* That Blush in
    their Prime;
Her *Lips* sweet as *Cherries* just Gather'd
    in Time.
To Gaze on her *Eyes* might an *Hermit*
    inflame;
And Who *Looks* on her *Moles* but Thinks
    o' *That same*?
Her *Bubbies* so prettily heave up and
    down,
The Sight wou'd Please All from a *King*
    to a *Clown*.
Her *Waist* is as Taper as MERCURY's
    Rod,
And the *Treasures* below were a Prize
    for a *God*.
Those *Beauties* are Hid ---- but my *Fancy*
    can trace
SHE's a VENUS when *Naked*, as *Drest*
    She's a GRACE.

Now, CUPID, Divine ---- Who's This
    Charming Fine *Thing*?
Well! for once You've Guess'd right: 'tis
    Dear MOLLY SPRING.

                      SONG.

S O N G.

I.

CÆLIA, Conscious of her Beauty,
    Treats her Servant with Disdain,
Like a Tyrant claims his Duty,
    Yet Rewards his Love with Pain.

II.

CUPID, O Survey Thy Quiver!
    And Address the *Keenest Dart*;
Pride no longer will Deceive Her,
    When She feels a *Bleeding Heart*.

D 3   *Writ*

Writ on a Bench in the Glade of a Wood.

Wou'd You Know how We Live in
    our *Rural Retreat*,
You Who Think All are *Wretched* but
    They That are *Great*?
The *Field* and the *Study*, by Turns, vary
    the Scene;
Or *Girls* and a *Bottle*, when in *Love* or
    the *Spleen.*
Thus in *Ease not inglorious* our Hours
    glide away,
Soft falls the *calm Evening*, gay Springs
    the *Young Day.*

Carving

Carving her Name on the Bark of a Tree.

FOrgive Me, Hospitable Tree!
And if beneath Thy friendly Shade
Thou e'er shalt View the lovely Maid,
For whom I Bleed with *secret Smart;*
Tell Her, the Wounds I gave to Thee
Affect Alone thine *outward Part* :
But Those her Eyes have giv'n to Me
Sunk *deeper far,* and Pierc'd my *Heart.*

A Question put upon the Bench in the HIDE.

FAIR, Auspicious, Gentle MAIDS!
Sweet Oracles of *These Blest Shades* !
Tell Me (for I Know You can)
What will Make a HAPPY MAN?

D 4

Is

Is it *Wisdom*, *Wit*, or *Wealth?*
Ancient Blood? or *Youthful Health?*
May *Conqu'ring Chiefs* That Title Boast?
Or is the WORLD *for* LOVE *well* Loft?
Fair, auſpicious, gentle MAIDS!
Sweet Oracles of *theſe Bleſt Shades!*
Tell Me (for I Know You can)
What will make a HAPPY MAN?

An Anſwer by ------

I Will Tell You, if I may,
What will make a HAPPY DAY.
Bring back the *Rovings* of Thy *Youth*
To bear with the *Important Truth:*
'Tis None of All That *Wanton Train*
Summ'd up in Thy *Poetick Vein;*
Neither is it VENUS' *Theft*,
But it is *The* WORLD *well Left.*
I will Tell You, if I may,
What will make a HAPPY DAY.

Occaſioned

Occasioned by the foregoing
VERSES.

A NIGHTINGALE That fought This
 * Grove,
The Seat of *Music* and of *Love*,
Was wont in Artleſs Strains to Sing
The *Bloomy Beauties* of the SPRING;
When, lo! She heard a ſolemn Noiſe
From the dark RAVEN's fatal Voice,
That bid the *Wanton* change her Note,
And Tune to *Graver Airs* her Throat:
Sighing the *Am'rous Bird* Reply'd,
Sung This ſhort *Dirge*, and then ſhe
 Died.

 " *Severe are Theſe Cenſorious Days,*
' *When* SATIRE *leſs Offends than* PRAISE.

An

* *The* HIDE

An EJACULATION.

YE Pow'rs supreme! Who rule this
    Vassal Earth,
Why to my Wretched Being gave Ye
    Birth?
Is *This to Live?* in Endless Care to roam
A *Pilgrim* from the *Cradle* to the *Tomb?*
In our *Uncertain Voyage* below, tho' *Few,*
Yet *some* attain the *Port* their Hopes
    pursue:
My feeble *Barque* by raging Storms was
    Tost
O'er the *rough Billows* on a *Dreary Coast*
Whilst Happier Mortals *Fair Possessions*
    got,
The Vale of Tears, alas! *was all my*
    Lot:
There Doom'd to Wander, I neglected
    Moan,
By FORTUNE Jilted, and by LOVE Un-
    done.

Inscribed

Inscribed on a Drinking-Glass.

VENUS no more shall be MOUNT
    IDA's Pride !
The Queen of *Beauty* now frequents the
    HIDE,

Writ on a Seat in the Glade of the HIDE.

STAY PASSENGER, Whoe'er Thou art,
    And, if Thou bear'st a Gentle Heart,
Pray for the Soul of ONE *in Love*,
That often *Haunts* this Gloomy Grove.
The *Wretch* was in a *State of Grace*,
    Whilst He cou'd View Bright CÆLIA's
      Charms ;
(For *Paradise* is in her Face,
    And *Heaven*, I trust, is in her Arms.)
              But

But from That GODDESS far Remov'd,
He hovers between *Hope* and *Fear*;
And *Death-like Absence* having Prov'd,
Now Mourns in PURGATORY Here.

CANTATA.

RECITATIVO.

AN Am'rous poor Unhappy Swain,
  Who long a Slave to CÆLIA's Pride,
That haughty MAID had Sued in vain,
  To CYTHERÆA thus Apply'd:

ARIET.

HAIL Propitious Deity!
  All Nature does Thy Bounty Bless:
Hear then an humble Votary
  Relieve the *Faithful* in *Distress!*
Subdue That Unrelenting Fair,
Or let Me *Die,* Who now *Despair.*

RECITATIVO.

RECITATIVO.

VENVS, his heavy Woe beguiling,
   Hopes infpir'd and gay Defire;
So, Night difperft, AURORA fmiling
   Cheers the Soul with *Genial Fire:*
Come, YOUTH, faid fhe, take *This*
      Advice,
When WOMEN prove *Coquet,* or *Nice.*

ARIET.

FIckle is the FEMALE MIND,
   LOVE, like CHANCE, *Perverfe* and
      Blind.
Sigh no more the Nymph purfuing;
   Wild and Wanton ftrive to Pain Her,
Leave thy dull officious Wooing;
   Make Her *Jealous,* That may gain Her.
Range among the Sex and Rove;
   All have not obdurate Hearts:
From the *Palace* to the *Grove,*
   LOVE at random throws his *Darts.*

An

An *ELEGY.*

I DREAMT but Now (for oh! 'twas All
    a Dream,

The Nymph, I fear, ne'er meant That
    Kind Extream)

Some Tears of Pity from MYRTILLA
    ftole,

That Dropt like Balm upon my wounded
    Soul.

Methought, She faid, " Arife, Dear in-
    jur'd Swain!

" And reap the full Reward of All Thy
    Pain:

" What You Defir'd, Unwilling I De-
    ny'd;

" And Liv'd a Wretched Slave to Fame,
    and Pride:

" Defend Me, Shepherd! from Thofe
    Falfe Alarms,

" O Take Me, Hide Me, Hold Me in
    Thy Arms!

My

My Heart, exulting with Approaching
    Bliss,

Sprung forth to Meet Her in an Ardent
    Kiss,

While *Fancy* sporting, Bold and Un-
    confin'd,

In Thousand Am'rous Folds our Limbs
    entwin'd :

Through all the Mazes of Delight I
    rov'd

By *Nature* form'd, and *Wanton Wit* im-
    prov'd :

Till the *Fierce Tide of Joy Tumultuous*
    broke

The Bands of Sleep, When I surpris'd
    Awoke ;

Found my Whole Frame Dissolv'd in sweet
    Excess,

But no fond *Partner* in the *soft Distress.*

    Venus ! Propitious Queen of young
        Desires !

Must I then Languish still in Hopeless
    Fires !

                    Or

Or was This *Flatt'ring Omen* not in vain?
O Join our *Loves,* or Equal our *Difdain!*

Epilogue to the ALCHYMIST. As Acted by the young Gentlemen of Bury-School, 1721.

OLD Surly BEN, to Night has let
    us know,
That in this ISLE a Plenteous Crop did
    grow
Of *Knaves* and *Fools* a Hundred Years
    ago.
Chymifts, Bawds, Gamefters, and a Nu-
    merous Train
Of humble Rogues, Content with mode-
    rate Gain.
The *Poet,* had he liv'd to fee *This Age,*
Had brought *Sublimer Villains* on the
    Stage;

Our

Our *Knaves* Sin higher now than those of
    Old

Kingdoms, not Private Men, are *Bought*
    and *Sold:*

Witness the *South-Sea* Project, which
    hath shown,

How far Philosophers may be out-
    done

By Modern Statesmen that have found
    the Stone.

Well might it take its Title from the
    Main,

That *Rose* so swift, and *Sunk* so soon
    again.

Fools have been always *bit* by artful
    Lyes;

But here the *Cautious* were deceiv'd, and
    Wise:

And yet, in these Flagitious Monstrous
    Times,

The *Knaves* detected *Triumph* in their
    Crimes;

E   Wallow

Wallow in Wealth, have all Things a_t
     Command,

And Brave the Vengeance of an *Injur'd*
     Land.

Well! since we've Learn'd Experience
     at our Coft,

Let us preferve the *Remnant* not yet
     Loft,

Though *Law* from *France* be landed
     on the Coaft

By Sober Arts Afpire to *Guiltlefs*
     Fame,

And Prove that *Virtue's* not an empty
     Name.

To

To *Mrs.* MARY SPRING *with the* SPECTATORS.

REceive This Gift , nor, Gentle Maid,
    refufe
The fond Addrefs of an Officious *Mufe*;
That of her meaner Store can little
    fend,
And *Abler Wits* would to your choice
    commend.

In *Thefe nice Finifh'd Pieces* You may
    find
Each *Beauty* trac'd and *Blemifh* of the
    Mind.
The *Diff'rent Airs* in Humankind that
    rife
From VIRTUE, PRUDENCE, IGNORANCE
    and VICE,

With all *Those Signs,* so Few have Understood,

Which mark the *Real* from the *Seeming*
Good,

Are to Your View expos'd with happy
Care,

Just the *Designs,* and *Sweet* the *Col'rings*
are.

What Grave PHILOSOPHERS could never Teach,

Nor heavy PARSONS in their Pulpits
reach,

In short Excursions, *here* You will Attain,

Without *laborious Search,* or *studious*
Pain.

Through all the MORALS artfully are
spread

A *Thousand Graces* That invite to
Read.

So

So the bleſt ANGELS, When they leave
  their Skies,
Aſſume ſome *Fav'rite Form* to Greet our
  Eyes.
With *Winning Eloquence* then Charge
  Diſpenſe,
And both *Inſtruct* the *Soul,* and *Charm*
  the *Senſe*

May Pleaſing Truths your *ſoft Inqui-*
  ries crown,
And YOU grow WISE, nor *Wrinkle* know,
  nor *Frown.*
Uneuvy'd, whether VIRGIN *Eaſe* You
  ſhare,
Or *take* a HUSBAND to *Divide* Your
  Care,
May *Fortune* ſtill on All your *Vows* At-
  tend,
Preſerve Your LOVER, and Confirm your
  FRIEND.

To a young Lady in Danger of making a Mistake for Life.

CAN then my *Dove* forsake this faithful Breast
In such a *vile Retreat* to Build her Nest?
Forgive Me, Dear unthinking Fickle Maid!
That thus severely I *Thy Choice* up-braid.
'Tis fond Concern these harsh Reproaches draws:
My Heart, oh! Bleeds in *Love*'s and *Beauty*'s Cause.
Unjust to Me, and to Yourself Un-kind!
Tho' Deaf to *Love*, be not to *Prudence* Blind.

More

More for your Int'reft than My own I
    Fear .

Your *Husband,* not my *Rival,* gives me
    Care

Should fome Brave Youth, Whom *Worth*
    and *Truth* commends,

(But, ah ! how Rare Such Lovers, or Such
    Friends !

Who Knows to Prize the Merits of your
    Charms,

By long Perfuafion win you to his
    Arms.

Tho' *Griev'd,* Submiffive I might *then*
    Refign

Your Blifs would make Amends for Lofs
    of *Mine.*

But if, feduc'd by low Defires of Gain,

You, who might *Give, Receive* the *Mar-*
    riage Chain.

Too foon, Unhappy, (and without Ex-
    cufe,)

You want that *Pity,* which you *Me* Re-
    fufe

Prologue to the MERRY WIVES OF WINDSOR. *Acted by the* Young Gentlemen *of* Bury-School, 1723.

IN Those Blest Days e'er Peevish *Reformation*

Deny'd Poor *Priests* the Rights of *Fornication,*

Our Good Lord ABBOT, and his Sons of Grace,

Enjoy'd sweet Quarters in This Happy Place.

He and his *Monks,* like FALSTAFF, and His Set,

Took All for *Fish* That came into their Net.

Mar-

Marriage They did Abjure, ſo Heav'n
    Defend 'em!
Yet Each cou'd Hold a *Damſel* in *Com-*
    mendam.
But left Grave Men might ſeem to Play
    the Fool,
Their Frolicks all were laid on a *Mad*
    Bull.
Not *Bulls* from ROME ſuch *Miracles*
    have ſhown,
As That *White Bull* from neighb'ring
    * HABYRDON.
No *Virgins* then 'till *Fifty* ſtuck o' Hand,
No *Barren Matrons* mourn'd within our
    Land.

Love

---

* *The Manno*r *of* Habyrdon *was held by the Te-
nure of furniſhing a* White Bull *to the Abbey, which,
at certain Times, was carried in Proceſſion to the Bier
of* St Edmond, *where Ladies who complained of Bar-
renneſs, after the Ceremony of* Stroaking *the Bull,
made their Offerings.*

Love was like *ready Money* in the Nation,
And *Their* * *Exchequer* gave it Circulation.
But Raillery apart —— This Jolly Town
For Acts of *Gallantry* was always Known.
Not that the *Ladies* were less *Chaste* than
       Fair :
True *Rigour*'s in the *Heart,* and not the
       Air.
In gen'rous Freedom *Virtue* shou'd be
       plac'd ;
By servile Chains her Honour is Debas'd.
The *Formal* often lead the *loosest Lives*,
Then —— *Merry be your Hearts* My
       MAIDS and WIVES.
While *Conscious Merit* justifies your
       Claim,
Assume the Pride That's Due to *Beauty*'s
       Fame.
For *Heroes*, WINDSOR does the World
       excell :
For *Toasts,* Our BURY *bears away the*
       Bell.

               Epilogue

---

* *A Place* so called, *belonging formerly, to the* Abbey

Epilogue on the same Occasion.

ILLIB'RAL *Souls,* to sordid *Av'rice*
    bred,
With Jealous Thoughts the SCHOOLS of
    Science dread :
They look with Envy, when Those
    Forts arise.
To Combat *Error,* and Extirpate *Vice :*
But All whom *Honour,* or whom *Worth*
    commends,
Are to Good *Discipline* and *Learning*
    Friends.
The Favours They for *Those just Ends*
    bestow
Grace the *Receivers,* and the *Donors* too :
No *Structure* rais'd upon the *Noblest*
    Plan,
Yields half the Credit, as to *Build* a
    MAN.

For

For *This,* of old, were COLLEGES
   endow'd,

And large *Immunities,* and *Gifts* allow'd.

We too can Boaft a ROYAL FOUNDER
   Here,

Who Thought *Our* MUSES not beneath
   His Care.

But *now* the *Tuneful Nine* are forc'd to
   Dwell,

Like poor old *Alms-Women,* within a
   Cell.

* Of EDWARD's *Bounty* little *Fruit*
   appears,

Through *Fraud,* or *Folly,* of Succeeding
   Years.

Well! Various *Schemes* o' late have *drain'd*
   your Fence,

Subfcribe —— for once —— to VIRTUE
   and to SENSE.

   Re-

---

* EDWARD VI *founded* Bury-Schoo

Reſtore the *Splendor* that the SCHOOL
    has Loſt;
And let Your SONS grow *Wiſe* —— though
    at *Your Coſt.*
So ſhall MINERVA on Your *Labours* ſmile,
And BURY be The ATHENS of *Our*
    ISLE.

Written

Written June 5. 1724. *up-on my Surprising Recovery from a Dangerous Illness by the Care of* Dr. Mead.

WHEN lately Ling'ring with Con-
      fuming Pain,
That *Drank* my *Blood,* and *Scorch'd* my
      tortur'd *Brain,*
My *Hands* and *Knees* in trembling Con-
      cert joyn'd,
Feeble my *Body,* and as *Weak* my *Mind,*
Idle the WITTY feem'd, and *Dull* the
      WISE,
The FAIR *Themfelves* look'd *Faded* in my
      Eyes,
Reftlefs and Faint, I found no Help from
      Art
To *Cool* my *Head,* or *Cheer* my Droop-
      ing *Heart,*
                     Till

Till my Good Genius pointed to my
    Aid

Thy Happy Counsel, O Judicious Mead!

The Foe, That long with Scorn had kept
    the Field,

At Thy Approach was quickly forc'd to
    Yield.

So swift your Progress, and withal so
    sure,

It shew'd more like a *Miracle* than *Cure.*

And yet I took, to Drown the *Fell
    Disease,*

No *nauseous Draught :* At once You
    Save and *Please.*

    So When the *Pulse* of Conscience
        from Within

Has giv'n *Strong Symptoms* of some
        Deadly Sin,

To Learned Tillotson I've told my
        Grief,

And sought from *His Dispensary* Relief.

                                    The

The Sickly *Soul*'s Great ÆSCULAPIUS,
 He
Soon from each *Fev'rish* PASSION fet
 me Free.
His foft *Infufions* fteal upon the Mind,
His *Elocution* moves; his *Reafons* bind,
Each fhort *Inftructive Page* more *Skill*
 can fhow,
Each *Sound Prefcription* furer *Health*
 beftow,
Than all the *Drugs* That from GENEVA
 come,
Or all the *Gilded Pills* They fell at
 ROME.

An

An Extempore Epistle to Mrs.
MERIOLINA SPRING.

THE Bards of Old, so Learn'd and
      Wise,
Nine *Female Muses* did Devise,
When at the same Time They thought fit
To name but One *Male God* of Wit;
And still the Charming Sex We find
The Noblest Part of Human Kind;
Whilst double Influence They Dispense,
Victorious by their Eyes and Sense:
They Guide our Heads, and Rule our
      Hearts;
Refine our Manners, and our Parts.
Among the Men the Few who claim
To Wit, or Worth, a lasting Name,
All That, or Give, or Merit Praise,
From Those bright Stars derive their
      Rays.

F   'Tis

'Tis by their Happy Genial Light
The *Painters* Draw, the *Poets* write.
Ev'n I, the Meaneſt of the Tribe,
An Humble *Sonneteering* Scribe,
Waim'd by your ſoft Poetick Fire,
To loftier Numbers may Aſpire,
Who Now in haſte my Thoughts convey
In This Familiar Doggrel Way.
More greedily your *Lines* I Learn,
Than Graceleſs Parſon ſtuffs his Barn,
Or Lady's Chaplain crams his Belly
With Whipt Cream, Marmalade, or
    Jelly.
More I would ſay, but here Comes
    Dinner,
And I muſt Eat, as I'm a Sinner.
Commend me then in ſhort to All,
Who *Live* and *Laugh* at HENGRAVE-
    HALL,
From little DILLY * ſly and ſleek,
To MOLLY with her *Dimpled Cheek* :
                But

---

* De la Riviere.

But naming MOLLY, *à propos*,

How does the Pretty Cripple do ?

I fwear That ugly wicked Blow

Juft broke my Heart, That bruis'd her
     Toe.

If *Kiffes* wou'd Allay the Smart,

I wou'd *Kifs* That, or ---- Any Part.

For 'tis no Wonder I fhould *Love* Her,

When Both *Coquets* and *Prudes* Approve
     Her.

Peace, Plenty, Pleafure, from his Soul

HE Drinks to All, who Signs This Scroll.

R. P.

The

The SPECIFICK.

To a Young Physician, whose Mistress was likewise his Patient.

WOU'D You the FAIR both *Cure* and
                    Please,
And merit, DOCTOR, *Double Fees?*
With *happy Care* your *Skill* Employ
To mix the *Seeds* and *Flow'rs* of Joy,
Free from each vile Polluting Weed,
That *Hate, Distrust,* or *Scorn* may breed:
Let solid *Sense* Gay *Humour* join;
And with Good *Manners Wit* refine;
To vig'rous *Health,* and comely *Youth,*
Add *Honour, Tenderness,* and *Truth;*
Then in *Love's Limbeck* 'Still the Whole ·
The *Cordial Drops* will *Cheer* her *Soul.*

An EPITAPH.

THE Man, who lies beneath This Stone,
Liv'd no One's *Foe* besides his Own :
The *Faults* He had were not a Few,
But moſt of a *Good-natur'd Hue* :
When ſudden Guſts his *Anger* mov'd,
With *Zeal* He *Hated*, as He *Lov'd*,
But Gentler Pow'rs ſoon rul'd his Mind,
The *Peeviſh* yielded to the *Kind* ·
Where He found FRIEND, or MISTRESS
True,
He Melted like *Deſcending Dew* :
Free from all mean *Diſtruſt*, or *Art*,
Sincere and *Open* was his *Heart* :
He *Honour'd* MERIT in *Diſgrace*,
And *Scorn'd* a VILLAIN in *high Place* :
To GOD, and CÆSAR *Tribute* gave,
Yet neither BIGOT was, or SLAVE ;
And in three Words, to Sum the Whole,
Was a *Warm, Honeſt, Am'rous Soul.*

F 3   *The*

The REVOLUTION.

I.

FICKLE once, and Changing,
    Wild as Wanton Air,
Thro' the *Whole Sex* ranging
    None cou'd give Me Care;

II.

When by Chance Pursuing
    IRIS to the Grove,
I in Idle Wooing
    Talkt to Her of Love:

III.

Tho' her Eyes lookt Killing,
    Soon I found her Heart,
Was extremely Willing
    To Relieve my Smart:

IV.

Prompted by Occasion,
    Urg'd by strong Desire,
I indulg'd my Passion,
    She Renew'd my Fire:

V.

V.

Lips She had Excelling
   All I've Kift or Seen;
And What's more worth Telling;
   You know, what I mean.

VI.

Such a NYMPH Careffing,
   Ah, You'll fay, how bleft'
No: Since the Poffeffing
   How much more Diftreft !

VII.

From an Happy Rover
   Free from Am'rous Pain,
Now an Anxious Lover
   Lo! I drag her Chain,

VIII

While She daily Changing,
   Wild as Wanton Air,
Through *our Whole Sex* ranging
   None can give Her Care,

IX.

CUPID makes, to Spite Us,
   Or becaufe He's Blind,
All, whofe Charms Invite Us,
   Cruel, or too *Kind.*   Albii

Albii Tibulli Elegia Prima a Verſu Primo ad Septem, deinde, ab Quadrageſimo primo ad finem.

D*IVITIAS alius fulvo ſibi congerat*
  auro,

Et teneat culti jugera magna ſoli :
Quem labor aſſiduus vicino terreat hoſte,
  Martia cui ſomnos claſſica pulſa fugent.
Me mea paupertas vitæ traducit inerti,
  Dum meus exiguo luceat igne focus.
Non ego Divitias patrum, fructuſque
  requiro,
  Quos tulit antiquo condita meſſis avo.
Parva ſeges ſatis eſt, parvo requieſcere
  lecto,
  Si licet, et ſolito membra levare toro.

Quàm

The First Elegy of the First Book of TIBULLUS, *from the First to the Seventh Verse, and from the Forty First to the End.*

LET Others share the Spoils *Ambition*
    yields,
Their treasur'd Gold, their Tracts of Fer-
    tile Fields;
Whom daily Fears of fierce invading Foes
Deny the sweeter Fruits of calm Repose.
Poor be my Lot, inglorious my Desires,
So my Hearth shine with constant Chear-
    ful Fires.
I crave not Riches, nor th' Extent of Land
My wealthier Ancestors did once com-
    mand
This Little *Farm* will All I'd Ask supply:
In This *lov'd Cottage* let me Live and Die.
                        What

Quàm juvat immites ventos audire cuban-
tem,

Et dominam tenero continuiſſe ſinu !

Aut, gelidas hibernus aquas cum fuderit
Auſter,

Securum ſomnos, imbre juvante, ſequi !

Hoc mihi contingat. Sit dives jure, fu-
rorem

Qui maris, & triſtes ferre poteſt plu-
vias.

O quantum eſt auri pereat, potiuſque ſma-
ragdi,

Quam fleat ob noſtras ulla puella vias.

Te

What *Pleasure* 'tis each Night at *Home*
    to Reſt,
Like *Birds* frequenting our *Accuſtom'd*
    Neſt!
What *Pleaſure* 'midſt the *Warring Winds*
    alarms,
To *claſp* a Gentle Mistress in our
    Arms!
Or when the *Breezy Clouds* in Murmurs
    Weep,
Lull'd by the *Noiſe,* to ſink to *ſounder*
    Sleep !
Thus *Bleſt* ; Unenvy'd be their *Hopes*
    (for me)
Whom Av'rice tempts thro' *Toils* and
    Storms at *Sea.*
Ah ! never in Love's *Annals* be it ſaid,
That I thus *wander'd* from a *Plaintive*
    Maid.
Not *Orient Pearl,* not *Gems* of higheſt
    Price
Avail one *Precious Drop* from *Female*
    Eyes.

                     War,

Te bellare decet terra, Meſſala, mari-
    que,

Ut domus hoſtiles præferat exuvias.

Me retinent vinctum formoſæ vincla
    puellæ,

Et ſedeo duras janitor ante fores

Non ego laudari curo, mea Delia : tecum

    Dummodo ſim, quæſo ſegnis, inerſque
    vocer.

Te ſpectem, ſuprema mihi cum venerit
    hora,

Te teneam moriens deficiente manu.

Flebis & arſuro poſitum me, Delia, lecto,

    Triſtibus & lacrymis oſcula miſta dabis.

Flebis · non tua ſunt duro præcordia ferro

    Vincta, nec in tenero ſtat tibi corde ſilex.

Illo

War, Great MESSALLA, may thy *Rank* become,

And *Hoftile Trophies* fhould Adorn Thy *Dome*.

A *Slave* to *Love*, on *Beauty*'s Call I Wait;

My *Poft* of *Duty* lies at DELIA'S Gate.

The *Bufy* World thefe *Idle Cares* may Blame;

But, DELIA! *Life* with *Thee* is more than *Fame*.

Ev'n in *Fate*'s Gloomy Hour on Thee I'd *Gaze*,

And *Dying* feebly reach one Fond Embrace!

And Thou (for well I know, fo Kind Thou art,

The Sight would Pierce Thy *foft-impaffion'd* Heart.)

Wilt Weep to fee me on the *Fun'ral Bed*,

And mingle *Kiffes* with the Tears you fhed.

Nor

Illo non juvenis poterit de funere quif-
    quam

    Lumina, non virgo ficca referre do-
    mum.

Tu Manes ne læde meos, fed parce fo-
    lutis

    Crinibus, & teneris, Delia, parce genis.

Interea, dum fata finunt, jungamus
    amores.

    Jam veniet tenebris mors adoperta
    caput.

Jam fubrepet iners ætas, nec amare de-
    cebit,

    Dicere nec cano blanditias capite.

Nunc levis eft tractanda Venus, dum fran-
    gere poftes

    Non pudet, & rixas inferuiffe juvat.

                   Hic

Nor YOUTH, nor gen'rous MAID, who views *my Urn,*

Will with *dry Eyes,* I weet, from Thence Return.

But THOU reftrain Thy *Grief,* and, oh! forbear

To *Wouud* thofe *tender Cheeks,* Thofe *Locks* to *Tear.*

And Now, whilft yet our *Day-light* does remain,

Let us contrive it may not fhine in vain.

DEATH in his *Sable Veil* fteals on apace.

AGE too robs LOVE, you know, of All its *Grace.*

Grey Hairs and *Gallantry* but ill agree:

Catch, catch the fleeting Hours, e'er yet They Flee.

YOUTH is the lucky Seafon of Addrefs,

When LOVERS *Arms* can only hope *Succefs.*

Defign'd by NATURE for *This am'rous Fight,*

Here lyes the *Skill* I boaft, and here my *Might.*

Colours

Hìc ego dux, milesque bonus; vos signa, tubæque

Ite procul, cupidis vulnera ferte viris,

Ferte & opes. Ego composito securus acervo

Despiciam dites, despiciamque famem.

Q. H

Colours, and *Drums*, and *Fifes* hence far
 Retire.
And reftlefs CHIEFS to *glorious Haz-*
 zards fire.
Intrench'd within the *Fortune* That I
 Prize,
I Fear no *Want*, and *Vanity* Defpife.

G   The

Quinti Horatii Flacci,
ODE II. LIB. III.

I.

ANgustam, Amici, pauperiem pati

Robustus acri militia puer

Condiscat, & Parthos feroces

Vexet eques metuendus hasta :

II.

The Second ODE of the Third Book of *Horace.*
Humbly Inscribed to his Grace the Duke of ARGYLL *and* GREENWICH.

I

TO *Discipline,* and *Dangers* Breed,
 And by the Hardships, *Camps*
endure,
The *Sturdy Boy,* my FRIENDS, inure
With Patience *pinching Want* to bear
 Teach Him to Mount the *fiery* Steed;
And, Dreadful with his Glitt'ring Spear,
 To Gall the PARTHIAN and the
MEDE.

II.

Vitamque sub dio, & trepidis agat

In rebus.   Illum ex mœnibus hosticis

Matrona bellantis Tyranni

Prospiciens, & adulta Virgo

III.

Suspiret : Eheu, ne rudis agminum

Sponsus lacessat regius asperum

Tactu leonem, quem cruenta

Per medias rapit ira cædes.

IV.

II.

Him if some *Royal Dame* Behold
    Advancing near the hostile Tow'rs,
    Ah Me! She'll cry, Forbid, ye Pow'rs!
The KING, my Lord, unus'd to Arms,
    Shou'd urge, unfortunately Bold,
Yon LION, Who the Plain alarms
    With *Rage* and *Slaughter* uncontroul'd.

III.

When in our COUNTRY's *Cause* We Fight,
    What *Glories* on a SOLDIER wait!
    How *Welcome* is the HEROE's Fate!
The Youth, who Timorous wou'd *Retreat*,
    Shuns but in vain grim DEATH's quick
        Sight;
The *Stripling* at each *Turn* HE'll *meet*,
    Or *overtake* Him in his *Flight*.

G 3   IV.

IV.

Dulce & decorum est pro patria mori.

Mors & fugacem persequitur virum :

Nec parcit imbellis juventæ

Poplitibus, timidoque tergo.

V.

Virtus, repulsæ nescia sordidæ,

Intaminatis fulget honoribus :

Nec sumit aut ponit secures

Arbitrio popularis auræ.

VI.

IV.

PATRIOTS no vile *Repulses* Know;
   They with *unsully'd Honours* Shine,
   Tho' FACTIONS in Their Fall *combine:*
The *Rods* and *Axes* of the BRAVE
   To none but to *Themselves* THEY
     Owe,
No *Popular Suffrages* They *Crave;*
   To VIRTUE 'tis Alone They *Bow.*

V.

VIRTUE's a Strong and *Piercing* Light,
   That ope's a *Passage* through the
     Skies,
   Deny'd and Hid to *Vulgar* Eyes:
SHE quits the *Dabbling Fowl* That Lye
In *Fenny* Bogs, and *Error's* Night;
But *Those,* who *Firmer Pinions* try,
   She Guides to HEAVEN's immortal
     Height.

G 4   VI.

VI.

Virtus, recludens immeritis mori

Cœlum, negata tentat iter via :

Cœtusque vulgareis & udum

Spernit humum fugiente penna.

VII.

Est & fideli tuta silentio

Merces. Vetabo, qui Cereris sacrum

Vulgarit arcanæ, sub iisdem

Sit trabibus, fragilemque mecum.

VIII

Solvat Phaselum.   Sæpe Diespiter

Neglectus incesto addidit integrum :

Rarò antecedentem scelestum

Deseruit pede pœna claudo.

VI.

VALOUR and WISDOM claim Respect:
    RELIGION too Demands your Care;
    Whose *Rites* * with *Silent Awe* Revere.
Who sacred *Mysteries* Reveal,
    Shou'd Judgments from the GOD's ex-
        pect:
With such at Sea I'd fear to Sail,
    Lest *Guilty Commerce* shou'd Infect.

VII.

By PROVIDENCE, severely Just,
    Join'd in one *Common Ruin* We,
    The *Pious* oft and *Impious* See:
But *Instances* are *very Few*
    Of Men *abandon'd* to their *Lust*,
Whom *Vengeance* does not *close* Pursue,
    And *Scatter* Them, as *Wind* the *Dust*.

C A N-

---

* *This refers to the Mysterious Ceremonies practised in celebrating the Feasts of* CERES, *a Custom derived from the* GREEKS, *among whom to Divulge Those Rites, was lookt upon as the Highest Crime, and accordingly punished with Death, and They who heard, were adjudged as Guilty.* See DACIER

CANTATA.

Set feverally to MUSICK.
By *Colonel* Blaithwayte,
Mrs. Margaret Robifon,
and Mr. Green, *Organift*
of St. Paul's.

RECITATIVO.

BENEATH a *Beech*, as STREPHON laid
   Reclin'd on CLOE's Breaft,
She *Blufh'd* —— and thus the *Gentle Maid*
   Her tender Fear confeft.

ARIET.

ARIET.

WANTON *Shepherd* ! Prithee
   Leave Me ;
You but Court Me, to Deceive Me.
Men, alas ! are ftill Purfuing
Poor unhappy *Women's* Ruin.
Wanton *Shepherd !* Prithee leave Me ;
You but Court Me, to Deceive Me.

RECITATIVO.

THE *Swain* hung o'er the *Panting*
   Fair,
With Rapture viewing e'ery Feature :
 Fondly He *footh'd* each *rifing Care,*
And thus Addreft the *Pretty Creature.*

ARIET.

CLOE ! I can ill Diffemble ——
  You may Truft my *Heart* and
  Eyes ——
Lo ! I *Languifh, Burn,* and *Trem-*
ble ——
 Is This *Nature,* or *Difguife ?*

But

But *These Symptoms* (Tell Me True)
Are, perhaps, Unknown to *You.*

D U E T.

*A*H ! *We Neither* can Diſſemble.
    We may Tiuſt our *Hearts* and
        Eyes
Lo! I *Languiſh, Burn,* and *Tremble,*
Nature Triumphs o'er *Diſguiſe.*

THE

THE
MYRTLE.
TO A
LADY.

Floridis velut enitens
Myrtus Afia ramulis,
Quos Hamadryades Deæ
Ludicrum fibi rofcido
Nutriunt humore. - - - -

         Catull. Epithal. Juliæ & Manlii.

PHÆBUS the *Laurell,* BACCHUS chofe
     the *Vine;*
The tender *Myrtle's* VENUS' *Tree,* and
     THINE:
As *Her Bright Charms* adorn *Thy Hea-*
     v'nly Face,
So the *Same Enfigns* fhou'd *Thy Vot'ries*
     Grace

                        Each

Each Morn *Thy Gift* I Place before my
 Sight,
And Think of THEE, the *Giver,* with
 Delight:
Then from the ſtreaming Urn I gently
 Pour,
To *Cheer* the *Plant,* a ſoft *refreſhing*
 Show'r.

 But, Happy HE!
Who thus might daily, Gazing on Thoſe
 Eyes,
Pour out *ſweet Pleaſure,* and *bleſt*
 Sacrifice.
May, Lovely Maid! each ſmiling *Branch*
 appear
With *op'ning Bloom* in each returning
 Year,
The *Leaves unſully'd,* as *Thy Native*
 Truth,
And *Fragrant* as *Thy Beauty* and *Thy*
 Youth.

      Catullus.

Catullus ad Lesbiam.

V Ivamus mea Lesbia, *atque amemus,*
    Rumoresque senum severiorum
Omnes *unius æstimemus* assis
Soles *occidere,* & *redire possunt ·*
Nobis cum semel occidit brevis Lux,
Nox *est perpetua una dormienda.*
Da mi basia mille, deinde centum,
Dein mille altera, da secunda centum,
Deinde usque altera mille, deinde centum :
Dein cum multa millia fecerimus,
Conturbabimus *illa, ne sciamus,*
Aut ne quis malus invidere possit,
Cum tantum sciat esse bassiorum.

Imitated in English.

L ET us, Lesbia, *Love* and *Play,*
    Careless what the *Grave Ones* say.

             This

This *Ev'ning* Sun at *Morn may* rise:
    But Life's short transitory *Light*
Knows no *new Dawn*, to Glad our Eyes
    When once 'tis *Set*, 'tis *endless Night*

A Thousand *Kisses*, Gentle Maid!
    An hundred Thousand Thousand more
Give me, nor Dearest! be Afraid,
    Lest I grow *Cloy'd*, or Thou grow *Poor*

When *They* to such a Sum amount,
    As *Numbers* can't record, or *Art*,
We'll *huddle* up the *long Account*
    With *One close Kiss* from *ev'ry Part*.

Let Us, Lesbia, *Love* and *Play*,
Careless what the *Grave Ones* say,

To

To a Free-Thinker.

YOU Who like HERACLITUS seem,
 And for Us *merry Mortals* weep,
Is LIFE then but a *restless Dream?*
 And DEATH *one long continu'd Sleep?*

Ah *Wretch Profane!* did You but Know
 The *Bliss* in CLOE's *Arms* I prove,
You'd own the *Joys* of *Love* Below
 Were *Earnest* of a HEAV'N Above.

H   *ELEGY.*

ELEGY.

WHEN I cou'd Boaſt the gentle
   happy Air,
That us'd to Guide Me to the *Female*
   Heart,
In Joys I *Revel'd*, and in Rapture *Writ*,
The FAIR, Who crown'd my *Hopes*, in-
   ſpir'd my *Wit*.
But ſince That *Summer-Fruit* of Life is
   Paſt,
(The ſweeteſt Fruits, alas! the ſhorteſt
   Laſt)
Since her I held moſt Dear, Unjuſt I find;
Since *Vows* are *Words o' courſe*, and *Sighs*
   are *Wind*,
Adieu PARNASSUS, and the CYPRIAN
   Groves!
Farewell, at once, the MUSES and the
   LOVES!

        Yet

Yet oh, by FATE, *Devoted* to the Sex,

What *soft Inquietudes* my Soul perplex:

Whilst gay BELINDA's *sparkling Eyes* I View,

I feel my Former *Passion* rage anew.

Tho' BEAUTY's *wand'ring Lights* too oft betray,

Led by *Those Stars* Who wou'd not *lose their Way?*

So charm'd th' Ingrate --- with such a *Grace* she *smil'd,* ---

Ah! with What Ease the *Honest* are Beguil'd!

Down the *smooth Tide* of TENDERNESS I sail'd,

Nor fear'd the *faithless Rocks* That lay conceal'd

Thus *ship-wreck'd Mariners* reproach the *Main,*

Yet, tir'd on *Shore,* soon put to *Sea* again.

No *Treach'ries*, no *Defeats* can Warn-
    ings prove

To make me quit th' *advent'rous Cause* of
    LOVE.

Sweet are his *Toils*, and *Pleasing* his
    Alarms ;

Ev'n *Death* were *Welcome* in BELINDA'S
    Arms.

    So the bold *Warrior*, tho' some *hidden*
       Mine

Foil'd his *Attack*, refumes his *brave*
    Design ;

Still *Bent* the *Rampart* of the Foe to
    Reach,

Urges his *Fate*, and *Falls* within the
    Breach

The

The Western Wonder.

WHEN sprightly Young *Colleton*
　　firſt ſtruck my Eye,
She look'd like ſome *Angel* juſt dropp'd
　　from the Sky :
The *Church* was the Place ; and I lov'd,
　　tho' 'twas *Lent* ;
I may *Faſt,* and may *Pray,* but ne'er can
　　Repent.

Seeing her in a Chaiſe, with a Cap and Feather, and Riding Habit.

SHE Who but now as *Love's* Bright
　　Goddess ſhone,
In This *Diſguiſe* ſeems that *Arch Youth*
　　her Son.

　　　　　　　And

And well she does their diff'rent *Emblems*
    prove,
Her *Eyes* are *Arrows*, and her *Heart*'s
    the *Dove.*
Blest *Nymph!* Who both the GODHEADS
    act with Eale;
Who *Wound* like CUPID, and like VENUS
    Pleafe.

To

To Miss COLLETON, Playing on the SPINET.

WHEN MYRA Sung, and ISABELLA
    Play'd,
Two noble *Bards* their grateful Tribute
    Paid.
The diftant Names ftill Triumph over
    Time
In * WALLER's Verfe, and GRANVILLE's
    happy Rhyme:
Had *Either* Heard thy well-tun'd *Spinet*
    found,
Or feen *Thofe Eyes* That do fo *fweetly*
    Wound.

H 4   But

* See, the two celebrated Poems. One writ by
Mr Waller on Lady Ifabella's Playing on the Lute
the Other by my Lord Lanfdown, on Myra's Singing

The *Poet*'s aided by the *Lover*'s
Flame,

As Thine the *Merit*, Thine had been the
Fame.

But we no more a Courtly WALLER
Boaft ;

And GRANVILLE too in Foreign Realms
is Loft :

NATURE did THEE with ev'ry *Charm*
Befriend,

FATE Grudg'd a MUSE That might thofe
Charms commend.

Thus ALEXANDER'S Lot and Thine are
One,

Each *Conquer'd* All, but cou'd be *Prais'd*
by None

On Her *Entring her* Room.

SEE ! See ! She Comes ; with Grace-
    ful Eafe She Treads ;
And all around a fhining Glory fpreads :
Officious Cupids fwift ; by Ways
    Unfeen,
Advance like *Harbingers* before their
    Queen
And, of each fond Beholder's Heart
    poffeft.
Lodge fome *Attendant Charm* in ev'ry
    Breaft.
Her *Eyes,* Her *Cheeks,* Her *Lips,* Her
    Shape, and *Air*
Love's Empire o'er her *Willing Captives*
    Share ;
Each fmalleft *Feature* might her *Pow'r*
    maintain,
And ev'ry *Hair* would weave a Lover's
    Chain.

Her

Her Diff'rent Beauties, Diff'rent Men
   enthrall.
But, Oh! I feel th' united Force of All.

  - - - - *in me tota ruit* Venus.

Writ on a GLASS, *under her* NAME.

WHO on her *outward Form* alone
   wou'd Look,
Seems but to Read the *Title* of the
   Book:
Confult her *Soul*; and NATURE then,
   you'll find,
In a *Fair Volume* bound a *Fairer Mind.*

Soliloquy. *Walking in a Church-Yard.*

HARD is the Lot ordain'd to MAN
    by FATE,
Few are his *Joys,* and *short,* alas! their
    Date!
All That can *Charm* the *Taste,* the *Touch,*
    or *Eye,* - - -
Ev'n SPRING shall *Fade,* and COLLETON
    must *Die.*
Tormenting Thought! and yet in ME
    how Vain,
Who *Fear* to *Lose,* What I can't *Hope* to
    Gain?

F I N I S.

THE
TABLE.

The TABLE.

The TABLE.

SOME

Remarkable Passages

OF THE

LIFE

OF

Mr. *WYCHERLEY.*

By Mr. DENNIS.

APPENDIX.

To the Honourable

Major PACK.

S I R,

Have lately had the Satisfaction to read over your MEMOIRS of Mr. *Wycherley,** which I had laſt Week from Mr. *Curll,* and found the Relation very entertaining, and the Reflections juſt and pathetick. If I give you Hints of ſome particular Paſſages which ſeem either to have ſlipt from your Memory, or to have eſcap'd your Knowledge, I flatter myſelf that you will receive them kindly, ſince they are only ſent with Intention to give you an Opportunity whenever you have a mind to re-touch your Memoirs, to make them more compleat, tho' they cannot be more agreeable.

I

And

* *See, Major Pack's former Volume of Miſcellanies.*

And now, Sir, to enter upon the Subject, without any more Ceremony. I never could learn, either from Mr. *Wycherley* himself, or from Mr. *Dryden*, or Sir *Harry Sheers*, or Mr. *Walkenden*, or from any of those who had been longest acquainted with Mr. *Wycherley*, that he had ever resided at either of our Universities. About the Age of Fifteen he was sent for Education to the Western Parts of *France*, either to *Saintonge* or the *Angoumois*. His Abode there was either upon the Banks of the *Charante*, or very little remov'd from it. And he had there the Happiness to be in the Neighbourhood of one of the most accomplish'd Ladies of the Court of *France*, *Madame de Montausier*, whom *Voiture* has made famous by several very ingenious Letters, the most of which were writ to her when she was a Maid, and call'd *Madamoiselle de Rambouillet*. I have heard Mr. *Wycherley* say, that he was often admitted to the Conversation of that Lady, who us'd to call him

him the Little *Hugenot*; and that young as he was, he was equally pleas'd with the Beauty of her Mind, and with the Graces of her Perfon.

Upon the writing his firft Play, which was *St. James's Park*, he became acquainted with feveral of the moft celebrated Wits, both of the Court and Town. The writing of that Play was likewife the Occafion of his becoming acquainted with one of King *Charles*'s Miftreffes* after a very particular manner. As Mr. *Wycherley* was going thro *Pall-Mall* towards St. *James*'s in his Chariot, he met the forefaid Lady in hers, who, thrufting half her Body out of the Chariot, cry'd out aloud to him, *You*, Wycherley, *you are a Son of a Whore*, at the fame time laughing aloud and heartily. Perhaps, Sir, if you never heard of this Paffage before, you may be furpriz'd at fo ftrange a Greeting from one of the moft beautiful and beft bred Ladies in the World. Mr. *Wycher-*

ley

* *The Dutchefs of* Cleveland

ley was certainly very much furpriz'd at it, yet not fo much but he foon apprehended it was fpoke with Allufion to the latter End of a Song in the foremention'd Play.

When Parents are Slaves
Their Brats cannot be any other,
Great Wits and great Braves
Have always a Punk to their Mother.

As, during Mr. *Wycherley's* Surprife, the Chariots drove different ways, they were foon at a confiderable Diftance from each other, when Mr. *Wycherley* recovering from his Surprife, ordered his Coachman to drive back and to overtake the Lady. As foon as he got over-againft her, he faid to her, *Madam, you have been pleafed to beftow a Title on me which generally belongs to the Fortunate. Will your Ladyfhip be at the Play to Night? Well,* fhe reply'd, *what if I am there? Why then I will be there to wait* on your *Ladyship, tho' I disappoint a very fine Woman who has made me an Assignation.* So, said she, *you are sure to disappoint a Woman who has favour'd you, for one who has not.* Yes, reply'd he, *if she who has not favour'd me is the finer Woman of the two. But he who will be constant to your Ladyship, till he can find a finer Woman, is sure to die your Captive.* The Lady blush'd, and bade her Coachman drive away. As she was then in all her Bloom, and the most celebrated Beauty that was then in *England,* or perhaps that has been in *England* since, she was touch'd with the Gallantry of that Compliment. In short, she was that Night in the first Row of the King's Box in *Drury-Lane,* and Mr. *Wycherley* in the Pit under her, where he entertain'd her during the whole Play. And this, Sir, was the beginning of a Correspondence between these two Persons, which afterwards made a great Noise in the Town.

But

But now, Sir, I fhall proceed to remind you of fomething more extraordinary, and that is, that the Correfpondence between Mr. *Wycberley* and the forefaid Lady was the Occafion of bringing Mr. *Wycberley* into favour with *George* Duke of *Buckingham*, who was paffionately in Love with that Lady, who was ill treated by her, and who believed Mr. *Wycberley* his happy Rival. After the Duke had long follicited her without obtaining any thing, whether the Relation between them fhock'd her, for fhe was his Coufin-Germain, or whether fhe apprehended that an Intrigue with a Perfon of his Rank and Character, a Perfon upon whom the Eyes of all Men were fix'd, muft of Neceffity in a little time come to the King's Ears, whatever was the Caufe, fhe refus'd to admit of his Vifits fo long, that at laft Indignation, Rage, and Difdain took Place of his Love, and he refolv'd to ruin her. When he had taken this Refolution, he had her fo narrowly watch'd

by

by his Spies, that he foon came to the Knowledge of thofe whom he had reafon to believe
his Rivals. And after he knew them, he
never fail'd to name them aloud, in order to
expofe the Lady, to all thofe who frequented
him, and among others, he us'd to name Mr.
Wycherley. As foon as it came to the Knowledge
of the latter, who had all his Expectations from
the Court, he apprehended the confequence of
fuch a Report, if it fhould reach the King. He
applied himfelf therefore to *Wilmot* Lord *Ro-
chefter* and to Sir *Charles Sedley,* and intreated them to remonftrate to the Duke of *Buckingham* the Mifchief which he was about to
do to one who had not the Honour to be known
to him, and who had never offended him.
Upon their opening the Matter to the Duke,
he cry'd out immediately, *that he did not
blame* Wycherley, *he only accus'd his Coufin.
Ay, but,* they reply'd, *by rendering him fufpected of fuch an Intrigue, you are about to*

ruin

ruin him, that is, your Grace is about to ruin a Man with whose Conversation you would be pleas'd above all things. Upon this Occasion they said so much of the shining Qualities of Mr. *Wycherley,* and of the Charms of his Conversation, that the Duke, who was as much in love with Wit, as he was with his Kinswoman, was impatient till he was brought to sup with him, which was in two or three Nights. After Supper Mr. *Wycherley,* who was then in the Height of his Vigour both of Body and Mind, thought himself oblig'd to exert himself, and the Duke was charm'd to that Degree, that he cry'd out in a Transport, *By G---- my Cousin is in the right of it*; and from that very Moment made a Friend of a Man whom he believ'd his happy Rival.

The Duke of *Buckingham* gave him solid sensible Proofs of his Esteem and Affection. For as he was at the same time Master of the Horse to King *Charles,* and Colonel of a Regiment;

ment; as Mafter of the Horfe he made him one of his Equeries, and as Colonel of a Regiment he made him Captain Lieutenant of his own Company, refigning to him at the fame time his own Pay as Captain, and all other Advantages that could be juftly made of the Company.   I remember that about that time I, who was come up from the Univerfity to fee my Friends in Town, happen'd to be one Night at the Fountain Tavern in the *Strand*, with the late Dr. *Duke*, *David Loggan* the Painter, and Mr. *Wilfon*, of whom *Otway* has made honourable Mention (in one of his Poems) and that after Supper we drank Mr. *Wycherley*'s Health by the Name of Captain *Wycherley*.

He was, not long after this, in fuch high Favour with the King, that that Monarch gave him a Proof of his Efteem and Affection, which never any Sovereign Prince before had given to an Author who was on-

ly

ly a private Gentleman. Mr. *Wycherley* happen'd to fall sick of a Fever at his Lodgings in *Bow-Street, Covent-Garden,* during which Sickness the King did him the Honour to visit him, when finding his Fever indeed abated, but his Body extremely weaken'd, and his Spirits miserably shatter'd, he commanded him, as soon as he was able to take a Journey, to go to the South of *France,* believing that nothing would contribute more to the restoring his former Vigour, than the gentle salutiferous Air of *Montpelier* during the Winter Season. At the same time the King was pleas'd to assure him, *that as soon as he was capable of taking that Journey, he would order five hundred Pounds to be paid him to defray the Expence of it.*

Mr. *Wycherley* accordingly went into *France* in the beginning of the Winter of 1678, if I am not mistaken, and return'd into *England*

land in the latter end of the Spring of 1679, entirely reſtor'd to his former Vigour both of Body and Mind. The King receiv'd him with the utmoſt Marks of Favour, and ſhortly after his Arrival told him that he had a Son, who he was reſolv'd ſhould be educated like the Son of a King, and that he could make choice of no Man ſo proper to be his Go-vernor as Mr. *Wycherley*; that for that Ser-vice he ſhould have fifteen hundred Pounds a Year paid him, for the Payment of which he ſhould have an Aſſignment upon three ſe-veral Offices, whoſe Names I have forgot, to which the King added, *that when the Time came that his Office was to ceaſe, he would take care to make ſuch a Proviſion for him as ſhould ſet him above the Malice of the World and Fortune.*

And now, Sir, is it not matter of Won-der, that One, of Mr. *Wycherley*'s extraordi-nary Merit, who was eſteem'd by all the

moſt

moft deferving Perfons of the Court of King *Charles* the Second, and in high Favour with the King himfelf, fhould in a little time, after he had received thefe gracious Offers which feem to have made and to have fix'd his Fortune, be thrown into Prifon for bare feven hundred Pounds, and be fuffer'd to languifh there during the laft four Years of that Monarch's Reign, forfaken by all his Friends at Court, and quite abandon'd by the King? 'Tis no eafy matter, Sir, to find a more extraordinary Inftance of the Viciffitude of human Affairs, and if the Caufe of fo ftrange an Alteration is unknown to you, I dare promife myfelf that you are very defirous to hear it.

It was immediately after Mr. *Wycherley* had receiv'd thefe gracious Offers from the King, that the Water-drinking Seafon coming on, he went down to *Tunbridge* to take either the Benefit of the Waters or the Diverfions

of

of the Place, when walking one Day upon the Wells-Walk with his Friend Mr. *Fairbeard* of *Grey's-Inn*, juſt as he came up to the Bookſeller's, my Lady *Drogheda*, a young Widow, rich, noble, and beautiful, came to the Bookſeller and enquir'd for *the Plain Dealer.* *Madam*, ſays Mr *Fairbeard*, *ſince you are for the* Plain Dealer, *there he is for you*, puſhing Mr. *Wycherley* towards her. *Yes*, ſays Mr. *Wycherley, this Lady can bear Plain Dealing, for ſhe appears to be ſo accompliſh'd, that what would be Compliment ſaid to others, ſpoke to her would be Plain Dealing.* No, truly, *Sir*, ſaid the Lady, *I am not without my Faults any more than the reſt of my Sex, and yet notwithſtanding all my Faults, I love Plain Dealing, and never am more fond of it than when it tells me of my Faults.* Then, Madam, ſaid Mr. *Fairbeard, You and the* Plain Dealer *ſeem deſign'd by Heaven for each other.* In ſhort, Mr. *Wycherley* walk'd with her

her upon the Walks, waited upon her home, vi-
fited her daily at her Lodgings, while fhe ftaid
at *Tunbridge,* and after fhe went to *London,*
at her Lodgings in *Hatton-Garden,* where in a
little time he got her Confent to marry her,
which he did, by his Father's Command, without acquainting the King, for it was reafona-
bly fuppos'd, that the Lady having a great Independent Eftate, and noble and powerful Relations, the acquainting the King with the intended Marriage might be the likelieft way to
prevent it.   As foon as the News of it came to
Court it was look'd upon as an Affront to the
King, and a Contempt of his Majefty's Offers.
And Mr. *Wycherley*'s Conduct after his Marriage
made this be refented more heinoufly.   For feldom or never coming near the Court, he was
thought downright ungrateful.   But the true
Caufe of his Abfence was not known, and the
Court was at that time too much alarm'd, and
in too much Difquiet to enquire into it.   In
short,

short, Sir, the Lady was jealous of him to Di-
straction, jealous to that degree, that she could
not endure that he should be one Moment out
of her Sight. Their Lodgings were in *Bow-
street, Covent-Garden,* over-against the *Cock,*
whither if he at any time went with his Friends,
he was oblig'd to leave the Windows open,
that the Lady might see there was no Woman in Company, or she would be immediately in a downright raving Condition. Whether this outrageous Jealousy proceeded from
the excess of her Passion, for she lov'd her
Husband with the same Violence with which
she had done her Lover, or from the great
Things which she had heard reported of his
manly Prowess, which were not answer'd by
her Experience, or from them both together,
Mr. *Wycherley* thought that he was oblig'd to
humour it, and that he could not be too indulgent to a Lady who had bestow'd both her
Person and her Fortune on him. This, Sir,

was

was the Cause that brought Mr. *Wycherley* all at once into the utmost Disgrace with the Court, whose Favour and Affection but just before he possessed in the highest Degree.   And these, Sir,   are the Particulars of Mr. *Wycherley's* Life,   which seem either to have slipt from your Memory,   or to have escaped your Knowledge.

I am, Sir,

Your most Obedient

Humble Servant,

Whitehall, Sept 1
1720.

JOHN DENNIS.

CATULLUS

Ad Amicam

FORMIANI.

*Alve, nec nimio, Puella, nafo,*
Nec bello pede, nec nigris ocellis,
Nec longis digitis, nec ore ficco,
Nec fanè nimis elegante lingua,
Decoctoris amica FORMIANI.
Tenè Provincia narrat effe bellam?
Tecum LESBIA noftra comparatur?
O faclum infipiens, & inficetum!

CATULLUS *ad Amicam* FORMIANI.

Applied in *English*.

Adeste Hendycasylabi!

THOU Dear Droll Dowdy *Dandiprat*,
With *Nose* of *Mastiff*, *Eyes* of *Cat*,
Fingers like *Toes*, *Feet* flat and long,
Wide *driv'ling Mouth*, and *drawling Tongue*.
Shall EXON *Beaus* Thy *Beauty* boast
With COLLETON's my *Darling Toast* ?
Well! Mercies on Thee, *little Brute!*
The *Lovers* and their *Mistress* suit.

ERRATA.

PAGE 19 Line 1   after Humane a *Semicolon*
    Idem. ibid dele the *Semicolon* after Manners.
    Idem   2   after Affable a *Comma*
    Idem.   4.   after Freedom a *Sem.colon*

POETRY, *Printed for* E. CURLL.

I THE Honourable Major PACK's (former Volume of) *Miscellanies*, in Profe and Verfe, *viz* 1 Original Poems upon feveral Occafions 2 Tranflations, *&c.* from *Virgil*, *Ovid*, *Catullus*, *Tibullus*, &c 3 An Effay upon *Study* 4 An Effay upon *Converfation* 5 An Effay upon the *Roman* Elegiac-Poets 6 Memoirs of the Life of *William Wycherley* Efq, The Second Edition Price 6s 3d

II Mr Secretary *Addifon's* Miscellanies, in Verfe and Profe. Price 3s

III The Poetical Works of the late Earl of *Halifax*, with his Life, and a true Copy of his laft Will and Teftament Price 5s

IV His Grace the Duke of *Buckingham's* Poems on feveral Occafions, collected into one Volume Adorned with Cuts. Price 3s 6d

V Mr *Creech's* Tranflation of the *Idylliums* of *Theocritus* To which is prefix'd, *Rapin's* Difcourfe upon *Paftorals* Price 2s 6d

VI The Works of *Anacreon*, *Sappho*, and *Bion*, made *Englifh* from the *Greek* By feveral Hands Price 1s

VII Dr *Young's* Poem on the LAST DAY Adorned with Cuts Price 1s

VIII The *Force of Religion* : Or, *Vanquifh'd Love* A Poem In two Books. Illuftrated in the Hiftory of the Lady *Jane Gray*. By Dr. *Young* Adorn'd with Cuts Price 1s

IX *Mufcipula* · Sic, *Cambro Muo-Machia* Authore E Holdfworth, e Coll Magd Oxon With a Tranflation of it By Mr *Samuel Cobb*, late of *Trinity College, Cambridge* Price 1s

X Mr *John Philips's* Poems *viz* The *Splendid Shilling, Blenheim Cyder, &c* With his Life By M. *Sewell* Price 4s in 8vo 2s 6d in 12°

CPSIA information can be obtained at www.ICGtesting.com
Printed in the USA
LVOW03s0815111114

412947LV00007B/40/P

9 781170 796344